She Married a
Narcissist and Survived

Alice Connor

Dedication

To my three sons who have supported and encouraged me.

Acknowledgement

To my sister and my very good friends who have supported me through many dramas.

About the Author

Kath, who writes books under the name of Alice Connor, has lived and worked on NZ farms or in the Agi business all of her life. She has gone against the acceptable roles for women and has endured resistance. She has always planned to write books from an early age. Many have been started, only to be abandoned due to reality.

Now that she has raised her family and survived emotional turmoil, she has time to write the books based on her experiences in rural NZ.

PART ONE

Chapter One

The Blind Date

Lisa was working as a banking rural manager in a town on the west coast of the north island. She had recently moved to the area, so didn't know anyone outside the office. Her job involved visiting farms and talking to the farmers. She had to sell products to the farmers, but at the same time, she had to ensure they were profitable. The job was demanding both emotionally and mentally.

Some of Lisa's clients were struggling financially. They had been over-lent to or had suffered financial hardship. It was difficult to tell a hard-working family that their dreams were ending in failure. Every month, Lisa had to visit them to monitor their progress. She went home at night emotionally drained and mentally tired. It was a lonely job as you couldn't discuss anything outside the office due to confidential requirements.

Lisa would just blob out in front of the TV or go for a long bike ride along the country roads, passing rolling hills with grazing dairy cows. Lisa would come back physically tired. One night, she had a phone call from Matt, an old friend: "I have a mate who is looking for a partner for a ball. Would you be interested in going?"

Lisa was very surprised, as it was the last thing she expected. "What is he like?"

Matt then explained, "Simon is a nice guy who lives on a farm and just needs a partner for the night. He doesn't get to meet many girls, living where he does."

"Okay, if he asks and seems OK, then I will go. I'm not doing anything else that weekend." Lisa replied

"Great, I will give him your phone number."

Lisa got off the phone a wee bit excited and a bit apprehensive. A blind date could go well or be a complete disaster. Either way it would make a change to her routine.

Lisa had never gone out much socially, so this was quite exciting. A few nights later, Lisa got a phone call.

"Hi, It's Simon. I'm a friend of Matt's. He gave me your phone number."

"Oh yes."

"So, how's things?"

"Oh, pretty good, busy at work."

"That's good. I live on a farm over the ranges from you. It's sheep and beef so just doing the normal winter stock work at the moment."

"Well, that will keep you busy. It's been a bit cold lately. We get a lot of wind off the sea, so we don't get many frosts."

"We get a lot of frosts, being down in a valley. They hang around for most of the day but at least the days have been sunny.

I have two tickets to a ball in a week's time. It's on Saturday night. It's a fundraiser for the local community. They are raising funds to build a squash court. Would you like to come?"

"Yeah, that sounds good." The ball was located three hours away from where Lisa lived, and being the middle of winter, the roads could be icy.

"I will need to stay somewhere for the night. It is too far for me to drive home afterwards".

"You can stay at my place for the night." Simon said.

Lisa wasn't so sure about staying at a strange guy's place, as she had no idea what he was like or what she was getting into. Lisa frantically thought, what would be a good option when inspiration struck.

"One of my friends lives in the town. You can pick me up from Linda's place, I could stay with her." Lisa gave Simon the address. All the time, Lisa's fingers were crossed that Linda would be home; otherwise, Lisa didn't know what she was going to do.

Once the phone call ended, Lisa hastily rang Linda. Linda was the mother of her best friend, Rose, who lived in Australia with her husband and children. They had known each other for years.

"Hi, can I stay Saturday night with you?"

"Why? What's up?"

"I have been asked to a ball by a local guy."

Linda got quite excited. "Ooh, that's wonderful. Who asked you? What's he like?"

"I have never met him. His name is Simon and his parents own a farm south of you."

"Course you can stay. Can't wait to meet him. How exciting. The ball is going to be the social highlight of the year. Everyone is going to it."

Lisa and Linda said goodbye. Lisa heaved a sigh as she now had somewhere to stay.

Lisa set off on Saturday morning with everything packed. The route was on a main highway, so it was two lanes and sealed all the way. It was a very scenic drive along the coastline before it turned inland to follow river valleys and then over a mountain range. The valleys were surrounded by steep hills, making Lisa feel like she was driving a matchbox car.

The car radio turned to static once they entered the valleys. This gave Lisa plenty of time to lecture herself about how stupid this was. He could be a total nuthead, and it could be a terrible night! 'Why am I going to all of this trouble? It could be a horrible night. I could just turn around and go home. That would be cowardly and I did say I would go. But then he might be Ok. I wonder what he's like?' I could miss out on a good night out. Round and round, the thoughts spiraled in Lisa's head. Curiosity won out.

Linda lived in a small rural community, and her husband used to farm in the district. Linda wasted no time tapping into her network and finding out about Simon's family. She found out where they lived, how many children they had, what Simon was like and how big the farm was. Therefore, when Simon knocked on her door, she greeted him like an acquaintance and promptly struck up a conversation about the district, the state of the roads, the weather, who they both knew and what farms had sold.

Simon was polite with a dry sense of humour and won Linda over in the first five minutes. Lisa peeked through the balustrade to see what he looked like. Didn't look too bad; he was about her height, dark curly hair, and broad-shouldered with a ginger beard. He was wearing a dark suit and tie. He seemed to be coherent and was making Linda laugh. All good signs, perhaps the evening would be a success.

Lisa's ball gown was made from blood-red velvet. It had long-form fitted sleeves, a high neck with a Chinese collar and a fitted bodice. It then flowed into a full, knee-length skirt. The neck and cuffs had tiny seed pearls sewn on, which stood out against the blood-red colour. Lisa felt like a million dollars in the dress. When she twirled, the skirt flared out, and then it would swish back. Lisa loved it. Paired with black medium-heeled sandals. Lisa liked how she looked.

Lisa took her courage and walked into the lounge to meet Simon. The effect was everything Lisa could have hoped for. Simon promptly stood, and sotto voice said, "You're gorgeous." It was like he didn't mean to say it; it just slipped out. Lisa was gratified and smiled at Simon.

Simon took her hand and escorted her out to his car. Lisa was a bit surprised by the car as it was a small four door car, one would expect grannies to drive. As Simon held the door for her, he said, "This is my mother's car. I normally drive a Ford Ute, but it's a bit messy."

The ball was a lot of fun. It was held in the local hall, and it was packed. They had tables for eating over against one wall, a dance space with a lively DJ and an area where everyone seemed to gather to chat. It appeared the whole district had turned out. As soon as they were inside, Simon introduced Lisa to his mother and father. Lisa shook hands and said 'Hi', feeling a bit nervous. How often do you meet the boy's parents on the first date? She had the distinct impression that they were weighing her up.

Simon was very attentive and had Lisa on the dance floor for most of the night. He was a good dancer and seemed to enjoy squiring Lisa around. The food was excellent, and the conversation entertaining. As the night progressed, Lisa was introduced to more members of Simon's family. It appeared the whole extended family had attended. One Uncle kept topping up Lisa's wine glass. At times, it seemed he was chasing her around the hall to ensure she had a refill. Lisa gave up trying to remember who was who. Most of them just became a blur of faces.

Once they arrived back at Linda's, Simon rushed around to Lisa's side and helped her out. In the process, he got hold of her hand and didn't let go.

"I would really like to see you again". He had slipped his fingers into Lisa's and moved in closer.

"Yeah. I'm sure we could organize something at the weekend. I work all week."

"That would be great. I will give you a call."

Simon then reached in for a kiss on the lips. It was a warm, chaste kiss in the wintery night. Lisa smiled and went inside.

Chapter Two

Simon's Home

Simon was working for the manager on one of his parent's properties, an hour south of where they lived, on another farm. Both farms were located in the central north island on the opposite side of the mountain range from where Lisa was living.

Lisa agreed to visit Simon for the weekend. She set off on Friday night, after work, to travel over the inland route. Lisa had never been on the road before, so wasn't sure what to expect. Simon had said it was a good well maintained road and she wouldn't have any problems. Simon had been a bit sparse with the directions, "You can't get lost, just follow the road. When you come to a fork in the road, take the right-hand one and then keep going until you come to a major bridge. Turn right over that, then turn left. Keep going and I am in the first house on the right. You'll be fine."

Lisa turned onto the road from the main highway and just kept following it. It was a sealed two laned road, but very twisting. Every time Lisa went around a corner, she found another corner directly in front of her. She drove slowly along the road as it climbed up the ridge, only to find herself winding around the toe of another ridge before climbing again.

After an hour, she began to wonder if it would ever reach a destination or if she had made a wrong turn. 'How could I have made a wrong turn, there was no other road, but I am the only one on the road'. Lisa began to feel like she was lost in the never-ending hills.

An hour later, a sign for a town appeared. Lisa smiled with relief. At least she was coming into civilization, and she would be able to check where she was. She only had another hour of daylight left, and she really didn't want to be driving a strange, twisting road in the dark. 'I will be able to get something hot to eat and drink', Lisa thought.

She came round the corner off the hill and down into the valley where the town was. Lisa looked, blinked and looked again. No, it still looked the same. She couldn't believe it. She slowly drove down the main street, looking and looking again in shock. 'Perhaps I passed through a time zone in the hills and stepped back a 100 years'. Lisa wondered. 'I wouldn't be surprised if I had, considering the dark gullies and forest I have passed through. I have seen no other human being this entire trip.'

It was a complete town with stables, a blacksmith, a store, a pub, a school and a bakery. Everything was shut except for the pub and school. They were all showing signs of age, some more than others. The signage had faded or peeled, and the facade timbers were white and shiny with age. The corrugated iron roofs were rusty, and in places, they had peeled back, revealing the rafters.

She could see the counter in the bakery and the old red brick stove, the sign by the blacksmith door, with the black furnace in the background. The pub and school were the only buildings actually in working order. Lisa didn't see another vehicle or person, which just added to the deserted feeling. The whole town looked as if everyone had just packed up and walked out.

The school was painted bright colours and looked reasonably modern. It quite clearly was operating but deserted at the moment. The pub, a two-story timber-clad, rambling-looking building, would have fitted right into a horror movie, especially with the goat tied to the front veranda pole.

Lisa decided it might be safer not to stop for a hot pie. She may never be seen again if she passed through those doors. It had 'rocky horror story' written all over it, and god only knows where the food came from.

Lisa gave a final look at the town in her rear vision mirror and carried on, hopefully towards Simon's place. The road then became unsealed and only wide enough for one and a half vehicles. It had two wheel marks in the road like a track. If Lisa met someone, she would have to pull over to the side into the loose gravel to let them pass.

Lisa continued driving, wondering just how much longer and where the hell was this fork in the road. 'Have I missed it?' she wondered. The road continued onwards into a thick bush as it followed the river.

Lisa was very impressed with the beautiful scenery. Dramatic rocky faces and green-covered hills stretching back like folded linen. The ridges blended into blue-coloured hills in the far distance. The river bank was edged with native trees and ferns as the water gurgled over the rocks towards the sea.

The river could only be viewed in short stretches as it would drop down into steep gorges while the road climbed over the next ridge. Lisa only dared quick glances at the river as most of her attention was on the winding road. 'It would be lovely to bike', Lisa thought. 'Then you could take the time to view the landscape. Keep your eyes on the road, Lisa, otherwise, you could drive off it.' She lectured herself. 'Thank god the weather was good. Trying to do this trip in bad weather would have been a nightmare.' Lisa thought.

The road then straightened out to climb up a rise to a tunnel. The tunnel was old with no facing at all. Just rough cut edges, only wide enough for one vehicle. The sides were covered in tree ferns, vines and long grass and in the center was the dark entrance. In complete contrast, directly above the entrance was a yellow road sign stating the height allowance.

It was like a mythical land which matched up perfectly with the town Lisa had driven through. Lisa wouldn't have been surprised if a Hobbit suddenly appeared. It was a wild, forgotten area showing the scars of a past life. In the last two hours, Lisa hadn't seen another vehicle. It was just her and this magical landscape, which never seemed to end.

Lisa passed through the tunnel and then dropped down the other side to enter into another deep gully. 'I must come out somewhere', Lisa thought as she continued. After a corner she came up to where the road forked. 'Thank god I am in the right place'. The road became two lanes and sealed. 'I must be getting closer to civilization', She thought.

From then it didn't take long to find the bridge and the valley Simon lived in. The road to the house was a one-way unsealed road, which wound its way into the hills along a river valley. Lisa hoped that she was nearly at Simon's place cause she was over the drive. It was becoming a marathon.

The road passed through native bush, causing the road to darken, broken only by the sun dappled spots. It was beautiful with the sun rays passing through the trees, and there was Simon's house, finally. 'Oh my god, we have finally arrived!" Lisa thought. Lisa was tired after a full day of work, followed by a dramatic three-hour car trip. Simon gave her a big hug and said, "Good trip? It's a good road, isn't it?"

Lisa just looked at him, wondering what he considered a bad road. "Yeah, it was Ok."

Simon led her inside and gave her a glass of wine as she settled into a chair. Lisa relaxed and had a look around the house. It was an old, rambling single-story farmhouse with an open fireplace, four bedrooms, a large pantry the size of a bedroom and a large kitchen. It was where his parents first lived and started their family. Outside there was a lawn sloping down to the road. On the right-hand side, there was a large swimming pool. Simon hadn't done anything with the swimming pool, so it consisted of green-coloured water with floating vegetation.

During the day, they just hung out and enjoyed the quiet and peace of the property. The farm was a steep hill country block running sheep and beef. The river was just across the road from the house. On both sides of the river, there were irregular flats where sheep and cattle grazed. On the house side of the road, a few flats nestled at the foot of steep ridges. Little streams burbled along the narrow valleys between the steep ridges before they emptied out into the river. The heads of the valleys become steep-sided cliffs with narrow, flat tops. A classic volcanic landscape. Bush-clad hills reached back from the property in a series of steep ridges. The view from the top was more hills reaching back and back again until the foothills of the mountain.

Over the summer Lisa and Simon went swimming in the river pools, carved out by the river as it ebbed and flowed around the rocks.

They were completely alone in nature.

Peaceful, just what Lisa needed after spending all week surrounded by people at work. Lisa would be caressed by the water as she floated with the gentle current downstream. Lying on her back, she would graze at the trees overhead and watch the birds flutter between the branches. The bird song was constant, with glimpses of wood pigeons, tuis and wax eyes fluttering in the bush.

She would then swim back upstream to repeat the weightless, peaceful sensation. Paradise ducks grazed on the paddocks amongst the sheep before they came in to land on the river. Sometimes, they would touch down in their favourite spot only to see Lisa and Simon at the last moment. With a frantic flapping of wings, they would take off again, spraying water droplets everywhere. Lisa and Simon would get a fright and then laugh at the duck's antics.

Simon's hunting horse would gallop around the paddock amongst the original rustic buildings next to the house. They added charm and an old-world feeling to the property.

Apart from their mutual friends and the manager, they hardly saw anyone else. On Sunday, Lisa drove back to work and repeated the trip the following weekend.

Every time Lisa arrived for the weekend, Simon was very attentive and charming. He always had little gifts for her, a dozen apricot-coloured roses or a box of chocolates and always a bottle of wine ready to pour when Lisa arrived. It was lovely. Simon made her feel like he really cared for her and went out of his way to make her feel special.

Simon cooked dinner, which was always a roast with Vege's. After tea, they sat around the open fire, talked and drank while Simon's cat, Dixie, curled up on his lap. She was a pretty relaxed cat, but she ruled the house. She was black, with white paws, whiskers and nose.

Dixie saw Lisa as a rival for Simon's attention, and she would glare at Lisa while she flexed her claws. She made it quite clear, nonverbally, her feelings about Lisa.

One Friday, Lisa passed the manager on the road. They had a brief chat about the season, and then Jake laughingly asked. "Have you seen Simon mow his lawn? It's a sight, one you won't forget."

Lisa was a bit perplexed. What was so interesting about mowing the lawn? "The lawn?"

"Ooh, you haven't seen it yet! Simon mows it naked, except for his gumboots."

"Really?" It seemed a strange thing to do. Lisa didn't give it much thought as she headed to Simon's house.

Saturday morning, after a leisurely breakfast of bacon and eggs cooked by Simon, he decided the lawn needed to be mowed. Lisa sat in the lounge watching Simon strip off all of his clothes before going outside and donning his gumboots. Lisa rushed over to the door to watch Simon walk over to get the lawnmower. She was fascinated, watching Simon pushing the lawn mower around the section. It was the most bizarre sight she had seen.

He was marching along behind the lawnmower with his farmer tan. Tanned legs until his sock marks and, tanned arms to his biceps and a tanned triangle area at the top of his chest, caused by the opened neck shirt. The rest was all pasty, white and hairy. Simon was very hairy front and back.

It was almost like a cartoon. Not a pretty picture, but a funny one. Lisa kept thinking about the flying stones and grass getting into all of his personal spaces.

"Simon, why do you mow the lawn naked?"

"It feels good. I feel free instead of being restricted by the clothing."

"It doesn't bother you that someone might visit and see you naked? You are right by the road."

"Nope, that's their problem. They will have to wait for me to get dressed if they want to visit."

"If it makes you happy...I would have thought the sand flies.., would be a problem."

"Nah, they're fine."

"What about safety? A flying stone?"

"That's why I am wearing the gumboots. Can't get anything safer than gumboots. Simon started to sing as he marched off with the lawnmower.

Where would you be without your gumboots,

In the hospital or the infirmary."

With clenching buttocks, he went down the hill. Lisa went and sat on the front porch and watched him. It was a sight to behold.

Chapter Three

Kayak Trip

O ne Friday, Lisa was travelling over the bridge to Simon's place when she spied kayaks on the river. It looked like fun.

"Simon, where do the kayaks go that I saw on the river?"

"Oh, they go into the river, just below the town, and you can spend days on the river. A company runs it. They supply the canoes and pick you up at the end of the trip"

"It sounds like fun, why don't we do it?"

"Really, you want to do it?"

"Yeah, why not?. It's just down the road, so we don't have to travel far. We could do it over Easter. It should still be warm enough then."

"You have to camp along the river edge at night?"

"That's fine. Do you have a tent?"

"Yeah, I have a small tent. I suppose we could do it. Have you done any canoeing?" Simon asked.

"No, but it can't be that hard. You have, at the expensive boarding school you went too. You can teach me."

Simon wasn't too keen on the idea, but he gave in reluctantly.

They decided to do the three-day trip in a Canadian canoe. It held two people, plus two barrels, to keep their gear dry. Lisa left all the organization to Simon as she was working full time. Simon seemed to have most of the required equipment.

Lisa arrived at Simon's place on Thursday night to find the corner of the lounge full of camping gear and food. Simon had everything organized. Lisa was very impressed. She went over to have a closer look and started to nose around, seeing what he had.

'Don't touch anything", Simon said firmly as he rushed over to her to take the box from her hands and put it back.

"It is all organized, and I don't want it mucked up." Lisa was a bit surprised about how protective Simon was, but OK, he had it organized. She left it to him.

Lisa got her clothes sorted out and packed them into the plastic bag Simon gave her. The next day, they collected the canoe and had a practice run on another smaller river. The guys gave them directions and watched to make sure they knew what to do. Simon yelled at Lisa to paddle on this side or that, depending on the river. She started to get the hang of it.

Once they got back to the starting point, they packed the barrels. Simon was very particular as to what went where. Lisa tried to help, but Simon made it clear that he didn't want any help. Simon was packing the barrels carefully as he muttered to himself about days and requirements. Lisa went over the river edge to watch the other kayaks setting off.

They launched the canoe into the river, and they were off on their adventure. It was sunny and warm, and the river was low. Lisa was in the front of the canoe, and Simon at the back. To begin with, the river was shallow and wide; consequently, they had to get out a couple of times and push the canoe when they ran aground. The river then narrowed up, with channels, deep water, rapids and back eddies.

Lisa got the first view of the rapids. The water would start to swirl with the white water, and the waves would come rushing up to her.

"Simon, Simon, this is a big rapid." All Lisa heard from Simon was, "Paddle! Paddle! Paddle! Keep paddling. On the left, on the left, paddle on the left. On the right, paddle on the right. Paddle."

Lisa laughed with relief and excitement once they made it through the rapids and into the still water. They were both soaked too the skin due to the white waves breaking over them. Lisa, laughing, turned around in the canoe to look at Simon.

"That was fun." Simon grinned back at her as he gently dipped his paddle into the water.

The scenery was breathtaking as they cruised down the river surrounded by bird song.

Past dramatic bluffs, water falls and farm land. Birds swooped over the river, and ducks took off in quacking alarm.

Another rapid came up. "Simon, Simon?"

"Paddle! Paddle! Paddle! On the left, paddle." Simon yelled. Then he went silent. Lisa started yelling, "Paddle, paddle, paddle. What are you doing, Simon?" The back of the canoe seemed to be swinging around with the current with no direction.

They had veered off course and were heading towards the rocks in the rapids. Lisa was trying frantically to paddle around the rocks. It was getting really hard for her to get the paddle in the water. Lisa seemed to be quite high in the air, which didn't seem right. Nothing seemed to be happening from behind her. They were being pushed into a back eddy along the side of the river. "Paddle, paddle. Simon, why aren't you paddling?"

As they slid into the back eddy and the still water, Lisa finally looked behind her. Simon was sitting in the canoe, the paddle lying across his front. The water was up to his chest, and the sides of the canoe were well under water. Simon was just sitting there with a very complacent smile on his face. "Simon?"

"There was nothing I could do." Simon remarked.

They had swamped the canoe, which was why Lisa was so high in the air. The canoe was just about pointing skyward.

God, Simon looked funny. Lisa started laughing as they waited for the back eddy to drift them over to the bank.

All the water had to be emptied out of the canoe. They replaced all of their gear and set off again.

Lisa got better as they progressed and the communication improved. They safely negotiated the worst rapid. It had a major rock in it, which many kayaks got pinned on by the force of the current. As they went past the rock, they could see a kayak struck on the rock. The pressure of the water had bent it.

Down below the rapid they talked to the guy whose kayak was struck. He was still a bit shocked by what had happened. He just kept saying, 'The current hit him, and that was it. He was stuck.'

The company was sending a speed boat to collect him.

Lisa was still sitting in the front of the canoe and constantly getting drenched from the white water hitting her, as they entered the rapids. Lisa had an aerial view of the rapid as the canoe paused briefly before it tipped into the white water.

Lisa would yell, "Simon, Simon, this is a big one", and then waves would break over her. Simon kept yelling, "Paddle! Paddle! Just paddle!"

At the end of the day, they found a grassy bank above a rocky beach. They paddled slowly over to it and allowed the canoe to beach. Lisa got out as Simon held the canoe. It was good to stretch her legs after sitting all day.

They started setting up camp. Simon was very organized and did not want any input from Lisa at all. She tried to help with the food and started pulling some of the containers out of the barrel. "Not that one. It's the wrong one. That's for tomorrow. See, it's got the day written on it," Simon said in an aggrieved voice.

"Well, if it's for tomorrow's dinner, why can't we eat it today? It won't matter, will it?"

"No, I packed that for tomorrow." Simon said as he took it away from Lisa. "Just leave it alone. I will sort it out. I have it all planned out, and now you are wrecking it."

"OK, I won't interfere." Lisa was impressed, surprised and a little bit shocked that he was so rigid. He had every day's food packed and labelled. Simon had also packed a small spade, a container for first aid, including insect repellant, a gas cooker, and a small saucepan. In fact, Simon had it covered. He must have spent hours planning it all out.

Lisa sat back and enjoyed the scenery. The bush-clad hills, the clear blue sky and all of the bird life. The river was gently lapping against the bank as it carried on towards the sea. Simon put up the tent and found the right food container for dinner. Got the fire going and produced a bottle of wine. They sat beside the fire and ate a hot dinner cooked over the flames. The evening slowly settled on the land as the temperature dropped. The fire got brighter, and the view retracted with the night. Lisa and Simon talked in hushed tones as they relaxed by the fire with a glass of wine, snuggled up together in their little spot of light.

In the morning, Simon got the fire going and cooked eggs and bacon on his skillet before they got going. It was peaceful and quiet as they floated down the river with the odd splash from the paddle. The river passed through the back of large sheep and beef stations. At times, they saw cattle or sheep grazing on steep grassed hills, which folded into bush-clad gullies. Most of these stations had originally been serviced from the river by paddle steamers in the 1800's. The river had been the main highway for the early Europeans and the Maori.

They came to a historic site, which Lisa saw from the river. "Look, Simon, that looks interesting; let's stop and have a look."

"Na, it's just some poles; not that interesting."

"Oh, come on. It won't take long, and it's not like we will be here again any time soon."

"If you want," Simon said in a reluctant voice. He wasn't the least bit interested in it. They pulled onto the bank, and Lisa walked up the track to the site of the Hau Hau poles. They were impressive, being very tall with markings on them and a detailed inscription at the bottom. It was quite poignant, giving an insight into another time. She walked back down to the canoe where Simon was waiting. Lisa was a bit bewildered as to why Simon didn't come with her and couldn't understand why he didn't make the effort to make the short walk.

They carried on down the river through gorges, where the water was incredibly deep and slow. They could stop paddling and just let the current take them. In the calmness, they could hear the sounds of the river, overlaid by bird song. Then they would be back to the fast-moving rapids, with Simon yelling, "Paddle! Paddle!"

For their second night, they camped again by the river and ate the food labelled for that day. No wine left, but a peaceful evening. Simon was sticking to his organized routine.

The morning greeted them with bright sunshine but with an autumn twinge. In late morning, the wind got stronger, rippling the water, and the sky got darker. Big, black, purple clouds moved in, and it started to rain. The light changed from bright sunshine to an evening grey colour. Heavy, heavy rain started to fall; they could hear the rain drops landing on the river, constantly pattering. Where they hit the water, little hollows were created. The rain droplet would then bounce, creating many little droplets. Lisa loved it. The fine rain droplets, combined with the temperature difference of the river, created mist, which rose from the surface. They were in a magical world.

Mist rising around them as the rain fell. It was relaxing and peaceful as they slowly moved down the river. The sound of the river lapping on the bank and the splash of the paddles just added to the moment. All the sounds on the river amplified. They started to whisper, not wanting to disturb the magical world as they allowed the current to carry them down the river.

In late afternoon, they paddled through the heavy rain towards the landing, marking the end of the trip. Lisa was disappointed that it had ended, she had loved it. Simon was looking forward to going home and getting out of his wet clothes after the two-hour van trip back to the start.

Chapter Four

The Trip from Hell

Winter slowly crept forward, with early nights and colder temperatures. Driving back on a gravel, one-way, twisting country road in the dark wasn't much fun. The area was very sparsely populated, being large, extensive farm properties and large tracts of forest. A driveway into a property was something to be noted as a landmark.

The locals started to wave to Lisa as she went along the road. Lisa wasn't sure if they waved because she had become a regular traveller or whether they knew who she was visiting. Lisa waved back.

This Sunday evening, Lisa set off to head back to her flat. It had been raining all day and was quite cold. It was a pitch-black night as the low cloud blocked any starlight. Lisa set off knowing the trip was going to be slow, but not too worried as she was reasonably familiar with the road. The start of the trip was on a sealed two-lane road. Then she turned off onto the road called the Forgotten Highway to transverse the dividing range between the coast and the central area of the island. The road wound up and down over steep ridges before it dropped down to follow the river. It then rose again as it traversed another set of steep ridges.

On this night, Lisa travelled along, hunched over the steering wheel trying to see through the windshield while the window wipers went at maximum speed. They still weren't keeping up with the rain. Due to the hills, there was no radio, so she just listened to the sounds of the rain and the vehicle.

Lisa came around a corner where the road had been cut into the bottom of a steep ridge and braked. 'Bloody hell'. There had been a slip, and it reached right across the road. It wasn't deep on the side of the angry, churning river. Lisa sat there for a while contemplating her best option while rain drummed on the roof of the car.

The main slip was on the bank side and just the toe of it was on the river side. Lisa got out of the car for a closer look to see how wide and deep the slip was. It didn't look too bad, as the clay wasn't thick on the riverside, and it wasn't a wide slip. Clearly, she would have to be right on the edge of the river bank to get around. It looked stable. Lisa had no idea if the bank had been undermined by the river.

Lisa got back into the car, soaking wet and took a deep breath. She slowly edged the car forward, hoping like hell that the bank was stable. Her fingers were crossed that the car didn't get stuck in the mud or slide into the river. It would be a long walk in the rain if it did.

The car slid in the mud, but it kept moving forward. She heaved a big sigh and relaxed as she continued on her way.

The rain had gotten heavier, if that was possible. The drains and culverts along the road were struggling to cope with the water coming off the hills. Water was running along the edge of the road, and in places, the headlights reflected off the water running across the road.

Lisa slowly carried on trying to pinpoint where she was as the window wipers went whoosh, whoosh. With the constant twisting and turning of the road, her lights didn't reach very far ahead. The road straightened out in places where river flats occurred, and the headlights would be able to illuminate more than just five meters in front of her. Then, around the toe of another ridge and, the road would twist and turn following the river's path. If she saw a light, it was a farmhouse located up towards the hills. It would be one lone light in a sea of blackness.

Lisa wondered how much further before she got to the better road and she would be able to relax a bit? The road continued to twist in and out around the river valley. She could hear the river water rumbling down below when she wound the window down.

Thinking this trip will never end, Lisa headed around a corner, when through the windscreen, she saw some faint outlines directly in front of her. Lisa slammed on the bakes as her heart jumped into her mouth. The car slid on the wet road before it came to a stop. 'OH MY GOD', there were cattle in the middle of the road! They were within touching distance of the bonnet of the car. Some of them even knocked the car as they moved past it. Another 30cm and Lisa would have hit them. Trying to see black cattle in the dark is impossible. They just blend into the blackness. It was a miracle that she actually stopped in time.

Lisa sat in the car with a thudding heart and watched as the mob moved off the road into the scrub on the other side. "Shit. Bloody hell. I could have had a major accident. What the hell are cattle doing in the middle of the bloody road? Bugger the rain, bugger this bloody awful road. What a shit awful trip this is. I can't keep doing this. Why do I always have to do the driving!" Lisa muttered at the windscreen as she tried to calm herself.

"What next?" Lisa asked herself as she moved the car slowly forward. This trip was shaping up to be a journey from hell. Would it ever end? Her nerves were rattled, her heart still pounding, and the rain was still pouring down.

"If I had hit one of them, it could have been a serious accident."

Lisa remembered when her father had hit a black cattle beast with a car. It had been at night on a busy highway. It had landed on the bonnet of his car before it slid off. Her father was stopped by the side of the road trying to pull the car panels out when a traffic cop had stopped and asked him if he had seen a cattle beast. Dad had informed him very curtly that he had just hit it! The cop then asked him to get into the cop car to help track it down.

The beast had escaped from the local meatworks and was making a bid for freedom. With all of the traffic lights and noises, it must have been freaking out.

It completely wrecked the family car.

The rain didn't let up for the entire trip. Lisa made it off the gravel road through the ghost town and onto the two-lane sealed road. She heaved a deep sigh of relief. Still winding and twisting, but at least Lisa had a wider road to drive around the scattered rocks and streams. For the rest of the drive, she went over the trip and what might have happened. Lisa rapidly came to the conclusion that she didn't want to risk repeating this trip.

Lisa finally made it back to her flat, overwhelmed by turmoil and emotional exhaustion. If she had hit one of the cows, no one would have known until the next day at the earliest. She was used to driving on one-way gravelled roads. She grew up on 19 km of road, which wound its way along a river valley. But that trip took the cake. After that harrying trip, Lisa decided something had to give. She couldn't keep doing this each weekend. Simon would have to make an effort to see her.

Lisa talked to Simon on the phone and explained to him that they had two options. 'Simon, I had a hell of a trip back. There were slips on the road and black cattle; I nearly hit them. I can't keep doing this. Things have to change; either we break up, or one of us moves closer."

"I don't want to break up. I really enjoy your company, and I want to keep seeing you," Simon said in a panicky voice. "Like I said before, it is a good road. You are being a bit dramatic. The trip can't have been that bad. It won't be any bother for me to come and see you."

The following weekend, Lisa stayed home and caught up on household chores. Simon was busy, so couldn't come over.

A week later, Simon had friends visiting, so Lisa agreed to go over again. They had a great weekend catching up, with a roaring fire at night and roast dinners. They sat around the open fireplace in large old lounge chairs, talking and drinking. During the day, they went for bike rides and did target practice.

On Sunday, the plan was for all of them to travel back in tandem. They left the farm early afternoon as their friends Jessie and Matt had to get back down south for work.

Lisa set off in the lead, with Simon bringing up the rear in an old Ford Ute. It was a lovely sunny day with a wintry sun shining. After an hour of travelling, their friends Jessie and Matt, who were in a two-seater sports car, flashed their lights. Lisa pulled over.

Well, bugger me, they were not happy. They all piled out of the vehicles. "There's something wrong with the car", Jessie keeps saying. "I have to keep wrenching the steering wheel to get it to stay on the road."

Matt started walking around the sports car, checking the tyres.

"Since we left the seal, it has graded the road the entire time. It has been a hell of a trip, and we still have miles to go yet." Jessie complained as she swung her arms around, trying to ease the cramp.

Simon was not happy either. "It's a shit road, it's like trying to drive an oil tanker backwards up a stream!"

Lisa just stared at him in shock. "You said it was a good road!"

"I have never driven it! The manager told me it was a good road when I asked him."

"So you had no idea what it was like?"

"Nope"

"So every time you told me it was a good road, you had no idea! When I complained, you said I was overreacting" Lisa couldn't believe it. She had driven the road most weekends in foul weather. This was a good day for driving. Dry and sunny.

Simon started to come over to Lisa's more often, which saved Lisa a lot of driving. Lisa had a stressful job, so being able to hang around the flat was good. They had a lot of fun when he came over. On this night they were in bed when Simon started a discussion about women and their place in the world. He had read this article about how women should be chained in the house. The chain should be long enough to reach from the bedroom to the kitchen.

"Women belong in the house", Simon explained.

"So you believe that women should be the only ones to look after the house?"

"No, I am just telling you about the article I read."

"Really? So you believe it's right?"

"I am just saying what this article said."

Lisa bent her knees and moved her feet up the bed to rest gently against Simon's side. "So you agree with the article?"

"Well, it has a point, that women are better at looking after the house than a man", Lisa pushed with all of her strength. Simon shot across the bed, hit the wall on the other side of the bed and dropped to the floor. Lisa was very impressed with the result. Far better than she had thought it would be. Lisa peered over the side of the bed but couldn't see anything in the dark. After a short silence, Lisa heard this very pathetic voice ask. "Can I get back into bed now?"

"Depends on your opinion."

"I didn't say I agreed with the article. I was just pointing out what it said," Simon said in a shocked voice as he climbed back into bed.

Lisa brought her feet up again.

"No. No. I don't agree with it." Simon said in a very firm voice.

Lisa overheard Simon telling some friends what had happened a week later. He was laughing about it.

"It was like a cartoon. I shot across the bed and hit the wall. But I didn't drop right away. I had this moment when everything stopped, like Coyote on Road Runner. I knew what was going to happen. I knew it was going to hurt, and there was nothing I could do about it. Then I hit the floor."

Chapter Five

Turning Point

One weekend, Simon said, "Sarah, my sister, is in Queenstown. I thought I would go down and stay with her for a week. I haven't been to Queenstown before."

"That sounds wonderful. Queenstown is a cool place." Lisa said

"It would be great if you came."

"I will have to put an application into work to see if I can get the time off. It will probably take a week before I get an answer." Lisa explained

"I am going to book the ticket this week."

Simon went home, and Lisa went to work on Monday. Lisa put in her application for a week off. It was approved at the end of the week.

Lisa rang Simon and said. "I have heard back, and my leave has been approved, so I can come."

"I have booked my ticket."

"That's fine. I can book a ticket and come down on another plane."

"I have booked my ticket. I have not made arrangements for you to come." Simon said in a firm voice.

"What are you saying?"

"I have booked and you are not coming. Why can't I see my sister without you being there?"

Lisa was surprised by his attitude and hurt. "So you don't want me to come?" Lisa had gone to the trouble of applying for the leave, because she thought he wanted her to come.

"No, I don't have to do everything with you. This is my time."

"Well, if you feel like that, I hope you have a nice time." Lisa hung up the phone. She was surprised by Simon's attitude, especially as he had originally asked her to come. It seemed a bit weird, and Lisa pondered that as she got ready for work the next day. Lisa cancelled her leave application. Everyone in the office was surprised she was still at work. They couldn't understand why Simon didn't want her to go with him. Lisa was hurt about it but put on a brave face.

Not a word was heard from Simon. For the following five days, silence. At the end of the fifth day, on the way home, Lisa stopped and bought a bottle of white wine. Her flatmate was away, so it was just Lisa at home. She ran a bubble bath, got a glass of wine and climbed into the bath. It was lovely. Lisa had over done the bubbles, so bubbles went everywhere. She sat in the bath and drank her wine. She decided that Simon and her were over. He didn't want her to go on holiday with him. If he had a reason for not wanting her to go, then fine. Just 'I don't want you to come' wasn't really a reason.

Lisa drank some more wine and decided that her life was just fine on her own. If he couldn't even make one phone call, why was she wasting her time? Simon could go hang. Lisa felt a bit better after making the decision. She had spent the last five days hoping for some contact from Simon. It wasn't like it was impossible for him to contact her. Just one lousy phone call. How hard was that?

Lisa went to work the next day. The mail arrived and in it were 4 postcards, all from Simon. He was having a good time. He had been jet boating, skiing, and seeing the local sights. He had been to a maze and said it would be great to take the kids one day. He missed her and wished Lisa was there. 'Simon, if you hadn't been so fixed in your plans, then I could have been with you.' Lisa thought.

Lisa sat in the office looking at the postcards. They were dated consecutive days, so Simon had written them every day he had been away. She was pleased with the comment about taking the kids one day. Lisa was still pissed off about the trip and no phone calls, but at least he had written. She couldn't blame him for the postal service. Simon came back excited about his trip. He rang Lisa up and told her all about it.

"I really missed you. I kept thinking it would have been really cool to share everything with you," Simon said longingly.

"Oooh, it's nice that you missed me. I didn't hear anything from you for five days, so I was really pissed off with you." Lisa then went on and explained about the postcards. Simon laughed. "That's hilarious. You were going to break up with me, then all of the postcards arrived. Ha Ha Ha, bet you were surprised to get the cards. That's brilliant."

"I wasn't happy, Simon."

"Then you had to forgive me. Ha Ha."

One quiet weekend at Simon's place, he told Lisa about his interests.

"My most enjoyable time was wandering up the farm creeks looking for fossils. I loved finding old fossils and bringing them home. Dad never understood that. He wanted me to go farming; being the eldest boy, I was to inherit the farm." Simon sighed and looked really sad as he took a long drink from the beer bottle. "They completely ignored what I was interested in and called it stupid and rubbish."

"Don't you like farming?"

"No. Don't want anything to do with it." Simon heaved a big sigh.

"But you are here working on the farm? Why didn't you do something else?"

"I did. I left varsity after a year, where Dad had signed me up for an Agricultural degree, straight out of school and went and enrolled in electrical engineering at polytechnic."

"Well, what happened with that?"

"Oh, I did it for a year and decided I didn't like it. Then I took a year and pumped petrol at a gas station while living at home. That was when they owned a farm two hours north of here. Dad was pushing me to go back and finish the Agricultural degree, so I did. I had a good time. Daddy paid for everything, so I enjoyed myself. The money just kept coming." Simon smiled sadly at Lisa.

"With an Agricultural degree, you can work in all sorts of areas. You could go anywhere in the world with it."

"I don't have the degree. I haven't finished it."

"Why, what happened?"

"Oh, I was home when the results came at the end of the fourth year, and Dad saw them. He looked at them and said, 'You had better leave varsity and come and work for me', so here I am. I still have a year to go. It's a three-year degree. So far, I have been there for four years, and I have a year to go."

Lisa just looked at Simon, really surprised. She had put herself through Varsity and worked her butt off to pass everything. This whole relaxed attitude was completely foreign to her.

"What happened? You are intelligent, you could have passed."

"Ooh, yeah, weeell. I went to all of the lectures but never handed an assignment in."

"My god, it's a wonder you passed anything. The assignments make up a massive portion of the final mark."

Simon smiled. "I had to sit most papers twice to pass."

"So you don't want to go farming, but you are working for your father on his farm with no plans."

"It's what is expected of me. Something will happen. I have you now, so it will be alright."

Simon looked so sad and lost, so Lisa gave him a hug and a kiss. She felt so bad for him, but she was also having a hard time wrapping her head around the situation. All Lisa could see were opportunities. My god, how many sons have the chance to inherit a farm?

Simon took Lisa to his celebration dinner for a course he had finished. On the way, they passed an expensive private boarding school.

"That's where I went for two years. I was 10 when I started."

"Really?" Lisa replied as she looked at all of the mature trees and the stone buildings; she glimpsed between the trees. "Did you enjoy it?"

"It took a while for me to settle in, as I didn't know anyone, and all the other boys played sports. I had never played for a team, as my parents wouldn't take us in to play on the weekends. I only got to go home in the holidays, since we lived three hours away. I was quite lonely". Simon said in a sad voice and then heaved a big sigh.

A bit further down the road, they came upon a very expensive private high school. "I spent five years at that school."

"How did you get on at that school?"

"I made some good friends there, but the cool kids were in the top sports teams. I wasn't good enough for that. I did play hockey and my team won the third division one year. That was pretty cool. It was the year I was on the Spirit of Adventure." Simon laughed. "It was a good year that."

"That would have been exciting", Lisa replied, thinking she never did anything like that.

"I didn't really fit into any group in my early years at the school, so I was quite lonely. To make myself feel like I belonged, I began taking pictures. Dad bought me a good camera, and I became the unofficial photographer. It made me part of the group. I really enjoyed taking the pictures.

"I haven't seen you taking any photos."

"Nah.... I don't have a camera any more. I miss not having a camera." Simon looked over at Lisa and smiled.

"One of the cool things I did was go on the Spirit of Adventure. I loved it and never got sick. It's a sailing yacht and all of us had to sail it. We had to climb up the ropes to unfurl the sail, navigate, cook the food; in fact, we had to do everything. The instructors just told us what to do. It was so cool. I was even made captain one day and got to tell everyone what to do." Simon was smiling as he remembered his days at sea.

"That sounds like fun. I would never do anything like that. I get really seasick." Simon laughed. "Landlubber. I told Dad how much I liked it, so in the final year of school, Dad bought me a sailing yacht, which was stored at the school. I had my car licence so in the allocated periods, I towed the yacht with my car and went sailing on the local lake. It was some of my most enjoyable time.

"Did you go with anyone?"

"No, I just went on my own. I just sailed around the lake for two hours, then travelled back to the school."

"You weren't tempted to go other places?"

"No, it never occurred to me to do something else. I was allowed to sail, so that's what I did."

The dinner celebration went off well. There was good music and food. Lisa just followed Simon around as she didn't know anyone, but they all seemed like really nice people. During the speeches, they all had to sit around the room. Lisa was wearing a full skirt, which fell below the knee.

On one side, it had a split up the side to mid-thigh, so when she sat down, it fell open. Lisa didn't consider it too exposing, so she was a bit surprised when Simon kept picking up the back skirt to pull it over her knee to stop her thigh from being seen. He was quite obsessed about it.

Chapter Six

Taking the Boyfriend Home

Lisa's family lived on a sheep and beef farm in the south island. It was a lovely area with mountains, beaches, orchards and many alternative lifestyle people. She was a bit worried about taking Simon down to meet them; her mother could be really nasty, and he would be only her second boyfriend to be introduced to her parents. You never knew how they would react. She had rung her mother up and mentioned that it was quite a serious relationship.

Lisa had talked her sister, Judith, into coming up with her family to stay in the other house with them.

On the day they arrived they went up to see her parents to discover her mother had laid it on. She had her elderly aunt out from town; the tables were set up in the carport with napkins, little tea cakes and the best china. Lisa looked in disbelief. Her mother never did anything like this.

Her mother was running around being the perfect hostess. Simon loved it. He was encased in a chair with a cake and cup of tea, chatting to everyone. Her mother kept asking him if he needed anything else and made a great fuss of him.

Lisa's father caught up with Lisa and chatted to his sister. He didn't say much, which was unusual for him. The whole afternoon was a picture of how you would imagine a perfectly prosed loving family. It was totally unnatural and nothing like the family. It was like the beginning to a horror movie where everyone is perfect. Lisa wandered around, wondering when the storm was going to break. It didn't; her mother and brother stayed sweet the entire time.

Lisa showed Simon the farm and the local sights. He had a great time and loved it. David, her brother, took him out hunting for pigs and spotlighting for possums. The first day they went out they got a small pig. That night, they went spotlighting and Simon shot a possum, which fell out of the tree with a loud thump. Simon was blown away with how big it was. Twice the size of the North Island possums.

The next day, they went pig hunting again. This time, they got a bigger pig. Simon refused to go spotlighting again as he was scared the possum might be bigger still. Everyone laughed about it.

After a very successful week, they went home. Lisa was still in shock over how her mother and brother had behaved for the whole week. It was not normal behaviour for them. Simon thought her family were lovely and didn't understand why Lisa had been nervous about visiting them.

Chapter Seven

Changes

"I really don't like driving that road. It's a pain. We need to work something out before winter," Simon said one day.

"I don't suppose you have much option in moving?"

"No. Can't exactly move a farm," Simon said, grinning.

"I will look for another job, which is a bit closer", Lisa said, resigned to the situation. Lisa found a job with another bank in a town closer to Simon's parents, Mary and Robert. Still an hour away from Simon but on a much better road.

Simon's parents suggested that she stay with them, as they had a separate sleepout and it was close to work. Consequently, she got to know his parents quite well. Mary was a good cook and always provided large cooked meals, served with serving bowls, silver cutlery and tablecloths. They were very social and seemed very happy about the arrangement. Simon would drive up from the other farm, on a two-lane sealed road, and visit.

Lisa wasn't aware that they saw more of their son by doing this than they normally did.

The discussion around the dinner table centred on the farm, weather, economics and local gossip. Simon never said a lot, as his father would lead the discussion and make statements. Simon spent most of his time with his head down.

Lisa settled into her new job and got to know the area. It was very attractive, with rivers, limestone outcrops, caves, native forest and rolling farmland. Her area went right out to the coast, so she did a lot of travelling.

The community was very traditional, with some dairy farming in one area and the rest was large sheep and beef properties. Many of them were two or three-generation farms. The local town had 500 inhabitants and sported a club, a pub, two stock and station agencies, two garages, a vet, an engineering shop, a post office, two banks, a trucking company, a primary school, where everyone had gone and a high school. Everybody knew everybody, and most of them were related. She soon realized that she had to be so careful as to what she said.

They all knew who she was going out with and speculation was rife as to where they would live. The manager was concerned about their job and locals, who were friends with the manager, were expressing their concerns about the future. Lisa would be seeing them about work and end up in a discussion about the farm and what was going to happen. It seemed safer to say nothing.

Robert owned two farms both with managers on them. There was talk about purchasing another farm for Simon to run, but nothing had been decided, and Lisa didn't know how serious they were.

Simon came up for dinner one night when he said after tea, "It's a nice evening. Why don't we go for a walk around the garden."

Lisa was quite happy to oblige, as it gave them a chance to talk without his parents present. "Sounds good, just let me get some shoes on."

They went out holding hands and went around to the front to where some brick steps lead down to the lower terrace towards the driveway. At this point, Simon got down on his knee and asked, "Will you marry me?"

Lisa smiled. "Yes, definitely yes", Whereupon upon Simon gave her a big hug and kissed her. They headed back inside to share the news.

Mary asked, "What are you doing about a ring?"

"I thought you had one lying around here we could use", replied Simon.

Lisa was at a bit of a loss as to what was going on. Mary disappeared and came back with two ring boxes and Simon got to choose which one. The ring had belonged to Simon's great grand mother and was her engagement ring. It had a central diamond surrounded by many small ones.

Simon slipped it on Lisa's finger. It was a bit big.

Robert opened a bottle of champagne, and they celebrated the engagement. For the rest of the evening, Lisa kept noticing the diamonds flashing when they caught the light.

Simon took Lisa to the hunt club season-ending dinner. It was at a local's house and was very informal. They all sat around the lounge in chairs or on the floor and chatted. Lisa enjoyed meeting all of them and felt very welcomed.

She was congratulated on her engagement and told she had a good one. "Simon is so nice and always helpful. He will never do anything to hurt you." The hostess said to her. Lisa smiled and felt really good about her future.

Chapter Eight

Wedding Plans

Lisa knew that her parents would not contribute to a wedding. Her mother did not approve of weddings. She had repeatedly said. 'weddings were just a ceremony to sacrifice the girl on the altar of marriage. That was why the girl wore white.' Lisa's mother had been married twice, and her parents had paid for her sister's first wedding but not her second one. Lisa knew that if it had been left up to Mum, they wouldn't have paid for the first one. It was Dad who had insisted on doing it properly.

Dad was old now, and Mum made all the decisions. The wedding had to be low cost as that was all she could afford. It was pointless even asking if they would help. Based on past experience, it would end with her mother yelling down the phone at her. Lisa didn't expect Simon's parents to help as it was the bride's family who paid for weddings.

Mary asked Lisa about the wedding plans.

"I am going to try and do the wedding for $5000. I am thinking a potluck meal. If we could set up something on the farm with a marquee. Would that be OK?"

"Oh no, you can't do a wedding like that. We are not going to have our son get married in a cheap arrangement. What about your parents? Won't the wedding be down south?"

"My parents won't help with the wedding. My mother does not approve of weddings."

"Oh." Mary looked shocked. "You can't have a wedding like that. It's not suitable. We will pay for the wedding."

"Are you sure?"

"Yes, absolutely, we will cover the cost of the wedding."

"Thank you."

Wow, Lisa was going to have a proper wedding. She started to rethink the whole plan.

Lisa expected that they would end up on the farm where Simon was currently working. It was the general expectation of the locals as well. She was looking to find work in the closer town.

Robert decided that the current manager on the farm where they lived would move south and replace the manager down there. Simon would take over the running of the finishing farm under his father's direction. It all sounded practical and workable. Lisa was busy working, so didn't pay a lot of attention to what was being organized. Between the wedding and work, she had very little time.

Simon seemed happy and it all seemed to be falling into place. One day, they all went down to show Lisa where they would be living. It was a small cottage on a private driveway about a kilometre from

Simon's parent's house. Lisa wasn't terribly impressed with the house. It was very basic and needed redecoration.

The house was small with two bedrooms average size and one small bedroom which only fitted a single bed. All the bedrooms had built-in wardrobes and were carpeted, as was the lounge.

There was an open-plan dining, lounge, and kitchen area. The kitchen had an L-shape on one side with the 1950s Formica bench and cupboards below and above. There was a stainless steel benchtop and sink. It had cupboards underneath and wooden windows above it, which looked out onto the driveway.

The kitchen and dining areas faced east, so they got the sun in the morning, as did the main bedroom. The main bedroom and the other bedroom across the hall each had a wall facing north. The small bedroom windows faced west, as did the lounge windows next to the fire place. The predominant wind direction was west.

Looking out the windows you could see the wind sculptured trees in the paddocks. On the downward side, the trees looked like proper trees with straight trunks. You could see the struggle some of them had on the windward side as they were stunted, bent and twisted with the finer branches and leaves only present on the down wind side.

Beyond the trees, they looked out over grassy slopes, dropping down to a small valley being the neighbours and then rising again to roll away in the distance. All farmland, but no houses were visible, as they were all located over the rise. Beyond them were more hills slowly rising into steeper ridges covered in forest.

In the main bedroom, they could see the grease mark on the wall where the manager's head had rested. The walls were all marked and scratched and painted dark colours, which intensified the impression of smallness.

The bathroom was off the kitchen with a separate toilet. The basin was free-standing with a cupboard underneath. The bath had walls on three sides with a shower curtain. A small window fitted between the wall cabinet above the basin and the bath.

There was a 1950s back porch with a laundry off it and access to the toilet on the other side. The laundry had a double concrete tub, room for the washing machine and some shelves. It was dark and dingy.

The house looked tired, but Lisa felt sure with a fresh coat of paint it would look better. For them, it seemed OK, and it would be their own space.

It had a fenced-off area around the house with some mature trees. Apart from insisting the house being painted, Lisa didn't notice anything else. It was a basic small cottage, clad in white brick located on a farm. Nothing really stood out as being a problem.

Lisa was working full time and travelling up and down the country to get the wedding dress made, picking up bridesmaids, and organizing fittings, flowers and invitations. It was a blur. Lisa was so tired she was running on adrenaline only.

Lisa organized for Simon to meet her in a main centre, four hours away. Simon arrived a wee bit late, and they went and caught up with friends. They enjoyed the weekend and sorted out what Simon would be wearing for the wedding. He really wanted a top hat.

One weekend, Lisa was staying at Simon's place and noticed an open letter sitting on the side table. She happened to glance at it in passing and saw the name of a courthouse on it.

"Simon, what's this?".

"Oh, you don't need to worry about that."

"What is it?" Lisa started to read it. Simon had been caught speeding when he was going through the National Park. He had been caught by a cop and clocked at 152km/hr. That meant it had to go to court. Simon didn't attend the court session, but he wrote a letter.

"Simon, you kept your licence! You are so lucky, you could have lost your licence. How come you kept it?"

"Oh, I wrote a pleading letter." Simon gave a bit of a giggle and looked a bit shame-faced.

"What letter? Can I see it?"

"Oh, I just told them that I was running late. I was stressed cause of the wedding, and I didn't want to get into trouble with you for being late. Stuff like that."

"So you blamed me for the speeding?"

"Yeah, well, I got off, so all good."

Lisa was absolutely blown away that the court had accepted his argument about not wanting to upset his fiance by being late. He had just got a fine. A hefty fine, but just a fine.

It was getting closer to the wedding and Lisa was juggling the last fittings for the dresses. The dressmaker was six hours away, so it made for a long weekend of driving. Twelve hours round trip.

Lisa's bridesmaids were Simon's sister, Sarah and her best friend Rose. Her daughter was the flower girl. Sarah was still overseas, so all her fittings were done from measurements. They just hoped they were right.

Lisa and Rose were coming back from a fitting on a Sunday afternoon. They came through a small town when the Ute in front of Lisa suddenly stopped, with no indication at all. Lisa ran into the back of it as her reaction seemed to be in slow motion from being so tired.

Fortunately, all they hit was his tow bar. The front of the car got a dent in the bumper, but that was it. It made a loud banging noise and everyone on the main street was staring at them. It was a young farm boy who obviously didn't drive around town much.

Rose was worried about how little sleep Lisa was getting and insisted they stop at Simon's, who was very surprised to see them. Rose gave Lisa a massage, before she drove the last hour and a half home. Rose refused to drive on New Zealand roads. She was from New Zealand but had married Ross, an Aussie years earlier and they now had three children. Lisa had been her bridesmaid.

Mary was keen to get involved with the wedding, so Lisa passed details over to her like hiring the hall and the menus. They used a lot of local fundraising groups, and the local school sports group did the catering and waitressing.

One night a month before the wedding, Lisa got a phone call from her mother. "I was visiting your aunt (Lisa's Dad's sister) yesterday when I was in town. They asked me about the wedding. Aunt Florrie wanted to know what colour the bridesmaids' dresses are, how many bridesmaids you are having, and how many are attending. What your wedding dress is like? I couldn't answer any of her questions. It made me look bad. Aunt Florrie even said, 'You don't know anything about your own daughter's wedding' in a shocked voice. Now you tell me about your wedding so I have something to talk about, and I won't look bad."

Lisa thought, what a selfish thing to say. She didn't care a damn about her wedding, she just wanted to make herself look good. She had not made any offers of help or enquired about the wedding at all. Only when it made her look bad did she want to know about the wedding.'

Lisa didn't expect her mother to come to her wedding. She never had time to go anywhere. Lisa knew that her mother's focus was her son, not her daughters. They were a by-product of having a son. Everything had to be given to him.

The whole family had come to her graduation ceremony, five years earlier, which had surprised Lisa. That would have been Dad's doing. Lisa had graduated from the same university that he had graduated from. He was so very proud of her.

It seemed easier to provide some information about the wedding. It wasn't worth the row for not doing it. Lisa gave her mother a brief description of the bridesmaids, her wedding dress, how many were coming and where the wedding was being held. She seemed happy about that and said goodbye.

The wedding invitations had been designed with a picture of the church on the front. The local bookshop had printed them on pale yellow paper. In the evenings Lisa sat and threaded red ribbon through the pages to make a booklet. She then had to address all the envelopes, apply the stamps and post them. It involved a lot of licking. The pile of envelopes was slowly growing.

Lisa got another phone call from her mother a couple of days later. "I have not contributed anything to your wedding. There's not a lot I can do from down here, but I could post the invitations out. You send me the invitations and the list of addresses, and I will post them."

Lisa was stunned by her offer. She was also very, very scared.

"Mum, you don't need to do that. The invitations are nearly done." Lisa replied, as she looked at the pile she needed to finish. "Thanks for the offer but I've got it sorted."

"Oh, I thought I could help. Well, goodbye." The phone went dead.

Once Lisa got off the phone, she wondered what had prompted that. This was the first offer of help her mother had made. There was no way she was going to risk her mother posting out the invitations. She could seriously have screwed up the wedding if Lisa had given her the invitations.

She could clearly visualize the invitations sitting in her mother's car under the back window and never being posted. She wouldn't have had any guests at her wedding. Mum would have said something like, 'Oh, I don't know how it happened, I just forgot to post them. I'm so sorry, I was so busy I just forgot about them. You still got married, and that's all that matters'.

Lisa went back to addressing the invitations, thinking, 'There was no way she was going to trust her mother with them. She could have caused so much heartache'.

Lisa's wedding dress was cream silk with a fitted bodice and a full skirt. She had piping on the neck and sleeves and a bow at the back in the tartan colours of Simon's family. They were very into family history and the Scottish clans. The bridesmaids' fitted bodices also had the same tartan colours above a knee-length cream full 1950s silk skirt. They looked stunning and suited the girls. Lisa was delighted with them.

Lisa had a waterfall bouquet of flowers with red roses, and the bridesmaid had red roses mixed with other flowers. Both bridesmaids had a comb in their hair with red silk roses attached.

Lisa expected to walk down the aisle on her own since her father was in hospital. She was quite comfortable about it as it showed it was her decision to marry Simon. She wasn't property being 'given away'.

She got another phone call from her mother. "Your brother is going to come up to walk you down the aisle. It will be good for him to get off the farm."

"It's fine; he doesn't need to do that." Lisa said in a shocked voice. This was the last thing she expected or wanted.

"No, it will be a good experience for him. He will see new things and meet new people."

"No, really, it's fine." Lisa replied frantically, thinking of a reason why he shouldn't.

"Nonsense, he will be arriving, and I understand he will be staying with Simon."

Oh bugger. She had already organized it with Simon's family.

Lisa didn't want him to ruin her wedding. David could throw a complete screaming match over some minor detail and then smash things up. Lisa took a deep, shaky breath and weighed up her options. She really didn't want him at her wedding and, certainly, not to walk her down the aisle.

You never knew how he would react. You were constantly walking on eggshells around him. He could carry grudges for months about some silly little thing. Then, out of the blue, he would suddenly start yelling about some perceived insult. You would be wondering what the hell he was on about as he smashed things and threatened you. It was like dealing with an unpredictable time bomb, not knowing when it would go off.

He had made it clear that he couldn't stand his sisters. He wanted his sisters as far away from him as possible. Lisa was a threat to him, inheriting all of Mum and Dad's assets. This concern of his was aided and encouraged by their mother.

Their mother gave him everything she could and defended his actions no matter how in the wrong he was. Lisa had grown up with constantly being told it was her fault that David had attacked her or smashed up her property. She had upset him.

Lisa remembered once when she arrived on the motorbike and David was talking to their mother and sister.

Lisa had just come back from putting a mob of sheep back in the paddock cause David had left the gate open. 'Should I say anything to him or not?' Lisa thought. 'He may hit me or yell at me if I do, but he really needs to know.' She looked at her mother and sister and thought, 'He won't attack me with them present. I will tell him what has happened.'

Lisa stopped next to David and said, "You left the gate open down below, and the sheep had got out". David reached over and grabbed Lisa by the throat and, pulled her off the bike and threw her on the ground. He then walked away very angrily.

Lisa's mum rushed over to her and said, "What did you say to upset him? You must have said something to upset him like that."

Lisa had just looked at her mother, with her hand on her throat, where he had grabbed her and shook her head as she walked away. Judith, Lisa's sister, just stood there, probably in shock. David could do no wrong. It was never his fault.

Lisa didn't want him to ruin her day, but it looked like she was stuck. If she stood her ground, then she would have to explain to her future in-laws why, and Mum would launch into how she was being unreasonable and a liar.

It was true he had lived a very sheltered life, having left school when he was thirteen. He was supposed to be on correspondence, but reality was that he didn't do any school work. He just worked on the farm. Lisa was never sure why he left school then. Mum was still going to work, so why she pulled him out of school part way through a year she never understood. Perhaps there was a problem at the school. Perhaps he had gotten into trouble. It was never discussed.

David turned up two days before the wedding. Lisa didn't see him apart from the rehearsal, when he hardly spoke to her. Lisa didn't say anything to him at all.

"He's a bit strange. You can't sit down and have a conversation with him. He won't sit still. He's constantly on the move. He just takes off on foot or on the push bike. I never know where he is or when he will be back." Simon said in a bewildered voice. Quite clearly, Simon hadn't met anyone like him before.

"One night, we were watching TV, and he just suddenly leapt to his feet and started running across the paddocks. I had no idea where he was going or why. He came back about two hours later with no explanation or comment. He just sat down and started watching TV again. He's the weirdest person I have ever met."

Lisa was busy meeting aeroplanes and organizing final fittings in between, holding down a full-time job. Judith and their mother arrived the day before the wedding. Her relationship with her mother was at the point where she didn't care whether she came or not. She was a very difficult woman who had gone out of her way to be really nasty to her over the years. Judith, Lisa's sister, had gone to a lot of trouble to organise things so she could come.

They had got Dad admitted to the hospital, where he was safe. Dad wasn't immobile, but at the age of 87, he was at risk of falling and couldn't really be left on his own. Dad had recently suffered two major heart attacks, which had involved lengthy stays in the hospital.

Their mother, aged 68, was a calculating, manipulative woman who played games. Sometimes, she would yell, demand, threaten and throw major tantrums, including slamming doors, smashing crockery and bash saucepans up and down on the bench till they were dented. Once she got her way, it would all stop.

Other times, she would play the pathetic woman who couldn't do anything. She would just sit there and make you do all the explaining and encouraging. It was like dealing with a blob, which would make no effort at all. It made Lisa feel like she was wading through treacle. It was emotionally draining.

Lisa's Mum would sit in a chair and say, 'Oh, I couldn't do that, or I wouldn't know what to do' and play the poor defenceless woman who was incapable of making a decision. Everyone had to run around after her and show her options and, hold her hand, tell her how much they appreciated, loved her and plead or encourage her.

Judith had taken her shopping to buy an outfit. This involved driving her into town, talking to the sales ladies, choosing an outfit, talking her into it while her mother just lapped up the attention, all the while acting like an emotional lead weight.

Judith had organized the plane flights, a suit for David and the accommodation. Their mother had just sat back and let everyone do it all for her. She played the part of being an emotionally crippled, abused woman, who needs comfort, combined with an expectation that you owe her this. It's your duty to your mother.

The only one, apart from her sister, who Lisa wanted at her wedding was her father, and he couldn't come.

Chapter Nine

The Wedding

The wedding was in the autumn, which suited Lisa, as she loved the autumn colours. It had been a dry season, so the colours on the trees were brilliant. Driving to work each day, Lisa would watch the trees slowly change colours. Every time she went past them, she kept telling them. 'Just hold on a bit longer. Just a bit longer. Just another two weeks, another week, a few more days' Lisa really wanted the wedding photos to have the autumn colours.

The wedding was held in a small white church on the edge of town next to a park and just around from the hall. Two Rolls Royce, lent by Simon's family, were the bridal cars driven by Simon's cousins.

In the morning, Lisa and her wedding party excitedly went to hair appointments, did the make-up, dressed and checked the flowers. Linda's house was a bustle of exciting activity. Once everyone was ready after some minor dramas, Lisa was left on her own in the bedroom just checking the dress. The dress looked beautiful and fitted perfectly. The work her friend had put into it was incredible. She had arrived with the dress the day before, only to discover that Lisa had lost weight. It all had to be taken in. She had been working on it right up to the last minute.

It was a princess cut with splashes of bright red tartan colour. It was dramatic, and Lisa loved it.

Lisa looked in the mirror and saw this exquisitely dressed girl and wondered what the hell she was doing. Her heart was pounding, and she took some deep breaths. 'Did she really want to marry Simon? Were they right for each other? Was Simon who she hoped or thought he was'.

"In the time they had known each other, there were periods when Simon seemed to have a dark side. Should I just run away?' The thought of walking out the door and running for it was very attractive. She knew that Simon had issues with his family and didn't seem to know what he wanted. Just to walk away from all of the drama, work, stress and just disappearing with no concerns was appealing.

They had only known each other for a short period of time; it had been a fast-moving relationship. Lisa enjoyed Simon's company, and his family seemed fine.

Lisa had focused on work for most of her life and, apart from some very good friends, had lived a quiet social life. She didn't expect angels singing or butterflies. For her, life was practical, and individuals worked with what was available. Life was a struggle.

After her mother's and brother's behaviour towards her, she wanted a partner who wouldn't hurt her and would support her. She was always looking to build something; with Simon and the farm, she could see a lifestyle, which she would enjoy. 'Was that what Simon wanted? Am I marrying Simon for the right reasons?'

'Then there was Simon's past life. It had come as a shock when Simon had told her about the child. The baby. It was only six months old!' Lisa was getting very worried and wished her father was here. He was a good judge of character.

Lisa had never seen the baby or met the mother. Simon had only told her about the baby boy three months ago.

Simon had said, "I want nothing to do with the child and that the mother is a liar."

'What did that say about Simon? He had a child, and he wanted nothing to do with it. Didn't he care? Perhaps fellows don't care how many children they have? After all, history has shown that men have fathered children all over the world and have nothing to do with them. It just didn't seem right.' Lisa couldn't understand why he didn't want to meet the child.

The bridal cars arrived, which galvanized everyone into action for the last-minute checks. Lisa thought of all the guests, the arrangements made, the effort made by all of her friends and realized it was a bit too late to run. She had to go through with it all. The bridesmaids looked wonderful, and the little flower girl was a picture. She was so proud of her dress and little matching shoes. She kept pulling up her dress to look at the shoes with their little satin bows.

David turned up wearing a suit. He did a big thing about how Lisa's hand should rest on his hand while they walked down the aisle.

Apparently, he had seen it somewhere. Lisa saw her mother and sister sitting up at the front of the church. She hadn't seen or spoken to her mother since she had arrived.

The trees were a riot of autumn colours, which provided a spectacular contrast to the white and black of the wedding party. Simon was delighted with his top hat and kept holding it up or tilting his head for effect. He kept making suggestions to the photographer, who was very patient.

The meal was fully catered, which included a homegrown cattle beast. The caterers were all locals who all knew or worked with each other. Lisa would be sitting at the top table, while the waitress had a discussion about the farm with Simon, as her husband was the fencer.

The atmosphere at the reception was vibrant and full of positive energy. Everyone got on with each other as they all came from the same rural culture.

Lisa's mother, partway through the reception, decided that Judith, David and her would all go back to the motel for the evening. "It's time we leave, as it's late" Judith was accommodating and arranged for them all to go. Once they had Mum settled, Judith then said, "We are going back to the reception".

"No, you need to stay. There's no reason for you to leave me; it's nearly over anyway", said their mother, who had not expected them to leave her alone in the motel room. She expected to be able to talk about the night and make nasty comments about the other guests. This was something she always did. Halfway through something, she would suddenly decide everyone needed to leave now. It didn't matter if it was something you wanted to stay for, if she wanted to leave, then they all had to go.

Judith pointed out, "The reception is still going, and there is no reason why David or I need to miss it". Mum was gob-smacked that they actually left her.

At the reception, Lisa was very surprised to see her brother dancing with Mary. He looked like an octopus with his arms and legs at funny angles.

Simon and Lisa went off to the honeymoon suite at a historical hotel. It had been built in the early 1900s. The high-ceiling rooms had polished native wood panelling with ornate carving and plasterwork. A large carved sweeping staircase took them upstairs to the spacious bedrooms with en-suites.

Lisa and Simon just collapsed on the bed and slept late. They had to get back to the in-laws' open house.

They paid for the room on the way out. The clerk was itemizing the account when he came to the champagne bottle. After he explained the cost of it, Lisa promptly gave it back to him unopened. His face took on a look of utter shock, and he stammered. Quite clearly, it was rare for the bottle to be returned. It saved them a lot of money.

Lisa and Simon caught up with everyone at the in-laws and said goodbye to those travelling long distances.

They discovered that there had been some drama. Robert wouldn't say what had happened, but Mary, with help from Sarah, explained.

Simon's family had cleaned up the hall after they left. Robert was tasked with removing the decorations, which included many potted trees and plants, back to the house. As he drove slowly down the deserted main street with the Ute back filled to bursting, the police sirens and lights suddenly went off. Robert, a very conservative farmer, was shocked that two police cars were chasing him down the road. He pulled over wondering what on earth they wanted with him. He sat in the Ute as the police officers approached, thinking perhaps this was a random breath testing stop.

They then proceeded to question him very sternly as to where he had obtained the plants. Robert, who considered himself an upright pillar of the community, found himself a suspect in a crime wave at one am in the morning.

They accused him of pinching the council plants, which were quite clearly in the back of his Ute. They had the culprit and the evidence. It was an open-and-shut case as far as the police were concerned.

Once Robert got his head around the situation he then had to do a lot of talking and explaining to convince the police he was not a thief. It took a lot of explaining, which included producing the wedding speech, gift cards and invitations, before they would believe him. The police finally accepted that he hadn't pinched the council plants. His case was helped by the fact he was wearing a suit and they didn't find any digging equipment or any soil on his shoes. The family thought it was hilarious.

Lisa just crashed after three months of non-stop go. They pottered around their house unpacking and sorting things out. Simon had a look at the books Lisa unpacked. She had the complete works of 'The Clan of the Cave Bear' by Jean M Auel. Simon was fascinated and promptly gathered them up to read. That was his reading sorted for the next few months.

Simon had moved into the house before Lisa, so as far as Dixie was concerned, Lisa was once again interfering with her life. Dixie proceeded to defend her spot in the bed between them. She would sit there glaring at Lisa while she flexed her claws. Simon would have to put her outside.

Simon had organized a short honeymoon, and he was very cagey about where they were going.

Rotorua turned out to be their destination. Simon stood in the motel room and just started taking his clothes off. Lisa stood there wondering, 'What the hell'. Simon then collected a wine bottle, two glasses and disappeared through the door. 'What the hell!' Lisa followed him outside and discovered the room came with a large thermal heated spa pool. Simon was settled in for the evening.

"Well, what are you doing?" Simon demanded, "Get your clothes off and get in."

It looked like a good offer to Lisa.

Lisa went back to work the following Monday and life settled down to a routine. The weekends were spent on the farm or around the house. Lisa loved the freedom of being able to go out on the farm and helping where she could. In summer she would change her clothes and walk out to wherever Simon was working. It was good exercise and allowed her to relax.

One Saturday, Simon stopped at the house with the trailer full of sheep. "Where are you going?" Lisa asked

"Down to the neighbours. That's their sheep I am returning."

"I'll come with you. I haven't met the neighbours yet or been down the driveway."

"No, You don't need to come."

"Why? It will be interesting. I would like to go."

"No. You stay here. I won't be long." Simon said in a very determined voice.

Lisa was very surprised and disappointed, wondering what the issue was. She went back inside, thinking that's weird. Why wouldn't he want me to go?

Chapter Ten

Overseas Trip

Lisa's friend, Christine, an American, was getting married, and she was going to be her bridesmaid. It had all been arranged before she married Simon. This would be Lisa's second trip to California, and she was really looking forward to it. She loved Christine and her family. They were wonderful people who were fun and loving. This was to be their main honeymoon.

Simon had never been to America and was excited and nervous. In fact, he had never been out of New Zealand. Lisa was very surprised as his sister and parents travelled overseas every year.

Linda and Lisa had put together the trip. Linda had friends and family in America who were very happy for them to stay with them. Between Lisa's friends and Linda's friends, they had organized a very extensive trip. Lisa really liked it as they were going to stay mostly with the locals, therefore, they would get to see the real America, not just the tourist sites.

Lisa had plane tickets for leaving and arriving, plus a few internal travel tickets purchased. She had one motel booked partway through the trip but nothing else. There were long periods when nothing was booked. Simon had trouble with this. Lisa would get a phone call at work asking, "What are we doing this day?"

"I don't know, we will just see what happens."

"But you have nothing listed."

"Yeah, it gives us some free time to have a look around the town."

"But nothing's booked."

"It'll be ok."

When Lisa got home, Simon would bring up another time where nothing was booked. Simon was really struggling with the fact they were going to just 'wing it ' for different days.

"Simon, if we have every day booked, then we are locked in. It is good to be able to have free time to be able to see whatever's around. If it's all booked, you could miss out on something."

"But what are we doing on this day? You can't have nothing planned?"

"It will be alright, just wait and see."

Simon was struggling. He wanted it all planned out hour by hour.

Lisa packed, ensuring she had plenty of space to bring shopping back. Simon packed like he was trying to take the kitchen sink.

"You don't need to take the books; they are heavy."

"But I might need them to read."

"You can buy a book over there. Why have you got four pairs of shoes packed."

"I might need them."

"Simon, it's summer over there. It will be hot, you don't need your thick jacket."

"It might get cold."

"If it does, we can buy something."

And on it went. Simon did unpack a few things, but he still had too much stuff including one book.

Simon's parents took them to the airport. Simon was really nervous and got very quiet on the trip up to the point that Mary started to get a bit worried about him. The flight was good, and Simon didn't do any reading of his book, which he had insisted on taking. Once they landed in LA, the crush of people and the accents hit them.

"They've got guns!"

"Yep, it's America. They are all armed."

"That's a machine gun", Simon stated as he grazed in shock at the armed border guards.

Simon, with his dry sense of humour, decided to have a joke with the border security as they were processing their bags. "Hey, yeah, we got drugs with us."

Lisa couldn't believe it, as the guards started looking at them a bit more closely. Lisa hissed at Simon, "You don't joke with them. They do not have a sense of humour." Simon looked surprised as Lisa assured the border guard that it was a joke, they didn't have any drugs. Lisa couldn't believe that someone would try and have a joke with a fully armed man, who had the right to put them back on the next plane out of there. It was like dancing with death.

Once they got out of the terminal, the heat washed over them.

"They really do drive on the wrong side of the road." Simon said with wonder in his voice.

Lisa looked at him, thinking, 'What the hell? He has seen movies, why would they make something like that up?'

Christine and her family were delighted to see them and gave them a warm welcome. In amongst the visiting and the fittings, they went on a day trip to Monterey Old Fisherman's wharf in a friend's Ute, with Simon driving. Driving on the wrong side of the road is unnatural.

They missed the turn-off to Monterey Aquarian.

"Look, it's just over there, Simon. We will have to drive round the block again." Simon looked at the spot and saw a driveway for the exit.

"I'll just cross the lanes."

"No, you can't do that!" Lisa was looking frantically at the four lanes they had to cross.

There was currently no traffic, as the lights hadn't changed, but it would be coming soon, at speed.

"Simon, you cannot go across there. We have to go round the block. Look, the turn-off is just up there, by the lights, not a problem."

Simon ignored Lisa and turned the car across the four lanes of traffic and into the driveway. Lisa was angry and stressed that he would just disregard the road rules and risk the lights changing.

As they pulled into the car park, the security guard said, "If you were seen by the highway patrol, you would have been arrested for dangerous driving."

Simon looked a bit put out and didn't say anything. Lisa was still getting over the shock of what had happened. The remedy had been simple.

They had a lovely time looking at all of the displays. It had sections where the public could touch the shellfish. It was wonderful. Outside on the balcony, they could see Otters in the sea kelp, eating shellfish, using their tummies as a table. The sea breeze was cooling, and they just relaxed. Simon had the camera and was clicking away constantly.

On the way back, they stopped off and looked at some of the golf courses. They just oozed money. No expense was spared with immaculate grounds, driveways, landscaping, and that was before they even reached the clubhouse. Not a blade of grass was out of place. A totally different world from their small house, rough driveways, not to mention the rain and mud.

It was impressive, the display of money and how it was presented. It would have been lovely to spend a bit of time in their world and have it all laid on. Lisa recognized that long term, it wasn't what she wanted. It would have been so restrictive in how one was expected to behave and dress. Lisa liked being able to break loose and do what she wanted. Not be concerned about whether she had held her own in a presentation performance. She would have failed spectacularly anyway.

The wedding was wonderful. The bridesmaids were dressed in floral prints with puffy sleeves and a full knee-length skirt. Christine looked wonderful in a white full length dress. The groom was a lot older than Christine, but they shared so much in common. They were both teachers and enjoyed outside activities like mountain biking and tramping. Lisa found it a bit uncanny just how much the groom resembled Christine's father. In the distance, Lisa had trouble telling them apart.

Towards the end of their stay in California, Simon at night would be very quiet and wouldn't talk to Lisa. He turned his back on her in bed. He seemed upset. Lisa tried talking to him. He just shut her out. Lisa lay in bed, wondering if it was something to do with her. Perhaps he regretted marrying her.

Simon had promised Lisa that he would quit smoking after they were married. Lisa's mother had been a chain smoker. It had controlled her life. Lisa also hated the taste of stale cigarette smoke. Perhaps Simon was suffering from withdrawal systems. That could be the problem.

Lisa couldn't think of anything else that could be a problem. During the day, he seemed to be having a really good time, and then at night, he just shut off. This went on for a few nights. Lisa decided that he needed to work through it on his own. For Simon to give up smoking, it was worth putting up with the silence.

After Christine's wedding they packed up and got ready for their next leg of the trip.

They were off to Las Vegas for four days. That night in bed, Simon started crying. He was quietly sobbing. Lisa couldn't understand what was wrong.

"I don't want it to end. This has been the best time of my life. I didn't know life could be like this."

"Simon, I don't understand. This is only the start of the holiday. The rest will be fun, too."

"No, it can't be like this. I didn't know I could be this happy" More sobs as he turned over in bed, away from her.

"You don't understand what it's like for me. I have never been overseas before. I don't want it to end". Simon sounded so sad and lost.

Lisa lay in bed next to him as he sobbed. She was trying to be understanding, but she didn't get it. Simon was shutting her out and didn't seem to grasp that this was only the first stage of the holiday.

They had packed a lot into the week, with a trip to Yosemite National Park, a tour through a berry factory, a visit to a dairy farm, trips to outlet stores, my god, the shopping, plus all of the family's celebrations.

"Simon, their life isn't always like this. They have to go to work just like everybody else. This is what a holiday is like. It's not everyday life."

"I don't want it to end. I have been so happy, and I will never be this happy again" Simon carried on crying and pushed away from Lisa.

Lisa was worried, but there was nothing she could do. Simon wouldn't listen to her and kept pushing her away. At least it wasn't anything to do with her. Lisa went to sleep.

They got to the airport and flew into Las Vegas. It was fascinating, the lights, the buildings in elaborate shapes. They were staying in one of the large motels, which had all-day gambling. The food was good, cheap, and the service was brilliant.

They wandered through the gambling halls, completely overwhelmed by everything. They couldn't believe that they had gambling for children downstairs as well. They were starting them young. Parents upstairs feeding the Pokey machines, and the kids feeding the games downstairs. They put in a token coin and left.

Outside, the heat was unbelievable, and the wind blew grit right into their eyes. They struggled down the street and found a guided tour for the Grand Canyon. They flew out to the canyon in a small six-seater plane, which didn't seem to have any air conditioning. The temperature in the plane just kept getting hotter.

They flew over the Hoover Dam. It didn't look natural, being a large lake surrounded by a broken desert landscape. The aero view showed sharp, brightly lit ridges next to ravines in deep shadow. Lisa watched the plane shadow undulate as it moved across the landscape. The shadow buckled and stretched depending on the contour of the ground. The Hoover Dam looked small in comparison to the never-ending desert.

The Grand Canyon was impressive. The far horizon was blurred with the heat.

Outlines could be seen amongst the blended earthy colours. The closer faces were broken with rocky ledges and cliffs. The predominant colour was drought brown, but blended in are all the other earth colours. The movement of the sunlight caused the colours to be forever changing.

At the bottom was a deep chasm, which seemed to reach forever. The bottom is impossible to see. Standing on the edge of this forever cliff face makes you realize just how small you are and just how big the world is. Lisa watched the eagles rising on the thermals as they drifted along the canyon walls. At her feet, squirrels were looking for any dropped food.

Simon just kept clicking away with the camera, and Lisa looked at all of the local artwork. She wanted to go down the trail of the Grand Canyon, but Simon didn't even want to walk part of the trail. The donkey rides they discovered had to be booked a year in advance. Lisa left feeling that they missed out on the full experience of the canyon.

They cut their stay short in Las Vegas and travelled to the Rocky Mountains. They enjoyed a bus trip through the Rockies, and then they stayed with some friends of Linda's in the Rockies.

Until Lisa had seen the Rockies she didn't fully understand the size of them. She had read a lot of Western books and looked at the maps of the wagon train route. Trying to imagine what it was like to travel by horse-drawn wagons over the rough trails defiled logic. Those trips must have been incredible, scary and tough.

After some days of viewing the scenery and resting, the next stage was to fly to Wyoming. They got to the airport and lined up for the plane. Lisa was about two spaces behind Simon. The first five people got on the plane, and then they announced that no one else could get on the plane. Lisa couldn't believe it. Simon was on, but she was going to be left behind.

"We booked this ticket months ago," Lisa said to the airport personnel.

"Sorry, lady, the air pressure is too low, so we have to reduce the weight."

Lisa was having a hard time getting to grips with this. "We booked it months ago, why can't we get on?" Thinking they would have worked out how many could fly when they released the seats.

"It doesn't matter if you are booked, if the air pressure is wrong, we can only take a certain weight. You may still get on if the pressure changes. We need it to cool down."

Lisa had visions of being left at the airport while Simon took off on the plane. He was showing no signs of not getting on. Lisa felt like she was going to be abandoned. Fortunately, the air pressure changed so that Lisa could get on. Apparently, this happened quite a lot as the Casper airport is 5,300 feet above sea level. The average for the whole state of Wyoming is over 6000 feet.

Simon had a great flight sitting next to the Wyoming governor. Lisa was a couple of seats back with a very quiet neighbour.

They arrived in Wyoming and met Linda's cousin, Jody, who had married an American. When they were going out Mike had explained to Jody that he was a hunter. Jody, being a Kiwi, was OK with that. After all, her father and brothers had hunted. No great issue. Mike tried again, explaining that he was an Elk hunter and when the season opened, nothing interfered with the hunt. Jody still wasn't grasping the concept.

"Jody, when the Elk season is open, I hunt. That's all I do. Nothing interferes with that," Mike explained.

"That's fine", Jody replied.

They were married and Mike went hunting Elk. Wyoming has very cold temperatures in winter. Like very cold temperatures. They explained to Lisa and Simon that if the car breaks down on the road. Then, stay in the vehicle. People would get out in winter to try and find help. They weren't found again until spring when the snow melted. Bodies would be found along the side of the road, where they had frozen to death. A very sobering picture.

This particular time, Mike was going hunting when the house water pipes froze. Jody needed water, especially as they had a new baby. Mike was going hunting.

Mike cut a hole in the floor of the house with a chainsaw so that the pipes could warm up and he then left. For two weeks, Jody had a small baby in a freezing climate, with a large hole in her floor. Nothing interfered with his hunting.

Wyoming has dinosaurs. Many of them and a university dedicated to the study of them. Simon was in his element. Fossils galore. They gave Lisa and Simon the opportunity to go on a 'dig' with some varsity students. Jody was friends with someone who worked at the university, so they had organized it. The students and lecturers all travelled in the minibus to the site. The students kept throwing looks at Lisa and Simon, trying to work out who they were.

Simon didn't help the situation cause he had donned his safari outfit, which he had bought from NZ. He had found an early explores pith helmet and was playing up to the outfit. Putting on an accent and overplaying the role of being Doctor Livingston. The students decided to stay well clear of them.

It was interesting, but not really Lisa's thing. Simon loved it and spent hours unearthing a bone. Once they got back to the university, they toured the display sections, talked to the scientists and looked at the drawings of the past landscapes. Simon was beside himself with enjoyment.

Jody and Mike decided to show them the state of Wyoming. They put them in a car and drove across the state. They showed them every noted landscape except Jackson's hole. They said New Zealand had better, so didn't waste their time. The night before they left, Simon was in tears. Again, he didn't want the holiday to end.

Lisa and Simon were both a bit tearful at the airport, as they were great people and they had loved staying with them. Lisa would go back in a heartbeat. Wyoming has a small population and fantastic scenery. In many ways, it's like New Zealand, as all of the locals know each other or know someone who does.

They had non-stop connections from Wyoming to Auckland, New Zealand. They arrived exhausted.

After spending weeks travelling around America, they arrived back with a lot more luggage. Simon had discovered American shops. Lisa and Simon waited for their bags to arrive on the carrier, but there was a delay. The conveyer had broken down, and they couldn't get their bags. Not to worry the New Zealand guys on the flight crawled up the shoot and threw the bags down.

The airport staff kept saying, "You shouldn't do that. It could be dangerous. You need to wait for the maintenance to fix it."

Only in New Zealand.

Lisa and Simon got their bags, which included newly purchased bags to accommodate the increased luggage and left. Robert and Mary had left a car so they could drive home. They had dinner at the in-law's place the first night they were back on the farm. All seemed good. Simon went outside and didn't come back. Lisa went out to see what was up.

Simon was standing in the porch area smoking. The concrete under him was littered with butts, and he was dragging on the cigarette like he couldn't consume it fast enough. Lisa was completely shocked.

Three weeks of not smoking and now this. "Simon, what are you doing?"

"Go back inside. I just need to be out here."

"But Simon?"

"I need to do this. I can't stand being back and all of the same stuff. Go back inside" Lisa went back inside, very disappointed by Simon's actions. Robert and Mary had questions and wanted to explain what had happened while they had been away. Simon stayed outside and smoked. Mary kept asking why Simon wouldn't come in. Lisa just gave non-committed answers.

'Three weeks of not smoking and now Simon was back to square one. Why would he do that?' Lisa was so disappointed. She had put up with all of his mood swings on the holiday, thinking that it was worth it, now this.

Chapter Eleven

Back to Reality & Their First Baby

They got back to New Zealand on Saturday, and Lisa went to work on Monday. She was a walking zombie at work and heaven only knows what she did that day. By the end of the week, she was back on New Zealand time.

Simon's family were talking about setting them up on a farm. A lot of discussions revolved around how it would be organized and the structure of it. They all went out with a real estate agent looking at farms. Some of them were quite attractive and a reasonable size but none of them were as good as the farm they were already on. Lisa liked the farm they were currently on and could see potential with it.

Lisa was working half an hour away in the local town and helping out on the farm at the weekends.

Lisa would come home and cook tea. Afterwards, she would catch up with Simon about what was happening. Simon was effectively working for his father, who had taken over the running of the farm.

Lisa suspected that she was pregnant and took a test. It came back positive. Wow, a baby. She was excited about what would happen, how her body would change and what she would need. Lisa told Simon, who was quite happy about being a father. They told Simon's parents at dinner one night. They were all very happy about the future event.

Simon's father was very happy but did not want to know any details. If any discussion came up about the baby, he would leave the room. It was all just too embarrassing for him to deal with.

Lisa developed morning sickness. It wasn't really bad, but Lisa kept dry retching. At work Lisa sat in the office, listening to a client describe the latest financial problem they were having, hoping like hell she would make it through the meeting before she had to rush out to the toilet.

Lisa would then come back to greet her next client to repeat the procedure. The other staff in the office just laughed at her. They did make certain that there was a clear path between the office and the toilet. No one stood in the way.

Once Lisa got to the fourth month, she felt great. Lisa found a midwife and had her regular checkups. The midwife informed Lisa that, while she was pregnant, she shouldn't spend time near any sheep. Lisa just looked at her in amazement. She had just spent the weekend helping with dagging and dosing sheep.

"I think it's a bit late for that. I would have caught it by now if it was a problem" Sue, the midwife, gave her a surprised look and pointed out that being near sheep can cause abortion.

Lisa carried on working full-time and helping on the farm on the weekends. Lisa slowly got bigger and bigger through the winter months.

The bank organized a formal evening for its senior staff. It was held in one of the main centres about two hours away. Being 7 months pregnant, Lisa had nothing to wear. One of the staff lent her an evening gown. It was a lovely mauve colour, and the cut complemented the baby bulge. Simon looked very dashing in his suit. They had a wonderful evening with good food and entertainment.

On the way home, Simon and Lisa got into a discussion about women and their place in society. Simon was taking the stand that women are designed to be in the home raising the children. The conversation went around in circles for a while. By this stage, they were on the private driveway. Lisa was driving because she was definitely the sober driver.

Simon said, "It is a fact that women are designed to look after children and run the house. The man is meant to be the provider."

"Do you really believe that? You believe that women are incapable of being active providers in society?"

"I am just saying that it is an acceptable fact that women are better looking after the home."

"Really, if you are such a believer, then you can walk home 'cause you wouldn't want to be in a car driven by a pregnant woman. It would be so dangerous for you to be driven by such an incompetent person."

With that, Lisa stopped the car. "Get out". She wasn't angry, just making a point. If Simon was silly enough to make sweeping statements like that while his pregnant wife was driving the car, then he must expect some reaction.

Simon looked a bit surprised and got out of the car. Lisa left him staring after the car as she drove off.

Lisa was only a short distance from home, so Simon didn't have far to walk. It was a lovely winter night with a clear, bright sky. The Milky Way was lighting the path through the darkness, and the crescent moon was shining.

Lisa drove over the cattle stop, round the corner, down the short straight and up to their house driveway, over another cattle stop and into their section.

And there in the headlights, right by the carport, was one very large possum eating the rose bush. "You bastard, how dare you sit there and eat the rose bush". Lisa had been frustrated and pissed off about the rose bushes being eaten, and this was the final straw.

Lisa took off into the house, through the french doors, grabbed the gun and headed out the door. By this time, the possum had moved away from the rose bush and was sitting on the lawn in the car light, washing his face. He was licking his paws, then wiping them over his face and whiskers. Like someone after they have consumed a good meal. Lisa wasn't impressed. She moved a bit closer to the carport, took aim and fired.

"What the bloody hell are you doing? Are you trying to kill me? We had an argument, there's no need to try and shoot me!" Simon sounded really angry and shocked.

Lisa said, "I wasn't aiming at you. There was a possum."

"No, there wasn't, you are lying. You could have killed me." By this stage, Simon was yelling.

"No, I knew where you were, I heard you coming over the cattle stop."

"You're mad! Trying to kill me over a stupid discussion!"

"No, really, there was a possum" With that, Lisa went and picked up the possum by the tail and held it out, so Simon could see. Simon just looked at the possum, then at Lisa with a look of complete shock on his face. After a moment, he started laughing. "Bloody hell, you are a sight, Annie, get your gun."

Here, Lisa was in an evening gown, 7-month pregnant, with a possum in one hand and a .22 gun in the other.

Simon came over and gave Lisa a big hug, and took the possum away.

On reflection, Lisa supposed it was a shock to have a gun go off suddenly with no warning. Even so, Lisa was a bit surprised he thought she was trying to shoot him. They put the car away and went inside.

Lisa grew up on a farm, which did lambing beats. Each day, the ewes were checked for cast sheep or ewes having trouble lambing. Simon didn't seem to do this, which Lisa found surprising. She decided to take the quad bike out on the weekends and go round the sheep.

The ewes weren't due to start lambing for a couple of weeks, but Lisa picked up quite a few cast ones. She also found ewes stuck in the bogs. They walk in looking for some more feed and then can't get out. They don't last long, stuck in a bog.

On this day, Lisa found two ewes still alive in the bog. She crawled over to them, as that helped to spread her weight so that she didn't fall through the vegetation layer to get them out. One came out quite easily as she was close to the bank. She struggled to her feet with mud all down her legs and belly as she staggered away. The cold water makes their legs go numb. The second ewe was further in and very heavy. Lisa was struggling to get her out when she felt something move inside.

It felt like something was being torn. Lisa stopped moving as she was worried about the baby. She sat down and waited to see what happened. She then looked at the sheep and decided that Simon would have to get her out. Lisa went carefully home while reassessing the situation. She was only four weeks away from giving birth.

Getting comfortable to sleep became a major issue. Lisa would be waking up in the night to adjust position or with cramps. As she lay awake, carefully moving her legs, she would be listening to the rats in the ceiling. It sounded like they were playing tag up there with running and thumps. Then, to add to the noises, a possum would start to cackle on the roof. They are really loud, especially when they are just above the window. It was a noisy neighbourhood. Occasionally, a morepork could be heard hooting in the distance. Lisa would eventually drop back to sleep and then wake to hear the rats in the morning.

"Simon, you have to do something about the rats."

"I'll put Dixie up there. She will sort them out."

Dixie, who had been purring as she rubbed and arched against Simon's leg, was positioned in the ceiling. The manhole was just outside the bedroom door. Dixie just sat by the manhole and then jumped down. Not to be deterred, Simon collected her up again and put her back. This time, Simon put the lid back over the manhole. Nothing was heard for some hours. Then Dixie could be heard meowing for a while before she stopped.

Simon left Dixie up there for the night. In the morning, Simon checked on Dixie. No rats but one unhappy cat who wanted out. Dixie quite clearly wanted nothing to do with the rats. So much for cats catching rats.

"I suppose we could set traps, but I don't have any." Simon said. "I'll get some today in town."

Lisa arrived home that night with the rat traps. Simon looked a bit surprised as to how prompt she had been.

"You can put them in the roof, Simon."

Simon duly set them just beside the manhole with peanut butter as the attraction. It didn't take long. That night, while they were eating dinner, they heard them go off. "Simon, we got one. Get up and have a look."

Simon duly climbed up the ladder. Two big rats were caught in the traps. Simon started to pick one up.

"Aaaw Shit, it's still alive, I'm not touching that!" Simon shot back down the ladder.

"You can't leave them there. You have to get them out." Lisa said, laughing at Simon's reaction to the rat. Her big, strong husband was a wimp.

Simon headed over to the kitchen and got the tongs. Armed with them, he climbed back up the ladder. By this stage, the rat was dead. Simon very carefully used the tongs to carry the rats out of the house and threw them over the bank.

They were very big rats. Lisa could understand why Dixie wanted nothing to do with them. They caught a few more rats before the noises stopped.

Lisa's nights became a bit more peaceful if the possums weren't cackling.

In between work and the farm, Lisa started to get things together for the baby. Lisa had no idea how much stuff is out there for babies or the prices. The salesladies assured Lisa that a new mother needed this, can't do without that, must have this, this is necessary. It's amazing how much stuff mothers can't do without, according to the retail and marketing departments.

It is an unknown field of possibilities until the baby is born. A new mother is worried about being set up to care for the baby and not forgetting anything. There are lists, but they have everything on them. Change tables, nappies, bassinets, baby powder, wipes, hats, mitts, The lists go on and on. Then there are the baby clothes. Not all babies are the same size. So, a mother may buy a newborn outfit thinking it will fit. But no, it's way too small for the baby. It's a minefield, but really interesting and exciting, so items are bought, which in reality are not needed.

Lisa went home with all of these pretty things, thinking she would be a good mother. The picture in every new mother's head is a happy, chubby baby who will be a joy and sleep through the night. Haha!

At work, Lisa had targets to meet. The accounts had to be well managed, and she had to sell life insurance, deposits, retirement accounts, and make loans. Based on the success in meeting the targets, Lisa was graded. Above a certain grade, the company paid a bonus. The whole district was depressed. Lisa was having a hard time meeting some targets.

Lisa saw Robert one day, and he asked what interest rate the bank was paying on deposits. At the time, Lisa had a very competitive rate.

Robert liked it and said, "That sounds good. I have a million dollars, not doing anything at the moment. It could be a short-term home for it."

"That would be great. I could get you a better deal with that size of deposit."

In one move Lisa had now way exceeded her deposit target. Brilliant. Lisa went to work the next day and talked to the deposit rate guys.

That night at home, Simon and Lisa were talking over tea. "Your Dad deposited a million dollars in the bank today."

"Oh, I like that. Dad put a million dollars in the account today. That's brilliant," Simon said in a superior voice and laughed.

It appealed to his sense of place in the world.

"It means I will get a good grade now", Lisa replied.

Simon just repeated, "Dad put a million dollars in my bank today. Oh, I love it." and continued to laugh.

Chapter Twelve

Family Business

When Lisa met Simon, she was working professionally in the business area. After they were married, Lisa continued to work, and Simon was working for his father on wages. When Lisa was about six months pregnant, Robert decided to set his son up on the farm. Simon had been working for his father on the other farm further south.

Simon confided that he didn't want to farm and had other interests.

"I am the oldest boy, and they expect me to take over the farming operation. All my life, they have said that I would go farming. They told me to go to varsity and do a farming degree. I never had a choice. They never asked me what I wanted. They just assumed I would do what they wanted. I never had the opportunity to play with different ideas for a career. They told me what I would do."

"But you were at varsity, Simon, didn't you look at all the other courses? That university has courses in all sorts of areas. You could have done anything."

"It never occurred to me to look at another subject. They sent me there to do an agricultural degree, so that's what I enrolled in. I don't like farming. My best time as a kid was walking up the creeks looking for fossils."

"But you didn't finish the three-year degree. You still have one year to go."

"Yea, I was home when my results arrived, and Dad looked at them and decided it was better. I left and came home to work for the manager."

"I don't understand why you didn't finish the degree."

"Oh well, I went to all the lectures but never handed anything in. My friend said that I was exercising passive resistance. I didn't want to do it, so I just mucked around. I had a good time, and Daddy paid for everything. Flat, living costs, the money just kept coming, so I enjoyed it."

This whole concept of wasting time mucking around and not taking advantage of the access to knowledge and opportunities was just beyond Lisa's understanding. How could Simon be in an environment with access to so many different people and knowledge and not make use of it? It just baffled her. A totally foreign concept. "Look, I have a good job, and you can get a job doing whatever you want. We can move anywhere in the country." Simon didn't reply but looked remorseful.

Lisa liked farming. All she had ever wanted to do was go farming. She had grown up on a farm and had worked on it from the time she could walk. She had spent every day out with her father and knew it like the back of her hand.

One of her first memories was lambing a ewe on a bitterly cold spring day. She had smaller hands than her father, so she could reach past the lamb's head to grab the lamb's leg.

When she was a senior at boarding school, on careers day, she had asked the spokesman from a university about doing an agricultural degree.

The guy had stood at the front of the class and said "You don't want to do that. It's far too rough for you. We do farm tours, and you would have to work alongside some very rough guys. There are no girls in the classes, so you would be on your own." Lisa was very surprised about his attitude.

"We have a degree in landscape architecture. It would be more suitable for you". Lisa sat back in her chair, thinking she wanted to do a farm-related degree, not landscape. After the presentation, one of the other girls at the school confided that she wanted to go farming as well. She was off an isolated sheep farm. Her parents had told her that they would not allow her to go farming. If she wanted to be on a farm, she would have to marry a farmer. The farm was going to be left to the son.

Lisa left school and went back to her parents' farm. She signed up for a Trade Cert in sheep farming. It was a three-year course with exams, a task work booklet, which had to be signed off and workshops. Lisa was the only girl on the course, which meant at some of the workshops the guys wouldn't talk to her. Some of the instructors wouldn't help either, as they did not approve of her being on the course. It probably didn't help that she won the top cadet prize for three years running.

Lisa then went on to do the advanced TCI is sheep farming. Once she had completed that, Lisa looked at her options. She was running a small block of ground on her parents' farm and working on the rest of the farm. It was frustrating cause her father maintained control and wanted to do things his way. His age was becoming an issue, and he was getting frustrated. Lisa's mother wanted the farm to be run down and blocked any changes.

David didn't want her anywhere around and resented her doing anything. Lisa's mother was trying to ensure her son was the 'man' and was seen as the future. They all kept pointing out to her that they wouldn't leave anything to her cause her husband would get his hands on it. The bulk of the property had to be left to David cause he was the boy. David had to be in charge.

Lisa pointed out that the same applied to David. He could have a wife who would get her hands on it. They ignored her and went on about how it had to be left to the boy.

Lisa loved the farm and the area, but she couldn't stay. The family in fighting had made it impossible for her to stay on the farm and stay sane.

It was a big offer of Lisa's to go down another path away from farming. Simon decided to take on the farm, which complied with his parents' wishes. "Is that what you really want?" Lisa asked

"I have made up my mind. I am going to take over the farm." Simon said in a very firm voice.

Lisa couldn't see why he couldn't farm and also maintain his interest in whatever. Develop a hobby and study what he wanted. The farm had a lot of fossils on it, as did the local area, so the two could be worked in together. To Lisa, it looked like an ideal situation.

They all travelled up to the lawyers in two cars. Mary and Lisa stood out in the car park while Simon and Robert went in to sign the documents. This was the ambition of the father, to have his son take over the farm. Succession planning, family history, continuity of the business.

Mary kept talking to Lisa in the car park about nothing really.

Robert had a big concern about securing the asset from the potential risk of an ex-wife suing for her share. They had kept bringing this up in front of Lisa at family meetings. They made it very clear that Lisa had married into a wealthy family and they would do everything they could to protect their assets against a potential risk. At the time, Lisa didn't have any intention of leaving. But then, newly married with a baby on the way, why would she?

Simon had effectively bought the farm via a family trust. He had family debt for the property, as the trust did not cover the purchase price. Lisa and Simon had a stock loan from the family for the purchase of the livestock, already on the property. Interest was paid on the loans. It was below market rate but above the deposit rate. Simon and Lisa formed a partnership, which owned the stock and ran the unit. The partnership paid the interest for the term loan and rent to the trust for the use of the land. Well, they didn't actually pay rent to the trust. It accumulated on the books. The set rent wasn't affordable; it was astronomical.

While Lisa was working in town, they had some cash, which covered the living costs. It allowed Lisa to purchase things for the baby and basic things for the house. Lisa worked right up until two weeks before the baby was due. In the last month, just getting behind the steering wheel proved to be too difficult.

Once Lisa took maternity leave, they had no money. Shearing took place in June, and the wool money had to cover them right through till the next income in December. At that point, wool was still worth something. In a sheep and beef operation, the bulk of the income comes in over a five-month period. From May till December, there is basically no income. They took over on 30 June, the balance date. Lisa could not afford to spend any surplus money on anything. Even the cost of petrol to go to town was costed out.

Lisa was in charge of the budget, and she updated it every day, trying to make it work.

The computer and files were all jammed in the corner of their bedroom. No internet then, so there was a large paper trail. Over those winter months, leading into spring, there are a lot of animal health expenses, like vaccinations for pre-lambing and calving.

They took over in 1996 in the middle of the farming depression. It was said that if a rifle shot was let off down the main street, no one would be hit. Everyone was struggling. In Lisa's work, she knew just how much people were struggling. The high interest rates just added to the struggle farmers were having. It was a good time to buy, but a difficult time to make it pay.

Every time they saw Simon's parents, they got a lecture about how tough it had been for them when they started out farming. A young family and no income. How they didn't spend any money and lived very simply. Robert was very careful with his money. He spent very little on anything, house or farm.

Mary had her own personal income, which she had inherited from her father. It was attracting a very good interest rate. This allowed her to buy her own clothes and to go out and about. Even so, Robert would make cutting comments about how she had wasted money on an extravagant item. Lisa noticed that Robert did enjoy what she bought.

The farm purchase included the house which Lisa's in-laws lived in. It was a spacious home built in the 1970s. It had a large lounge with bifold doors, which opened into the kitchen dining area. A hall opened off this area, leading to three large bedrooms, a laundry, a toilet and a bathroom. Outside, there was a double carport and at the back was a sleep out with a separate bathroom. It was a very nice home with a large brick parking area out the front.

It still had the original 1970's kitchen and wallpaper. It was like stepping back in time. Robert spent nothing on the house.

Chapter Thirteen

Lisa's First Born

Lisa's plan was to have the baby in a large hospital with full access to medical care in case something didn't go to plan. Lisa wasn't into home births; being a farmer, she was well aware of what could go wrong. Lisa had pulled out enough lambs in difficult positions, to know what could happen. Plus, her family history pointed to complications.

Lisa went into what she thought was labour. The pains were certainly intense. She lived two hours away from the hospital and didn't want to run the risk of arriving late. Lisa and Simon left in the evening and travelled up to the hospital after ringing the midwife. They arrived around 11 pm at night and went to the after-hours entrance.

It was locked. They had to access the intercom and, spoke to the security guard on the camera and explain why he should let them in. Lisa was quite clearly heavily pregnant, but he didn't seem to see that as a reason to open the door.

They eventually let them in. Lisa was examined and was told it was very early labour. She had only dilated two centimetres, and it would be some time before she was anywhere near to delivery. They sent them home. Lisa was a bit upset about being sent home, due to where they lived. Lisa didn't know what to expect, and if she was in early labour, then wasn't it worth keeping her close? It was suggested they could hire a motel unit so that they were closer. With the farm and the cost, it wasn't an option. They started on the road home.

One of the effects of being pregnant is having to constantly wee. So, on the trip up, Simon had to stop many times for her to use the toilet. Traveling back home at 1 am in the morning, many toilets are locked. Simon would stop at the toilet and Lisa would waddle over to use it, only to find it was locked. Only option was to squat on the side of the road, trying to hide behind the car door to avoid being seen by the oncoming trucks. Many of them honked. The effort to lower her heavily pregnant body down to squat on the side of the road while in the early stages of labour was horrible.

It was a slow, difficult trip home. Simon stayed in the car listening to the radio as Lisa tried the toilets. They arrived home exhausted at 2 am in the morning. Lisa crawled into bed to sleep.

Lisa was not a happy camper and did not want to repeat that drama. Three days later, Lisa started to have very uncomfortable pains. Not full labour pain, but constant muscle pain in her stomach area. Couldn't sleep. Not that she was getting much anyway with a kicking baby, a large belly and cramps. Lisa found the best position was on her side, with a pillow between her legs and one partially under her belly. Made turning over a real procedure.

Lisa's midwife, Sue, came out daily and ran her checks. Lisa was in early stages of labour. It could go on for days. On the second day, Lisa informed her that she was cancelling the whole thing. Lisa had had enough. No sleep, constant achy pains and being the size of a house. It was uncomfortable and frustrating.

"I just want this baby out, and I don't care how". This had gone on long enough, and Lisa was over it.

Sue became a bit upset about her statement. "You really need to stay with the plan. It is really important that you just relax and let things proceed as they should. It is all perfectly natural to be in early labour. This could go on for a couple of days and possibly up to a week before it really starts. The baby is fine, its heart rate is normal, and it's in the right position. All you need to do is allow nature to follow its course. It's important that you just allow it to follow through and wait for your time. Don't do anything else."

Not what Lisa wanted to hear.

Once Sue left, Lisa wondered what she thought she was going to do. Here she was 9 months pregnant. Did she expect her to take the baby out and put it into a holding tank? Because if that was an option, Lisa would have done it months ago. What options did Lisa have? So why was she so upset?

That afternoon, Lisa decided she really had had enough and something needed to happen. So Lisa went outside and got on the quad bike. Simon became a bit concerned and demanded to know what she was up to. Lisa informed him that she was over it and this baby was going to be born.

They ran a lot of cattle, and in the wet, they pugged up the tracks and parts of the paddock. When it dried, it was like riding over Judder bars. Lisa's plan was to ride the bike over all of the pugged areas she could find. Plus, it got her out of the house. She was getting cabin fever. Simon didn't argue with her. Perhaps the look on her face stopped him, but he did decide he needed to come with her. So, with Lisa driving, they rode round all of the bumpiest places she could find for a good hour.

Lisa felt a lot better for having got outside. When they got back to the house, Mary was there and when she saw her on the bike, she just started shaking her head. Her sister had rang and wanted to know what was happening. When she couldn't get hold of Lisa, she had rang her. Mary didn't say much, other then she expected them for dinner that night.

At five o'clock, they went up to the in-laws and had a lovely dinner. Lisa really enjoyed it, which seems a bit bizarre since she kept having contractions. Lisa kept squeezing Simon's hand under the table as another large pain hit. After dinner, they drove to the local hospital.

Lisa was having regular contractions 7 minutes apart in the car. She suffered through one to then tried to relax back into the car seat. Sue had instructed Simon that he was to time the contractions, which he was diligently doing.

"Your next contraction will be in a minute, 30s, 10s. Now." Simon said as he watched the clock. He would then laugh as the contraction hit Lisa.

This really upset Lisa as she didn't want to know when the next contraction was coming. They hurt and being told to expect one in !!! just really upset her focus. "I don't want to know when the contraction is. Stop telling me!" Lisa said in a frustrated voice

Simon just laughed and said, "Sue told me to time them, and you are like clockwork."

"I Do Not Want To Know."

"Your next contraction will be in 20s, 10s Now." Simon started laughing again. It was like he had a new toy. Push here, and it will react.

Lisa suffered through another one. "Simon, stop telling me!"

He just laughed again as he watched the clock. Quite clearly, he was not going to stop for the entire trip to the hospital.

After another contraction, Lisa reached over and thumped him on the shoulder.

Simon started yelling at Lisa, "You must not touch the driver. We could have an accident if you hit the driver, it's really dangerous. What is wrong with you hitting me?" Simon glared at Lisa.

Lisa looked with surprise at Simon's angry face. 'Well, that was a turn-up for the books,' Lisa thought.

When they were going out, Lisa used to slide her hand over his thigh and up towards his groin while he was driving. He never complained about that being a distraction for the driver. In fact, he encouraged it.

At the local hospital, where they had a small birthing unit, Sue met them and assessed Lisa. The birthing unit consisted of a small room on the second floor, isolated from the rest of the hospital. Lisa was in full labour, and her water broke as Sue examined her. Lisa was lying on the bed, while Sue and Simon discussed over the top of her how they were going to get Lisa to the main hospital.

Lisa lay on the bed looking up at them and decided all the suggested options, did not appeal to her. Sitting in a car seat, having contractions, while they drove an hour and a half to the hospital did not fill her with enthusiasm.

"I am not moving!" Lisa suddenly said in a firm voice.

"Of course, that's fine. It's your choice. I will make arrangements for you to have it here." Sue quite clearly was used to mothers changing their minds.

Labour is hard work and painful for a good number of hours. Lisa just lived in the moment of the contraction, followed by a short break and another contraction. Her whole body was focused on the birth.

Sue offered gas to Lisa. "Take a good suck on the mouthpiece, and then let it out slowly."

Lisa tried. After a while, she decided it was a waste of time. It didn't seem to have any effect on the withering pain. Simon loved how it made him sound and had a great time playing with it.

"I don't need to be here. Dad wasn't present at my birth; he was down the club playing pool." Simon repeatedly said.

"This has nothing to do with me. I can't help. It's pointless for me being here. I could be having a beer."

"You could help by putting hot cloths on your wife's lower back. It will ease the pain for her." Sue told Simon as she gave him a hot cloth.

"Rubbing the lower back will also help."

Simon started to put the hot cloths on and rubbed. "Oooh, that's feels so good", Lisa said.

Simon continued, only stopping when Lisa was having another contraction.

Lisa wasn't happy that Simon didn't want to be at the birth of his child. She thought he would be excited about it. Again, Simon brought up how he shouldn't be there. "My hand is getting tired." With that, Simon stopped rubbing or putting hot cloths on and wandered around the room.

Lisa was disappointed that he stopped cause they really did make a difference.

At 7 pm, Lisa's dinner came up. The silly little pots they gave Lisa to vomit into did not hold everything. She filled the plastic pot, the back of the raised bed and the floor. Lisa was hanging over the back of the bed, holding the pot, when Sue noticed, "You poor thing, let me take that", and she whisked it away, changed the sheets and cleaned the floor.

Simon was slouching in the chair and wandering around the room in-between mentioning how his father had it easier. It then got to be entertaining for Simon. The local fire brigade turned up to carry out a full evacuation drill for the hospital. They had sirens going, lights flashing, which reflected on the windows and many fire engines (must have been a joint effort) all below the birthing unit.

Lisa was now pushing a walker around the room. Walking seemed to help with the contractions. As she passed the windows, she could see firemen in full fire gear, with hoses laid out and ladders.

All of the elderly were out, some in hospital beds with attached drips, nurses helping those that could walk out and healthier patients in hospital gowns, all being gathered on the grass area directly outside the window. There was a lot of excited talk and milling around. Simon was hanging out the window, watching everything. Since most of the fire brigade were locals, Simon knew many of them and was shouting to them, from the window.

Simon thought it was great. He couldn't have had a more entertaining evening. Far better than dealing with a grumbling wife who was in pain.

On one of Lisa's passes by the windows, she reached the conclusion that they were probably planning on evacuating her as well. Lisa made up her mind that fire or no fire, she was not moving. Walking down the stairs, to then moan with contractions outside in full public view, with the fire brigade looking on, was not going to happen. Many of them worked for the local trucking company, which picked up their stock. Lisa was not going to be their entertainment!

A nurse opened the door with a flourish, armed with the fire drill batten, took one look at Lisa and backed back out of the room.

Lisa hadn't said a word, but the look on her face must have been enough. Nothing was said.

Lisa moved to the shower, which was very nice. The warm water was relaxing, and then she moved to the bath and stayed there as long as she could. Most of it was a bit hazy, but Simon kept saying "I love you" over and over again, which was becoming a bit annoying.

In her haze of pain, Lisa registered Simon, saying, "Stop, stop, you have sharp teeth." A bit later, she heard him saying, "Please let go, please let go, you are going to break my arm."

Lisa made herself let go of Simon's arm, when the contraction eased. After that when Lisa grabbed for something to hold onto, Simon made sure he was out of reach.

Lisa then went into full pushing mode and was completely oblivious to anything else in the room. Lisa did remember moaning and withering on the bed, pleading for the pain to stop. It was at that point that Sue gave her an injection for pain relief.

Their son was born in early spring at 2 am, weighing 8lbs and 7oz. He needed oxygen briefly before he started screaming. Simon cut the cord and held his son for the first time.

Holding their baby for the first time is an experience they could not describe. This new being, which has slowly been making its presence known over months, is finally face-to-face with them. Lisa had spent months wondering what they would be like, what sex and if it would have hair. Then, it all became real.

Lisa finally got to see his screwed-up face while he lay in her arms. She counted his 10 toes, tiny little fingers, soft skin and admired his delicate finger nails. A perfect miniature human being.

Lisa was on a high and didn't even notice the needle going into her leg to help the uterus contract. All of her focus was on the baby.

Simon rang everyone he could think of in New Zealand and overseas. When he rang his parents, Jim screamed down the phone to them. At 2:30 in the morning, it was probably the last thing they wanted to hear.

After Lisa and Simon had collected themselves and had a drink and a biscuit, they moved down to the maternity ward with Lisa pushing the cradle. Jim slept in the nurse's room, and Simon slept next to Lisa in the chair.

In the morning, Simon disappeared and did a few things round town. Probably had a good feed somewhere. Simon came back and gave Lisa a beautiful pearl necklace, which he had bought. It was lovely. He stayed for a short while, held the baby, gave Lisa a kiss and left for home. They had stock which needed to be moved and dogs to be fed and let off.

Sue came and saw Lisa and checked Jim over.

"How did the fire drill go?" Lisa asked

"They are in discussion about developing a new plan on how to handle the situation if the birthing unit is being used. They had not factored in the need to deal with a woman in full labour. It's going to be interesting to see what they come up with".

"Good luck with that." Lisa replied.

Lisa got to grips with breastfeeding, which was a bit frustrating. She had no privacy and no spacial respect. All personal boundaries were gone. Lisa no longer had ownership of her body; it was just a production unit for the child. Sue was good and explained things well.

They tried to let Lisa get some sleep and took Jim into the nurse's room at night. But he just screamed. They brought him back to Lisa.

"You have a very determined little boy. Jim will not settle. We have tried everything." Sue said.

Lisa looked at her beautiful baby, who was screaming full blast and realized it was going to be a long night. Jim had very blue eyes, which seemed to follow Lisa. They say that babies can't focus, but Lisa didn't believe it.

Jim screamed a lot. Lisa was breastfeeding, and it was going well.

Lisa had some visitors from her next door neighbour, who lived down the driveway from her. They gave her a brown teddy bear for Jim, which was just as big as him.

Lisa wanted to go home on the second day and have her things around her. To be able to relax and settle in with the baby. In a hospital bed, she had no privacy.

"The best place for you is the hospital. It's pointless you coming home now", Simon stated on the phone when Lisa rang him.

Lisa was sure his mother had a hand in that. By the third day, Lisa was wondering who she could get to take her home. Simon hadn't been in to see her since the birth. Simon finally arrived to take her home.

Lisa's mother-in-law believed in cloth nappies, so being helpful, she had bought Lisa a whole bunch of them. Apparently, there is nothing more satisfying than seeing pristine white nappies hanging on the line.

She also made little woollen baby wraps, like they used to have in her day.

No onesies for Lisa. So the cloth nappy was put on the baby, then the plastic pants pulled up over the nappy. The wrap-around dress then got pulled down. Once the baby was dressed, it was wrapped in a woollen wrap. The baby was warm, no question of that.

Problem? It was not designed to fit into a car seat, with the strap going up between the legs. The other problem was the nappy stayed wet, so there was a sopping wet, sagging nappy, which then leaked. It had none of the modern design, which keeps the wetness away from the baby and contained, so there wouldn't be any leakage. The wees leaked out the sides and wet all the bedding. Same with the poos when it was runny.

In summer, it wasn't so bad, as Lisa was able to get the nappies dry, but in winter, with it being wet and damp, it was quite difficult.

The bucket with the wet nappies would sit in the corner, giving off an acid smell.

Mary did collect the nappies and wash them for Lisa for the first three weeks. It was very helpful of her.

Jim didn't have a basinet. He had a wooden cot with a drop side and wooden slates. It was made from recycled wood. It was a present from Mary on a long term borrow. It had a cot mattress, which Lisa placed towels under to create a gentle slope for the baby to sleep on. Then, Lisa rolled up towels to make a spot for the baby. It worked well, as the baby was in a well-protected spot and couldn't move. The bedding was placed over the top.

The first week at home was great. Jim was doing well and meeting all of his milestones. He regained his birth weight in the first 7 days, which was very good. Jim was a very strong baby and had excellent IGA scores at birth. He actually managed to lift his head off the table, which is unusual.

Lisa was getting broken sleep with the night time feeds, but that was to be expected. In the baby's room, there was a hard 1950s dining chair and Lisa would sit in that to feed Jim. Simon slept through the night soundly and didn't wake for a single reason. Even when Jim screamed. Lisa heard the first scream, and she was bolt awake, ready to face whatever the problem was.

Chapter Fourteen

The House

Once Lisa began living in the house, she noticed that it actually had some serious problems. It was a very cold house with no heating. It had a log fire, which just smoked. The house originally had an open fire, and somewhere in the past, a log burner had been installed. Lisa talked to Simon about getting it fixed.

"It can't be fixed." Simon said firmly and left.

They had an oil heater in the baby's room to keep it warm, but the rest of the house was cold. When Lisa walked past the windows, she could feel the cold draft blowing in. On a windy night, the curtains would lift over a meter off the floor, flapping as if they were hanging on a clothesline.

One night, it was really cold, and Lisa was looking to have some company/help with the nappy. She took Jim, who was screaming, into their bedroom and laid him on the bed, with his little angry rosebud mouth only centimetres away from Simon's face. Lisa proceeded to change his nappy and get organized to feed him. All the time watching to see if Simon woke up, twitched, turned over, or had any reaction at all!

Jim screamed. He would have been heard out in the paddock easily with that set of lungs and Simon slept. Not even a twitch. His snoring did not miss a beat. Lisa climbed back into bed, where it was warmer and fed Jim in comfort. From that point on, she no longer worried about being quiet so Simon could sleep.

The fridge freezer was at the end of the kitchen bench, so it protruded into the lounge area. In the lounge, there was a 1970s sofa, which folded down to make a very firm bed. It had bright orange synthetic covering and wooden arms. Apart from the stand, which held the TV, it was the only furniture that fitted in the lounge.

The Formica kitchen table was fitted between the door to the bathroom and the door to the outside porch. It was a neat fit. If anyone was sitting in either chair, they had to move to let someone through either door. The dining area had a four seater table and some large shelves rescued from the local stock firm, who were upgrading their display units. As the saying goes, 'you couldn't swing a cat without hitting something'.

The house was on piles with no underfloor insulation. Pink batts were installed in the ceiling, when Lisa and Simon moved in. God only knows how cold it was before that. It had french doors which opened onto steps, no porch. The putty in the doors had deteriorated to the point that the rain ran down the inside of the windows and onto the floor. Lisa would find puddles of water on the lino. They were dangerous if she forgot about them, when moving around the room.

When Lisa cleaned the dining room floor in spring, she had trouble getting thin strips of something off the floor. They would be stuck to the floor, and they had to be pried off with a knife. Then, one particularly wet day, Lisa worked out what they were. Worms would come in through the door gaps, wiggle so far into the room and die. They become dried-up strips, bit like kinky spaghetti.

The lino on the floor of the bathroom and toilet was old and started to crumble. It probably had asbestos in it, but Lisa and Simon didn't know that. Holes appeared, and the bare floorboards showed through. They discovered that there were holes in the floorboards. Some of the holes were big enough to put your fist through.

By the bath, there was a large hole in the floor, so in winter, the cold wind would whistle up through the floor onto Lisa's bare, shivering body as she got in and out of the shower. It was freezing cold. Once washed, Lisa dried rapidly and made a dash for the lounge/bedroom, where it was warmer.

The hot water cylinder was only 35 litres. Both of them had to have quick showers otherwise, they ran out of hot water. It was by the door into the bathroom and only fitted the cylinder. The linen cupboard was between two bedrooms and was two feet wide. Lisa measured it one day in frustration. She was trying to fit the towels onto the shelves. Lisa shut the door, which then popped open, and all the towels fell out. She was not happy.

The chest freezer and the clothes dryer lived in the carport, down two steps from the porch. Since the wind drove the rain into the carport, Lisa got wet feet trying to get dry clothes out of the dryer. She would be bent over, trying to shelter the washing from the driving rain, desperately trying to ensure nothing was dropped onto the wet concrete while she froze.

The house, sometime in the past, had experienced a house fire, so in the ceiling, they could see charred timber. The dining, kitchen and bathroom area had been replaced with cheap particle board. The windows and doors, had the look of being collected from a salvage yard, as they did not seem to match the rest of the house.

The house section had been carved out at the bottom of a long slope. Two sides dropped off into a steep bank above the road or a drain. One side went into a gentle slope above the driveway. The last side, which faced the french doors, had a rock and concrete wall.

All of the bank above the wall sloped into the house section. When it rained, the surface water would run down the hill and over the wall. This was OK, where the garden and grass area was. It would absorb the water over time. It didn't work so well with the driveway. The driveway came up a slope to the metaled area outside the house. They could then drive round into the carport.

The metaled area collected the surface water, plus the water from the bank, which would then run across the driveway and under the house. It was a stream, which would be over Lisa's feet. Consequently, the house was consistently damp in winter, spring and autumn unless there was a drought. This dampness would rise into the house, and everything in it would be damp.

On a positive note, due to the poor state of the joinery, there was a constant draft. This ensured good air movement. The mould only grew in areas behind beds, wardrobes or anywhere, it was sheltered. Lisa kept telling herself that the early pioneers had it worse. It became harder and harder to convince herself of this.

Chapter Fifteen

Hospital

In the second week of being home, after giving birth, things started to go backwards. Jim wouldn't feed and grizzled all the time. Lisa sat up all night trying to feed him. Jim's skin started to get wrinkly, like he had too much skin, to cover his little arms and legs. They started to look like little sticks. Lisa called Sue, who had been out just three days earlier, to come out. Lisa was very worried.

Jim had lost 200 grams, which is a lot. Sue sent Jim to the hospital. Lisa was distressed and worried, holding a baby which no longer looked chubby, but starved. Simon didn't seem bothered.

The local paper ran a monthly competition for the best baby of the month. The winner got some flowers, a box of chocolates and a photo in the paper. Jim had won, and Simon was very pleased about it. The newspaper wanted to take photos. Simon saw no reason why they shouldn't stop on the way to the hospital to do it. Lisa just wanted to get Jim to the hospital. She was upset and worried about Jim. She didn't care a shit about a photo.

Lisa and Simon had a discussion in the car on the way and Simon kept saying, "It's on our way. It will hardly take any time at all. They are waiting for us. It would be rude not to go."

"Jim is sick; we need to go to the hospital. It's important that we go as soon as we can. They can take the photo another day."

"No, they are waiting. We can stop on the way. It is organized and it will not take any time. You are making a drama about nothing. It won't make any difference to Jim if we arrive a bit later."

"Jim's ill and has lost a lot of weight. It's serious." Lisa said in a concerned voice.

"Jim will be fine. We are going."

"It doesn't matter if we have our photo in the paper or not. I just want to get Jim to the hospital."

"We are doing it. Stop being unreasonable. Just shut up about it." By this stage, Simon was getting angry about it.

Simon was driving and would not change his mind. He just drove into town and round to the newspaper office. It was the last thing Lisa wanted to do. Lisa got out and dutifully held the baby while they took the photos, all the time feeling worried sick. She just wanted it to be over with. Jim looked terrible. He looked like a third-world child that's starving.

They finally got to the hospital, which was two hours from home. Simon dropped Lisa and Jim off and left. They took blood tests, urine tests, x-rays. They said he was dehydrated. They treated Lisa like it was her fault. They accused her of not feeding him. Jim couldn't suck, so the La Leche people got Lisa to express milk and then held the little cup to Jim's mouth and expected him to lap the milk.

A 10-day-old baby really does not know how to lap, so most of the milk got spilt. Lisa sat there thinking, 'This is a complete waste of time as Jim, who desperately needed to be feed, was getting nothing'. The woman kept going on about how she had seen babies lapping and how easy it was for them.

"If we put the milk in a bottle, Jim would be able to get more milk. It could drip into his mouth, and then Jim could swallow." Lisa said.

"Never use a bottle to feed a baby! Breast is best. That is what they must have. Putting milk into a bottle will affect their future feeding. They won't go back to the breast. You must never ever use a bottle. It will give them buck teeth." With that statement, the woman continued to try and get Jim to lap the milk. To Lisa, it looked like a complete waste of time. Milk ran down his chin and dripped onto his wee chest.

Lisa was so worried about Jim not feeding and how he looked. She just wanted him to feed. Lisa sat beside the La Leche woman, watching in an emotionally frustrated mess.

They constantly lectured Lisa about 'breast is best.' Lisa would be sitting by Jim's bed, and a La Leche woman would come in and start lecturing her. Sometimes, there would be more than one of them. They would sit themselves down and start a lecture about breastfeeding and how Lisa must never use a bottle. The lectures included how Jim would fail at school.

"Do you want a boy who was stupid? Not being breastfed will affect his brain development. Your baby will become ill from not having the antibiotics from your breast milk. You will have a sickly boy. Do you want that?"

In fact, it would be Lisa's fault if anything went wrong with the baby in the future. They even said that it could cause him to end up in jail from Lisa not breastfeeding him. Lisa found that statement a bit far-fetched.

Lisa was tired and, stressed and worried about Jim. Lisa was oh so, so tired. Jim was in a bed in a ward, and she was expected to change his nappies, feed him, express milk and do anything that was required. The hospital did supply the cloth nappies and put them through the hospital laundry.

At night, they put down a camp stretcher in the common room for Lisa to sleep on. And every four hours Lisa was woken to feed the baby. The nurses seemed angry that they had to wake Lisa to feed him. So, she had a very broken sleep schedule. At 7 am, the doors opened for visitors, and the common room would be filled with families of noisy children who peed on the floor, screaming and loudly talking parents. There was no chance of sleep until they left at 8 pm at night. Lisa was tired when she arrived and got very little sleep at the hospital.

Simon didn't come to see Lisa at all. She didn't expect him to come and see her. It was spring on the farm, which is a busy time of the year.

Lisa had no family living anywhere near. She was completely on her own. The only phone was a pay phone on the wall, outside the ward, which Lisa had to feed coins into. She couldn't even get anything washed.

Lisa wanted to do everything she could to have a healthy baby. After the stress of giving birth, being home and looking after the baby, plus doing everything else she needed to do and then being in the hospital, Lisa wasn't thinking clearly. She was tired oh so, so tired and had all these determined women constantly lecturing.

She was not a good milker. Yes, Lisa had milk, but not a lot, and Lisa understood it did not flow that well. In other words, it was a hard suck. They talk about how women can feel the flow of the milk to their nipples. Lisa only experienced that sensation once. It is incredible and felt as if all Lisa's internal juices, were flowing in one direction. She was also incredibly thirsty, it's like she was dehydrating. Why it only happened once, Lisa does not know. She can only assume that one has to be fully relaxed for it to happen. Most of the time, Lisa wasn't relaxed but busy and/or stressed.

After three long days of being accused of not feeding her child and being lectured by the La Leche woman, Jim had not improved. The doctors were concerned about Jim's weight loss. They seemed scared of the La Leche women and would not say anything in front of them.

The tests came back positive for RSV. They promptly put Jim into isolation in another ward. Jim did not have a snotty nose, cough or any other signs of the flu. There was nothing to suggest he was ill. He just didn't feed, was dehydrated and still losing weight.

Once they had an answer, they began feeding Jim with a nasal tube after he had tried to suck from Lisa. At last, Jim was actually getting fed. Why they didn't feed Jim nasally before, Lisa didn't know. It didn't make sense. If the baby wasn't sucking, how was that the mother's fault. Lisa had spent three days being told that it was her fault by very determined women. Jim, in the meantime, had suffered.

They did test weights to see if he got any breast milk and then topped up with formula. Lisa expressed milk, but her flow had dropped. Not surprising, really. Lack of sleep, stress and haphazard eating.

The morning of the fourth day into their stay, a nurse came and saw Lisa. She explained that in the night, she had placed a test tube up Jim's nose and gently sucked. She was very surprised as to how much snot she had got out. It nearly filled a 30ml test tube with dark green snot. Once that happened, Jim started to feed better and coughed some more of it up. Jim was still suffering, but they had turned the corner. They sent Lisa and Jim home on Friday after two weeks in hospital.

Lisa managed to get a message to Simon to come and pick them up. Saturday and Sunday were good, with Jim feeding and sleeping. Monday night, Jim wouldn't feed from Lisa and started to vomit. Lisa fought all night to feed him. Jim just grizzled and fussed. In the morning, Lisa rang the doctors, and they readmitted Jim to the hospital. Mary drove them up as Simon was busy. They were re-admitted to the same ward. Jim was still below his birth weight.

The doctors had a meeting in Jim's private room, and it was decided that putting Jim on the bottle was the best option. The doctors were a bit apprehensive about it being made public in the ward. They kept glancing at the door and impressed upon Lisa that it would be best if she didn't say anything about it. 'The breast is best campaign' was implemented with ruthless determination across the hospital.

Jim was fed predominantly from the bottle, but Lisa made an effort to breastfeed him. This kept the raging campaigning women at bay. Jim was topped up with nasal feeding when he had trouble sucking. Jim's room had a fridge in it and a sink so Lisa could mix up the formula given to her by the doctors. Lisa fed Jim from the bottle unseen by the La Leche women.

Jim was in hospital for another week. Lisa was still very tired as she was caring for Jim and up all night feeding him. But at least she could sleep in his room, which made it a lot easier.

A group of La Leche women would come and sit next to Lisa and start in on advice as to how she should be behaving. They would lecture her about being a good mother.

It was a steady stream of criticism. They started in on how the baby would be taken away from her if she didn't improve. Lisa should be breastfeeding, and if Lisa didn't, then Jim would suffer from her poor performance. It all came down to it being her fault and she was a bad mother. Lisa was tired, worried and still getting over the stress of the birth. It all became overwhelming.

Lisa lost it after three days of this, on top of the previous two weeks. A total feeling of helplessness just overwhelmed her. Lisa could do nothing right, and it was her fault that they were in the hospital. Mary, on the trip up, had made it quite plain that Jim was ill because Lisa hadn't looked after him properly.

Lisa walked out of the hospital in tears. She didn't tell anyone where she was going. She just walked out. She walked into town, which was 1.5 kilometres away.

She went and sat in the cinema and watched Alaska while she quietly sobbed. She even rang her mother on a pay phone afterwards and cried down the phone to her. Her mother, who had not visited her once, who hardly ever enquired as to how Lisa was getting on and did very little for her.

She told Lisa she should go back to the hospital. Lisa was making it sound worse than it really was. All of the nurses were there to help her. She had overreacted.

Lisa then walked slowly back towards the hospital, quietly sobbing. On the way she saw a lake just below the hospital, so she walked around the lake in tears. Lisa just cried and cried. She didn't see any point in going on. Quite clearly, she was going to have the baby taken away from her. It was all her fault and Jim would be better off with someone else. Lisa was a bad person and should just leave. The La Leche women had made that quite clear.

Lack of sleep, on top of constant criticism, combined with the emotional roller coaster of giving birth three weeks ago and having a sick baby, was all too much.

Lisa really didn't have anywhere else to go other than the hospital. She had limited money and no vehicle.

When Lisa got back, Mary was waiting for her. The hospital had rang home when they couldn't find Lisa to feed the baby.

A nurse said, "You abandoned your baby when you walked out. No one knew where you were. If you hadn't come back when you did, we were about to report you to social services for abandoning your baby." The nurse quite clearly had a very low opinion of Lisa.

It was the first visit Mary had made to the hospital since she had dropped Lisa off. Lisa looked a mess and she decided to take Lisa home with her. The nurses were informed about what was happening.

Lisa went back with Mary and, slept in her bed and saw Simon. Simon had not visited or rang since she had been in the hospital.

The next morning, after an unbroken night of sleep, Lisa drove herself back in the car. This meant that she had a vehicle for the first time. It gave Lisa a chance to get out and do some shopping. She became an independent person who could buy food instead of being reliant on a spare hospital tray. Lisa was a support person, not a patient, so she didn't get meals. The only other option was the café down three floors.

Lisa's sister had a work meeting in the North Island and organized to come and stay a couple of nights. Judith had raised two boys of her own and, being a school teacher had a lot of experience dealing with people.

Judith arrived late afternoon and summed up the situation quite quickly. Lisa must have looked a mess because once she had got to grips with Jim and the situation, she sent Lisa off to her bed to get a good night's sleep. Judith had booked a room in the hospital hostel accommodation, for family members.

Lisa didn't know that was an option or that she would qualify to use it. Lisa made a small protest and pointed out that the nurses would demand her to feed the baby. Lisa was still expressing milk. Judith had no problem about that and assured Lisa she would sort it out. Lisa went off to her room and slept. It was so nice to sleep in a bed, in a quiet room with a door which shut. Lisa slept soundly.

Judith settled down in the chair in Jim's room for the night. Lisa's sister is an intelligent, capable, determined woman, so when the nurse came in in the middle of the night to demand Lisa's presence, she stood her ground. According to Judith, at 2 am in the morning, she had a nose-to-nose, aggressive discussion with the nurse about finding Lisa to feed the baby.

The nurse was demanding that Lisa be woken and brought immediately to feed Jim. Lisa's sister flat-out refused. The nurse then demanded to be told where Lisa was so that she could organize someone to get her. Once again, Judith flat-out refused to tell her. Judith pointed out that she was here and there was a bottle of formula in the fridge, which she would be heating. The nurse apparently started in on 'the breast was best' rant, and Judith pointed out that there was nothing wrong with formula, and that was what Jim was going to be fed!

Both of her boys were fed formula, and they were fine. Their mother had had very little milk, and all her children were fed formula.

The nurse left in a huff, and Jim was fed.

Judith stayed for the last two days of the week. It made such a difference to have some support and someone to talk to, not to mention the ability to sleep through the night in a bed. Lisa didn't feel so alone and isolated.

At the end of the week, they decided that Lisa should go into Mother Craft. The hospital nurses were not happy about it. They did not approve of the Mother Craft's policy and felt that all their work about breastfeeding would be lost.

Lisa wasn't happy about it. She didn't want to have another week of being told how bad she was and what a terrible mother she was. Lisa just wanted to go home. Her sister talked Lisa into it and took her over to see them. *Wow, good God, bloody hell, what a difference in attitude.*

Lisa arrived with Jim and their bags. Jim was taken from her. They sat Lisa down and asked what had happened. Lisa explained about RSV and the relapse. They were sympathetic. Told her she had been through a lot and showed her to her bed. When Lisa asked about Jim, they said they would look after him, and she could sleep. Lisa had uninterrupted sleep.

They took care of Jim. In the morning, Lisa was given a good breakfast and left to relax. Lisa didn't have to do anything for Jim. They put Jim into a routine, and if he cried, he cried. He wasn't picked up until he was due for his next feed. Jim was crying one day, and Lisa went to pick him up. They told her off. He was not to be picked up until it was time for his next feed. They had a sitting room with magazines, and everything was very calm and relaxed.

They had no issue with Jim being fed on the bottle. Lisa was there for three days where basically she caught up on sleep. After three days, Lisa drove home, armed with tins of formula, bottles, sterilizer, bottle brush and teats. Breastfeeding was over, and they were on formula! Thank God.

Once they got home, Jim just blossomed. He put on weight and hit his milestones. Smiled, rolled over twice, before three months. Up to three months, he had been arching his back and pushing with his legs, lifting his whole body off the floor. He pushed himself around on his back. It was like he was swimming on the floor, and somehow, his whole body moved forward.

Jim was on formula only up until his fourth month when he started on solids. Jim just loved the baby rice and consumed the lot. Once he started eating solids, he also slept through the night.

Oh, the wonder of a good night's sleep. Simon didn't once get up for the night feeds.

He never woke up. He just lay in bed, snoring through the entire night.

Jim always enjoyed his food, and today was no different. Lisa was feeding Jim tinned spaghetti for lunch. Jim liked spaghetti and was at a stage when he felt feeding himself was the way to go. Lisa was trying to get the food into Jim and not on him when the phone rang. In those days, they had a fixed phone in the bedroom. Lisa went and answered it. It was an agent ringing about stock.

Lisa could hear laughter from the kitchen. When she got back to Jim, she could see why he was laughing. Jim had spaghetti on his face, in his hair and all over the bib. Jim was mashing the food all over the tray and gathering up handfuls to throw across the room. There was spaghetti on the front of the fridge, all over the floor and the table. You would think someone had committed murder if you didn't know what it was. Lisa couldn't believe it. In the space of five minutes, Jim had wreaked havoc.

It was at this point that Simon came home. He just stood at the door and started laughing. He thought it was hilarious. Jim started laughing even harder and launched a handful at his father. Simon didn't think that was so funny.

Lisa began cleaning up the mess, starting with the highchair tray. It took a long time to clean the whole kitchen up, which included sponging some of the carpet.

Chapter Sixteen

Nappies

L isa was still dealing with cloth nappies. The more a baby consumes, means more comes out the other end. Lisa had reached the point where she was over wet bedding and soaking nappies. They were in this constant routine of washing and changing nappies. It felt like it would never end.

Lisa went to town and bought disposable nappies. Oh, the anticipated joy of having disposable nappies and dry bedding. Lisa drove home in a state of ecstatic joy. No more washing of nappies, sheets, blankets and underlays, all in a damp house. It would also mean that when they went somewhere, she wouldn't have to pack nappies, change of clothes, blankets and a bag to put the used nappy in. On a hot day, it stunk the whole car out.

Lisa put the first nappy on Jim with great delight. It was so easy with sticky tabs. No safety pins to worry about. Jim was happy, and after a few hours, she changed the nappy.

Lisa discovered that Jim had a really nasty-looking rash on his sides at the top of the nappy. Jim was allergic to the sticky tape on the nappies. Lisa was so disappointed. Disposable nappies were going to change her life, and now she was back to cloth nappies. Back to the piles of washing.

Oh, the satisfaction for Mary, who did not approve of Lisa putting her grandson in disposable nappies. Lisa was back to square one, soaking and washing nappies. Washing all of the bedding and trying to get it all dry.

Mary was not impressed with Lisa's washing of the nappies. Lisa's nappies had a brown tinge to them after they had been washed. She was accused of being a dirty washer, not soaking them long enough and/or not hanging them out in the sunshine. Sunshine removes the soiled colour from the nappies.

Robert and Mary were delighted with their first grandchild and that it was a boy. Traditionally, in the family, the first born was always a boy, so Simon and Lisa had delivered as required. Sometimes, Lisa would leave Jim with them for an afternoon so that she could go out on the farm. Lisa would walk out to where Simon was working and see how he was getting on. It gave her a break.

On this day in October, Simon was docking. He wasn't too far from the house. Lisa headed out, enjoying the sunshine. On the way, she walked past the paddock where the heifers were calving. Lisa was shocked, there were dead heifers lying in the paddock with a calf hanging out of them. It wouldn't have taken much to calve them. Lisa counted three dead heifers just lying at the top of the paddock. Lisa couldn't believe it.

How could he leave the heifers to die like that? Those poor cows and the lost calf. Lisa couldn't see all of the paddock so more could be dead elsewhere. What a waste. Lisa carried on walking and found Simon. He was about halfway through the mob and was laughing with the guys he had helping him. They were having a great time laughing and joking. It just grated on her nerves after what she had just seen. Lisa stayed for a bit and then left them to it.

As she walked back, Lisa saw the heifers again and thought, 'That's our future lying dead there'. Lisa was in partnership with Simon, and her financial security was lying dead in the paddock.

That night, over tea, Lisa asked Simon about the dead heifers. "When I walked out to see you, I walked past the heifers."

"Did you?"

"Yeah, I saw three dead ones, which could have been saved. Why didn't you calve them?"

"I haven't got time to calve the heifers. I am busy docking."

"Simon, you could check the heifers in the morning."

"I haven't got time. I can't do everything, just leave me alone." With that, Simon stormed out of the house. Lisa started cleaning up the mess, thinking, 'This cannot continue. Just leaving the heifers to die is not an option. Quite clearly, she was going to have to get more involved in the farm. This wasn't going to happen again.'

Chapter Seventeen

Presents

Sarah Simon's sister came and stayed with her parents. She had been overseas since the wedding. Sarah is blond, skinny, outgoing, very social and very beautiful. Sarah is five years younger than her brother and spends her time being a ski bunny. She travels all around the world, rubbing shoulders with the rich and famous. Going from ski season to ski season. Then, she would spend a month lying on a beach in the tropics somewhere to catch up on her sunshine.

Sarah only wears designer clothes and has her lifestyle supported by her parents. Mary had explained to Lisa one day why she paid for all of her daughter's plane flights.

When Sarah was younger, she had been taking a bus from the North Island to Queenstown to go skiing. While she was in Picton, using the public toilets, she overheard two guys talking outside the toilet window. According to Sarah, they were discussing how they were going to rape her on the trip.

Sarah rang her parents and told them all about it. From then on, Sarah was not required to use the bus as it was too dangerous for her. They paid for her to fly from Blenheim to Queenstown on that occasion. Most other people would have rang the police and filed a complaint. Not Sarah or her parents.

Lisa had doubts about how true the story was. It was all too convenient for Sarah's travel plans. Considering she travelled all over the world without any issues, and yet she had one issue, in a small country town in New Zealand on a public bus. Damn those buses.

During the ski season, Sarah provided for her daily living expenses by working at waitressing or being a short-term nanny to the super-rich. The parents loved that she socialised with the rich and famous. They want her to make a very advantageous marriage, to a wealthy family and be a socialite. To help with this the parents pay for all her travel costs.

Sarah had a constant string of boyfriends who seemed to come and go like the wind. They paid for her to travell from NZ to England, paid for holidays, took her shopping, and showered her with gifts.

Lisa and Simon were very short of money. With the farm and the new baby, every penny was carefully calculated. Sarah's birthday rolled around in November. The low point in their budget. Simon wanted to give her something for her birthday.

"I am going to give her $100," Simon said

"Really, you could give her something else that costs less."

"No, I want to give her a $100 note, it's my sister. Why shouldn't I give her $100?"

"Because we don't have any money."

"We can afford it. I am going to give it to her!" Simon stated in a very forceful voice. There wasn't much more Lisa could say. Simon had made up his mind, and that's what he was going to do. Simon didn't look at the budget. He left all of that up to Lisa, so probably wasn't fully aware of the cash flow.

Sarah was very happy with the $100 note, Simon gave to her. Lisa was a bit pissed off about it. He was giving it to a very spoilt girl who really didn't need it. Lisa could not remember a time when Sarah had given Simon anything for his birthday.

A few weeks later, Sarah was home, visiting her parents.

"Look what I bought with the money you gave me. Isn't it cool? I love it, and see, it's got a little diamond on the end." Sarah explained as she pulled up her top and pushed out her tummy to show Simon her belly button. She had got it pierced.

Seeing that his sister had pieced her belly button was a bit of a shock for Simon. He couldn't believe what she had spent the money on. As they went home Simon kept muttering about the piercing and what a waste of money it was. Simon stopped giving his sister money. Lisa was pleased with the outcome.

Chapter Eighteen

Dagging

In December, all of the ewes and lambs are shorn. Before they can be shorn, they have to be dagged. Many farmers do this themselves due to the expense. It is a busy time of year. Each mob of ewes and lambs needed to be brought in. The lambs are separated and are dosed for worms. They are both dagged and put back together and returned to the paddock as soon as possible.

If the lambs are in the yards too long, it will affect their growth rates. To speed up the process, the ewes are not emptied out before dagging. They are full of grass, which makes them heavier, plus they wee and shit on the board. It makes the board very slippery and dangerous. Robert came down to help with the dagging. He did it for both farms.

Lisa had dagged and crutched on the farm she grew up on, so was called into service. Lisa brought Jim up to the shed and made a nice protected spot for him to lie in with his blanket and bear.

Simon had gone to the stock sale in town. He had stood on a nail a couple of days before, so was limping quite badly.

Lisa and Robert were both struggling with the wet, fat ewes on the board, slipping and sliding. After about three hours, Robert said, between sheep, "There's a local guy who's developed a dagging plant. The sheep walk up a ramp, then it holds them while you dag them."

"Sounds like a good idea. Do you have his contact number?"

"Yeah, I got it at home. I can ring him when I go up for some lunch and have a yarn with him."

"Find out if we can see it working." Lisa thought anything would be better than this. Lisa took Jim home, fed him, cleaned him and got organized for the afternoon at the woolshed.

Back at the shed, while they were changing the gear, Robert said, "Peter is going to bring it out and set it up this afternoon. He's keen for us to see it in use."

"That was fast. I hope it works."

They went back to dagging. Jim was happy, watching the lights on the ceiling.

Mary arrived and collected up Jim. Her grandson was not going to spend his time in the woolshed.

Simon and Lisa were selling some heifers at the stock sale, hoping to make some money on the grass market. Lisa slowly worked out, while she was dagging, what price they needed to sell the heifers for in order to meet their costs. What they made over this, they could use to buy the dagging plant, if it worked. Lisa was really keen on the dagging plant idea. Dragging, wet, fat, full ewes, for the next three weeks, looked a bit bleak.

Peter arrived with his plant and set it up. It had to be plugged in and Peter had the extension cords for that. He also bought out an air compressor to run the plant. In fact, Peter arrived with everything they could possibly need.

They had a portable shearing plant, which they hung up. Peter showed Lisa how it worked, ran some sheep through it, adjusted a few things and it was all go. Lisa was impressed.

"How much is it?

"The price for the unit is $3000, but you will need to get the air compressor."

"I don't know if we can afford it yet." Lisa replied, wondering where they were going to get $3000 from.

Peter, looking quite happy about the situation, said, "I'll just leave it here, and you can trial it."

"You'll leave the air compressor and everything? It will end up really dirty, and I might break something."

"Not a problem. Give me a ring in a couple of weeks, and let me know what you think." With that, Peter left.

Lisa was a bit surprised and very pleased that she had a couple of weeks to play with it. It was like having a new toy. Wow, she was going to make the most of it and get as many sheep through it as she could.

Robert and Lisa went back to the woolshed. They had finished the ewes and were onto the lambs. Lambs are easier, being lighter and generally have very few dags. Simon came back from the sale, looking quite happy with himself. As soon as he got in the door, Lisa bombarded him with questions about what the heifers had sold for. The price was way better than they expected. They had enough money for the dagging plant and the air compressor.

"Simon, a local guy, Peter, came out with a dagging plant he has designed"

"What?"

"It's on trial. Come and have a look at it?" Lisa took Simon outside and showed him the plant.

"That won't work. You're wasting our time."

"No, it did work. Peter put some of the ewes through it and showed me how it worked. It's real easy to use. It will be so much faster than doing them on the board."

Simon angrily replied in a loud voice, "It's a complete waste of time. You have been mucking around with this when you could have finished the mob. What made you think you have the right to go ahead and organize something like this? What possessed you to think this would work?"

Simon was really angry about it and stalked back to the woolshed. "Simon, your father made the suggestion, and it worked."

"We don't have money to waste on silly gadgets like this," was Simon's parting remark. Lisa was left standing in the covered yards, looking at the new plant. Dagging ewes on the board was hard work and slow. This looked to be a really good idea.

Lisa was not going to give it up. All she could see were benefits. It could weigh sheep as well.

That night, Simon wasn't happy about the new plant. He refused to talk about it. Lisa was determined to make it work. Simon finally agreed to Lisa dagging the next mob of ewes in it. He seemed pretty certain that Lisa would fail and the plant would be returned.

In the morning, Simon brought another mob in to be dagged. Lisa took Jim up to Mary and then went down to the shed.

The lambs were drafted off and driven into the woolshed. Robert and Simon were going to crutch and dose them on the board. The ewes were left in the yards for Lisa to deal with. She was going to dag in the new plant, on her own, in a poor set-up. Simon was sceptical about the whole idea. He was humouring Lisa, sure in the knowledge that after today, he would be proved right, and the plant would go back.

The race had been designed for goats, so the sides were very high. Lisa would be off her feet as she hung over the side, trying to push the sheep up. It was also very long, so she had to do a lot of running up and down the race to get the sheep moving.

Lisa got her dog at the back and filled the race. She started dagging. It took her a while to get used to everything, but it was so much easier and faster. Lisa ran up and down the race, to push the ewes up, to be as fast as possible. She really wanted it to work and to show them that it was worth it.

Lisa finished the ewes. *Yippee!* Lisa was so happy to have them done, and her back didn't hurt, and she had finished them in record time. She kept smiling at the freshly dagged ewes out in the paddock. Lisa was very chuffed with herself.

Lisa could hear the shearing plants on the board going, so she had beaten them. Lisa was tired and sore but elated. She had proved the benefits of the new dagging plant. Simon couldn't get angry about it now.

Lisa went up to the shearing shed and leaned against the wall, watching Robert and Simon crutching the lambs. There's nothing better than watching a dagging gang, knowing you don't have to do anything. They looked up at her occasionally and carried on. Lisa just continued to lean against the wall.

Simon finally looked up and said, "Well, aren't you going back to finish them?"

"Nope, I'm finished."

They both stopped crutching and looked at her. Lisa didn't say how she had run up and down frantically to finish them. In disbelief, they both looked out the door to check if she had any left.

Robert looked at Lisa and said, "I'm going home. You don't need me."

There weren't many lambs left to do, so Simon and Lisa finished them on the board. "Well, that's it, we aren't dagging on the board any longer. The lambs can get done in it as well." With that, Simon walked out and took the mob back to the paddock. Lisa walked down to the house, feeling self-satisfied. She was really impressed with just how well it had worked. Life was going to get easier, so much easier. Lisa then compared the numbers of how many ewes and lambs were dagged.

Their lambing percentage was 90 to 110%, and she had dagged 250 ewes, which meant they would have had, at the very most, 275 lambs to crutch. There were two of them crutching, and lambs are easier to do, being smaller and cleaner.

So they had 138 lambs each, and she had still beaten them. Lisa was very pleased with herself. She had a quick shower, before collecting Jim from Mary.

From then on, they did all the dagging with the Racewell plant. They fixed up the race so it was easier to chase the sheep up to the unit. Lisa ended up doing all of the dagging. That hadn't been her plan. Simon explained to her that she was faster than him and they needed to get them done. Jim went up to his grandparents in the morning, and Lisa spent the day dagging in the covered yards. It wasn't such an issue dagging wet and full sheep as it was on the board. The yards got muddy, and Lisa got covered in mud and shit. Simon stood at the side of the race, watching in between chasing the sheep up.

Chapter Nineteen

Water

After Lisa moved into the house, she was told not to drink the water. Not a word was mentioned about the water before she moved in, but everyone knew about it. The manager and the previous owners had got sick from drinking the water. All of the water had to be boiled before it was drunk. No one understood why, as it came from the bore, so it should be fine.

Mary gave them a water filter, which sat on the very limited bench space Lisa had. It didn't boil the water, so Lisa wasn't sure how effective it was. Lisa didn't drink coffee or tea. She drank cold drinks or water.

Lisa used the filter for a while and then just started using the water out of the tap. She was reasonably sure it would take a lot to make her sick. Sometimes, the water was clear, and other times, it would be cloudy. It would have fine particles floating in it.

Lisa grew up on a farm, which had water issues. The house water came from a spring located up the hill behind the house. It was pristine, clean water. Dad had years earlier dug the spring out and put a concrete wall, around the front. It had an outlet pipe about a quarter of the way up the concrete wall. Round the back of the dam was a bank with Manuka growing on it. Mostly, it was good, except in a drought, when they ran out of water.

The down side was when sheep were grazing the paddock; they would push into the Manuka looking for that next bite of grass. Sometimes, one would fall off the bank and land in the dam. No one would check the dam unless something was wrong. Their first sign was when the water started to smell or/and bits of wool came down the tap. So Lisa, who drank cold drinks made from the water out of the tap, would be drinking the water when it had dead sheep in it. Her immune system was pretty darn good.

Judith used to tell stories. She was 13 years older when they lived in the older house on the flat below. It had a dam on the same system, except that dam was full of frogs and tadpoles. In summer, when they turned on the tap, part of a tadpole could land in the wash basin or saucepan. The tadpole would have been decapitated when the tap had been turned off the time before. Judith has vivid memories of turning on the bathroom tap in the morning to wash her face to find part of a tadpole floating in the water.

Lisa thinks the first time that happened, Judith had totally freaked out. It would have been a shock for a 12-year-old girl to face first thing in the morning when she was still half asleep. At least they didn't have that.

Consequently, the water wasn't a problem for Lisa. The baby's drinks Lisa boiled, so all good. Simon only drank hot drinks.

Lisa washed the nappies in the washing machine and hung them on the line. They had a brown tinge to them. She couldn't understand why they weren't white. They were soaked, bleached and washed on a full wash. Lisa doubled the recommended rate for the bleach, but they still came out brown. Sometimes, they weren't just brown but would have a harsh feel to them.

Local housewives would say, "Nothing gave them greater pleasure than seeing pristine white nappies hanging on the line. What joy and satisfaction it gave them." Lisa would look at them wondering, just how boring their lives must be. If that gave them their greatest pleasure, she didn't want a bar of it.

The family friends of her husband's that turned up to visit would look at Lisa's washing and say:

"Those nappies aren't clean, you need to soak them".

"I can't stand someone who is a dirty washer."

"Better care needs to be taken with cleaning the nappies".

"You have to wash them separately, you can't put them in with the farm clothes."

Some of them got quite worked up about the nappies and her washing. Mary would make tut-tutting noises and mutter about Lisa not washing correctly. Lisa assured everyone, that she did soak them and she did wash them separately. They just looked at her, sniffed in disbelief, put their noses in the air and walked away muttering.

Lisa would be left feeling chastened and frustrated. It got to the stage that she didn't care what they said any longer. Lisa did the best she could and she had no idea what she did wrong. It was just the way it was.

Lisa struggled with this concept of being a dirty washer. They all have washing machines. The washing is put into the machine, then add the powder and turn it on. The biggest mistake one can make is adding something, which has an unstable colour. Its not like they go down to the river and beat the clothes on a rock any more. In that situation, maybe someone is a dirty washer, less beating.

So Lisa wondered what she did wrong and carried on. She noticed that every time Simon put sheep in the yards, the water at the house turned brown. Sometimes, it was just a light colour and other times it would be a very dark colour.

Lisa mentioned this repeatedly to Simon, who really didn't pay much attention to it. He always drank tea or coffee, so he didn't notice. When it was really bad, Lisa would get large bottles of water from her in-laws' house. Lisa cooked the food in the clean water. When the spuds were boiled in brown water, they came out looking rotten. Not a good look. It really put them off eating them. Simon never commented on the colour of the spuds. He just added more butter.

Jim was four months old when Lisa ran him a bath. The bath water was clay brown, to the point the bottom of the bath couldn't be seen. Lisa was standing by the bathtub, looking at the bath water, wondering whether bathing Jim was going to have any benefit. Perhaps she should just give him a wipeover. Trouble was, it was the same water. Jim really needed a bath to clean out all his little folds of skin, but Lisa didn't want to put him into that water.

Simon came home and demanded to know what she was doing. "I am wondering if I should bathe Jim in the bath or not."

Simon looked at the bath water and said in a loud voice, "Don't be so stupid. You can't bath him in that, it's filthy."

"I don't have any other water. Every time you put stock in the yards, the water turns brown. What else am I to do?"

"Well, you aren't washing my son in that, so let it out and stop being an idiot."

Lisa let the water out of the bath, feeling hurt. She was only trying to do the best for Jim. It was the same water from the same water source she had used yesterday. Lisa had no control over the water.

Lisa really didn't want to take Jim up to the in-laws to wash him. It would have turned into a full visit and given Mary an opportunity to launch into her latest concerns over her child-rearing.

To bring enough water down from their house for a bath, would have been a nightmare. Lisa would have had to heat it on the stove and then cart it to the bath. Jim really did need to be washed. Lisa wiped Jim down with a flannel, using the same water, wondering if she would be better off going down to the creek. Simon watched her clean Jim and didn't comment about the water she was using. Quite clearly, he didn't connect the dots.

Simon had mobs of ewes in and out of the yards as it was time for the first pick of lambs for sale. The rest of the lambs were being dosed.

The bath water must have finally made an impression on Simon cause the next day, he got a farm water plumber out. Lisa and Simon had been living in the house for close to 16 months by this time. Over that time, Lisa had constantly mentioned the water. All to no avail. Something was finally happening.

Simon and the plumber spent five hours up the hill chasing water pipes. The dog kennels were in view of the kitchen and dining room windows. They were just up the bank from the driveway.

The previous owner had built some very impressive dog motels right up the bank, not far from the sheep yards. They had been cut into the bank with a concrete base. The base was all sloped with a drain so that all the dog shit could be washed out and run down the hill. On the uphill side was a tap, which a hose could be attached too. Above them was a gate into the holding paddock, around the sheep yards. The bore where all the water came from was just across from the gate. It fed the woolshed, house and the water troughs.

After much digging and turning taps on and off, they discovered that the dog water to the original dog kennels was straight from the bore. Pristine clean water.

The house water went via the sheep yards. So the bore pumped the water to the woolshed and on the way it fed the water troughs. The house waterline was T joined into this water pipe. The water troughs were right by the sheep yards.

These are the troughs that the dogs jump in to cool off. The troughs that they piss on the side of (and some in the trough) and they are the troughs that the sheep or cattle will jump in as they are being chased around the yards. It was the trough that the cattle might shit into. It was the trough that the sheath knife would be rinsed in to remove the blood after it had been used to kill a sick sheep. It was a foul mixture of just about everything one could imagine, and just looking at the water, there was no way anyone would consider drinking it. Just the thought would turn your stomach.

The water line filled the trough with water. However, when the water system had no pressure on it, the water in the trough would backflow out of it to the lowest point. When Lisa turned a tap on at the house, gravity created a suction on the line, and the water in the trough backflowed down to the house.

They were drinking water directly from the water trough and its cocktail of urine, shit, mud and blood. It was a bacteria haven. Like Lisa said her immune system was cast iron. Lisa didn't get sick once. As a kid, Lisa had every illness one could get, including Meningitis and Glandular fever.

Simon was shocked about the source of the house water. They spent the next day laying new pipe to tap into the house line so the house would work directly off the bore. From then on, they had pristine, clean water.

Guess what? The nappies turned white, and they stopped going on about Lisa being a dirty washer. She would have done better taking them down to the river and beating them on a rock.

Lisa happened to see the daughter of the previous owners a few months later. They used to live in the same house. Lisa asked them about the water, and they confirmed that it was bad. It was not drinkable. Lisa explained what they had found out. They didn't seem surprised and said they used to cart drinking water from the other house. Lisa went home wondering why no one had thought to fix the problem over a 20 year plus period, which included two previous owners and a manager. One would think that one of them might have looked at it, including her in-laws, who had owned the farm for 10 years. It did take them 16 months, before they fixed it, but at least they did.

The improved water made a big difference to Lisa and the house. It was so much nicer and easier to have clean water come out of the tap. Lisa still had some concerns. One day, when she was up with Simon, Lisa asked about the offal holes. Offal holes are deep holes drilled into the ground where dead animals are dropped. It has a concrete lid on top for safety. The issue Lisa had was that they were by the sheep yards and close to the Bore.

"Simon, do you think the offal holes are to close to the bore?"

"No."

"But the bore taps into the groundwater, and the Offal holes are in the same area."

"They are completely separate. Don't be so silly. The groundwater flows in a different direction."

"Oh," Lisa struggled with that. How did Simon know which way the ground water flowed? It made no sense to Lisa. She didn't say anything else, but each time she was around the bore, she wondered. Lisa tried to get any future offal holes drilled elsewhere, just in case.

Chapter Twenty

First Xmas with Jim

In December they weaned, picked lambs for sale, dosed the remaining lambs and shore everything. Finally, they had some income.

The house started to dry out with the sunshine and warmth. The water was clean. Things were looking good.

Simon found a Xmas tree on the farm and bought it home. They set it up in the corner next to the fireplace. They didn't have any Xmas decorations and Lisa couldn't afford any. They were a luxury. Jim had a lot of stuffed toys his friends had given him.

Lisa collected them up, except for Bear, and put them in the branches of the tree. She was quite tearful that she didn't have any tinsel or lights. She wanted their first Xmas with Jim to be special. Mary came down and visited and made a comment about it being a bear tree. Lisa got a bit tearful again. Lisa was so focused on the fact she didn't have tinsel that she missed the fact the tree looked pretty good. Lisa didn't realise that until some months later when she looked at the photos.

Robert and Mary didn't have a Xmas tree, and they didn't believe in giving presents. The wider family would do a Xmas luncheon at each other's houses. Robert had three brothers, two of which farmed, in the area with their families. The other brother, was an accountant, who they didn't see much of.

Jim, being nearly four months old, was quite happy playing with cardboard boxes. The whole Xmas thing was too abstract for him.

Xmas morning, they gave Jim a plastic truck and some wooden jigsaw puzzles. Jim was happier with the wrapping paper. At 10 o'clock, Jim and Lisa went up to the in-laws' house to go to the family luncheon. Simon didn't come. He said he had stock to move.

Lisa had never been to the family Xmas luncheon before, so she was not sure what to expect. This year, it was just one brother's family and them.

They all went in one car, so Sarah, Jim in his car seat and Lisa were all crammed in the back seat. Sarah was very nicely dressed, as usual. Jim was at the stage when he just wanted to play with whatever he could get his hands on and cry when he couldn't have it. Sarah decided that to keep Jim entertained, she would let him play with her make-up bag. Lisa didn't think this was a good idea and tried to stop Sarah, but was over-ridden. Jim got the lipstick cap off and proceeded to spread lipstick all over himself and whatever else he could reach.

They managed to wrestle that off him and minimise the damage. Sarah was a bit upset cause some had got onto her.

Lisa kept thinking, 'In what world is it sensible to give a child a makeup bag to play with?' It could have been so much worse.

Robert, in the meantime, thought it was really good to give Lisa a lecture about child-rearing, the farm and how she should behave. Lisa was relieved when they arrived two hours later.

It was a lovely bungalow house set in amongst mature trees. Carol had prepared an extravagant Xmas luncheon. It consisted of nibbles followed by a three-course meal served on fine china with silver cutlery and napkins, plus all of the table decorations. Jim, by this stage, was moving around on his tummy and able to pull himself up on things, to a sitting position. He could then reach for shiny objects. At home, this was fine, as Lisa had moved everything up. Carol had not. Neither did she have a highchair. In the open-plan dining lounge area, there were display shelves, which started at the floor and reached to waist height. On these were lovely and expensive-looking china cups, sauceboats, figurines and plates.

Lisa fed Jim at the table, sitting on her lap. She tried holding Jim on her lap as she ate. It didn't work. All Jim wanted was to move about and grab everything. Since Lisa needed both a knife and fork to eat the meal, it was beyond her.

Lisa put Jim down in the middle of the lounge floor to play while she ate. Jim moved a lot faster than she thought he would. Lisa was in constant terror that Jim would break something. She was up and down, shifting Jim away from the latest attraction. All the other adults made comments, about how well Jim was moving. He wasn't far away from crawling. Not one of them suggested anything which might help with limiting Jim's ability to reach the expensive china.

During the first course, Lisa wasn't paying much attention to the conversation. She was looking around the room and outside trying to find a solution, which would save the china. Through the windows at her back, she spied a deck outside the french doors.

When it came to the second course, Lisa decided that leaving Jim on the floor was not working. He always seemed to be able to move further and faster than she expected.

Lisa stood up. "I'm going to take Jim outside so he can play on the grass."

Lisa collected her plate and Jim. Everybody else at the table looked a bit surprised and just looked at her.

Lisa went outside. There was a wide wooden deck with a table and chairs. It was in the shade, and just down below was a shaded grass area. Lisa put Jim down there, with his toys and sat down at the table and had lunch. It was very pleasant. Unbeknownst to her, she had caused a drama inside. Apparently, they were all distressed that she had left the table and gone outside.

Robert kept asking, "Why has she walked out? Why would Lisa just walk out? How rude of her. What is wrong with her?"

They felt that she did not appreciate the hostess's efforts. Lisa was trying to save her expensive china from a sticky end.

Once the main course had been finished, Lisa was looking forward to spending the rest of the afternoon, on the deck with dessert. It was very pleasant, and she was relaxing while watching Jim roll around on the grass. The conversation inside about people she didn't know held no interest for her at all.

Lisa was surprised when Mary rushed out. "I will watch Jim now, you can go back inside and have the rest of Xmas lunch."

"No, it's fine, you go back and enjoy it with your family. I'm fine out here, and Jim is very happy."

"No, no, you must go back inside. Everyone is waiting for you. I don't want to have anything else to eat."

Lisa went back inside reluctantly. She was happier outside. Apparently, Mary had rushed through her meal so that she could go outside and look after Jim.

In Lisa went to spend the rest of the afternoon playing ladies with dessert, followed by cake and drinks. Carol, when Lisa went back in, said, "The house isn't really organised for a toddler, is it?"

Lisa replied, "No."

At the end of the afternoon, they all packed back into the car and travelled home. Jim slept, thank God. Once again, Robert felt he had a trapped audience and launched into another lecture about the economy, farming and family.

Lisa took her tired and scratchy child home to find Simon sitting on the sofa with a cup of tea, looking quite happy and relaxed.

"How did it go?" he asked.

"I am never repeating that again. Next time you have a family get-together, I am not going on my own. This is your family, not mine, and you can go."

"That well."

Lisa then went off to start tea and get Jim changed and fed. Lisa began to wonder, 'if Simon actually did have stock to shift or if it was an excuse.'

Chapter Twenty-One

February the 14th

Valentine's Day arrived. Nothing was said or discussed. They were still struggling financially and spending any spare money on the farm. They wished each other happy valentines in bed, kissed and started their day.

About mid-afternoon, Simon arrived home with a dozen red roses with babies breath. They were lovely, and they contained a card wishing Lisa, Happy Valentines. Lisa was very surprised, pleased and at a complete loss. They smelt divine and looked gorgeous. Lisa knew they were also very expensive. She put them in a jug on the kitchen table. They looked completely out of place in an old, faded kitchen.

They had a joint account, so she knew where the money came from. It meant she couldn't get other household things. Simon was really pleased with himself and told everyone he had bought Lisa a dozen red roses. Lisa was pleased that he had thought to do it, but there were other things he could have done. Fixing the windows to stop the water coming in, cooking her dinner, or one single rose would have been more than satisfactory.

Every time Lisa looked at the roses, she was conflicted. The wasted money won out and they just became a symbol of her sacrifice.

Lisa's Dad, who felt all funds should be spent on the farm and resented any money being spent on the house, would have been shocked. Lisa remembers, when he had bought hay from a local farmer. The bloke had just given his wife a large diamond ring. He was telling everyone what he had done. How it was important to show 'the old girl' how much she was appreciated.

Well, Dad happened to stop at the house and saw the wife. She was in the laundry doing the washing. The only washing machine she had was an old mangle. It's one of those machines which has an open bowl with an agitator. Once the water is drained out, the clothes are pulled out and threaded through the rollers to ring them out. They are then put back into the washing machine to rinse, then repeat. Mum used to have one. When Lisa was a kid, she tried to help with the washing and managed to put her arm through the rollers. They had to unscrew the rollers to get her out.

Dad was shocked that the husband could leave his wife struggling with an outdated washing machine and spend the money on a ring. He told everyone he saw how he felt about it. Not sure what the husband thought, when it got back to him, as it would have done. It was a small community.

Lisa kept thinking about the roses in the same category as the washing machine. Her husband was going around telling everyone what he had done and basking in the adulation. Robert saw it as a waste of money and was very verbal about it. Lisa couldn't say anything cause it would have just caused conflict.

The petals slowly fell off the roses and drifted to the floor. When the last petal floated to the floor, Lisa looked at it, thinking, 'They were nice while they lasted, but what a waste.' Lisa liked flowers, but it was not the right time to spend money on them. There were so many other more pressing issues. There was still a hole in the bathroom floor and the leaking windows. Lisa tried to make potpourri from the petals, but they just went mouldy.

Chapter Twenty-Two

Wedding

S imon's cousin on his mother's side was getting married. It was four hours away on the east coast. The plan was for them to travel over for the day, attend the wedding and travel back that night.

They left in the morning with nappies, baby food, blankets and toys for Jim. The car's air conditioning was the windows being wound down. It was a hot, humid long day with Jim being car sick.

They arrived at the beach, which was cooler, and all stood around waiting for the service. Lisa hadn't met any of Mary's extended family before. She spent her time trying to entertain Jim, changing and storing cloth nappies and feeding him. Simon was off catching up with relatives and having a good time.

The bride wore a cream-flared dress with cream roses around the neckline. It was a simple, elegant wedding. The after-function was afternoon tea on a deck overlooking the ocean.

Lisa wanted to go home as Jim was scratchy, and it was a long trip back. She was pushing the pushchair around, looking for Simon. Couldn't see him anywhere. He had disappeared. Mary kept talking to her and asking what was wrong with Jim. Lisa felt totally alone and had no idea where Simon was. Other guests were leaving and still no sign of Simon.

A bunch of guys started walking towards them, and Lisa saw Simon. They all made a lot of fuss over Simon as he had been helping them move all of the chairs. Simon looked very happy with himself and demanded that Lisa be ready to leave. She felt totally alone.

Chapter Twenty-Three

Immunity

One day, Lisa was in the kitchen when Jim was 7 months old. He was crawling with speed. He would be playing on the floor next to Lisa, and then he would be gone. On this day, Lisa was placing the formula bottles in the steriliser after they had been boiled. It was a real rigmarole and took up her limited bench space. Lisa had just put the last bottle into the sterilising liquid when she looked out the window.

Jim was sitting outside in the middle of the driveway, sucking rocks. He had got himself out of the lounge, down the steps, into the carport and out to the gravel. Lisa rushed outside and collected Jim up. Fished the rock out of his mouth and headed back inside. The driveway was a mess. It was where the quad bike was ridden after it had been round the farm covered in shit and mud. The dogs pissed on the driveway and walked all over it. It was a toxic bacteria mix.

Lisa came back inside with Jim and looked at the sterilising bottles and then looked at the rock Jim had been sucking.

"It's a complete waste of time doing this, isn't it, Jim?"

From then on, the steriliser got put into storage, and the bottles didn't get boiled any longer. They got washed and rinsed out with boiling water. Jim's health didn't alter, and Lisa's life got easier. Jim's immune system probably improved as well.

Sarah

Sarah would stay with her parents in-between her trips. She enjoyed playing with Jim at Simon's and Lisa's place or when Jim stayed with his grandparents. Mary did all the cooking and Sarah enjoyed all the play. She refused point blank to change nappies or to clean up any mess.

It was nice that she came and stayed and caught up with her brother. One day when they were visiting Simons parent's, Sarah was sunbathing on a deck chair out by the bedrooms. She proudly showed Lisa and Simon her latest purchase. A pair of leather boots, which cost $800/boot. They were impressed. She had also bought a leather jacket but didn't say what that cost. It was very soft leather with a very pretentious designer label. Simon was a bit shocked.

Lisa and Simon were very broke, and he explained to his sister that they were getting $800 for a whole 300kg (carcase weight) steer.

After Sarah showed them, she said, "Don't tell Daddy. I want him to pay for my plane trip to Whistler in Canada next month." Daddy paid.

Lisa and Simon went home to their cold, damp, mouldy house with their son after having a glimpse of how the other half lived.

Chapter Twenty-Four

Out and About

After Jim's checkered start, Jim and Lisa got out on the farm. It was nice to escape the damp house. Lisa wrapped Jim up warmly and got him into the Macpac with Bear. Jim loved it. He had a great view of the world and free access to Lisa's ears and hair. Baby fingers can pull with a surprising amount of strength.

In the first year, they raised Frisian bull calves. It was the cheapest way they could improve their stock numbers and get into running bulls. Simon had been feeding them in early spring when Lisa was busy with Jim. Lisa had been helping out when she could. The woolshed and covered yards were just up the hill from the house, so it was easy for her to go up.

Once Jim was older, Lisa started feeding the calves in the morning. They were housed in the covered yards used for dagging and for shearing. Not designed for calf feeding at all. They had about 120 calves, with 15 per pen. The pens had sawdust on the floor, and water troughs, and Simon had made hay feeders out of netting and battens. The calves were fine. The problem was feeding them. Lisa had to cart 15-litre buckets through pens to get to the other pens. This meant that once Lisa fed one pen, she had to move rapidly to get the next pen fed before the first pen decided they wanted a second feed. It was a battle.

Jim loved it, he would be laughing at the calves and was fascinated. One day, Lisa had Jim on her back and two 15-litre buckets in her hands as she struggled through one pen of calves to reach the other pen. Lisa was nearly to the next gate when Jim, who had been laughing, suddenly let out a blood-curdling scream. Lisa nearly dropped the buckets in shock. It sounded like her son was being eaten.

Lisa was hanging onto the buckets, trying to stop the calves from knocking them and desperately twisting around, trying to see what had set Jim off. Jim didn't let up on the screaming.

Lisa laughed with relief when she saw what the problem was. Jim's feet hung down each side of the Macpac. An enterprising calf had decided that his foot looked promising. It had all of Jim's foot in its mouth and was sucking madly. Calves will suck on anything that they can reach and have a very strong suck with a rough tongue. Jim was still screaming and probably thought the calf was eating him.

Lisa calmed down and focused on getting both of them out of the calf pen. Once she got the gate shut, she took Jim out of the backpack and gave him a big hug. He was so upset, with tears running down his cheeks and gasping breaths.

Lisa hoped the calf enjoyed Jim's sock cause it was never seen again.

After that Jim was a bit wary of the calves and tended to keep his feet up high so they couldn't reach him. Lisa started to leave his backpack hooked on the rails when she carted the buckets. Jim was quite happy watching the calves and seeing her passing back and forth in front of him.

Lisa took Jim with her when she checked the stock on the bike. Jim loved it. He came home with pink cheeks, hugging Bear. Cause he was in a backpack, he was really warm, being protected by the canvas sides and tucked in against her back. His feet were warm in their little red band gumboots.

Jim loved to play in the creek. There was nothing Jim liked better than throwing rocks into the creek and watching the splashes.

Bear had to go everywhere, but Jim wasn't very protective of Bear. Bear got thrown into the cattle yards and came out a soaking shitty mess. Bear got dropped in the sheep yards and thrown in the creek. Lisa was always fishing Bear out of things and washing him. Jim would laugh as he threw Bear, but then he would get upset if Bear disappeared.

God help them if Bear wasn't available at night for bed. It would be a screaming match like no other. If they forgot Bear, then they had to go back and get him. Lisa went to the local town to do some shopping. Lisa had organised to leave Jim with her friend Linda. She enjoyed spending time with Jim.

This day, while Jim was having his nap she washed his bear. Bear needed a wash. Bear always needed a wash. Trouble was Jim woke up to discover Bear had disappeared. Linda tried in vain to explain to Jim that Bear was being washed. Jim continued screaming for Bear.

Finally, Linda took Jim out to the washing machine where he could watch Bear, through the plastic panel, going around and around and around in the washing machine.

When Lisa got back, Jim was sitting on the floor watching Bear. Every so often, he would reach out to touch the clear plastic. Jim was not moving. He was quite upset about Bear being in the washing machine. Once the washing machine stopped, Jim got Bear. There was no way Bear was going to be put into the drier. They took Bear home, spun but wet.

Chapter Twenty-Five

Fire

The first summer after Jim was born. Lisa happened to see the past manager. "Jan, did the fire work when you lived in the house? All it does now is smoke."

"It works; it's a good fire, and you need it in that house. The only trouble is the bricks move around with the heat. You have to reach up and re-adjust them. Just fiddle with them, and they will slide back into place. You will know when they are right."

"Thank you so much, 'cause it is a very cold house without any heating."

"Yeah, it is. The fire makes all the difference."

Lisa did what Jan suggested that autumn and the fire started working again. It was wonderful to have warmth throughout the house. The house stopped being so damp, and Lisa didn't need to use the oil heater in the baby's room so much.

Chapter Twenty-Six

Work

After a long think and a visit to a work meeting, Lisa decided she would resign from her job. Lisa had taken maternity leave, unpaid back then, and the time was up. She cost out the cost of child support and the wages of a worker against her wages if she went back to work. It turned out Lisa would be working to clear $5000/year. That was before travelling costs. Lisa resigned.

The bank appointed another manager, who Lisa had worked with before. Ted came and saw Lisa after he had been on the job for about four months. They had a catch-up about the economy and the district.

Ted then got down to the reason he had come out. "Last year, there was a million dollars deposited into the account."

"Yeah, Robert, my father-in-law deposited it."

"Is there any chance it will come back to the bank?"

"Sorry, no, Robert has invested it."

"There's no way it will come back? Because of that deposit my target has been substantially increased. There's no way I will come anywhere near to meeting the target."

"Sorry. The whole area is depressed, so unlikely another large deposit will be made at all."

Ted left. Poor bugger, he was going to have a hard time meeting his targets.

Chapter Twenty-Seven

Relationships

Lisa's mother was a trained speech therapist. Lisa understood she was really good at her job. The development of children and their language was a passion of hers. One day, on the phone they talked about Jim. Mum wanted to know what he was doing and if he was developing correctly.

"I could do up an exercise booklet for Jim. I would put pictures, and he could do little exercises. You would have to write down what he said. You could then post it back to me, and I would add some more to it."

"Oh, OK, that sounds fun. Jim could get a parcel in the mail. I am sure he would like to do that."

Mum then posted the book to Lisa with some pictures in it. Jim had fun colouring in one picture and telling Lisa what the things were in another. Lisa posted it back to her. This was repeated for some months. After a while, it stopped happening, and just died a death.

Lisa visited Mary one day after the play centre. Jim was playing on the floor quite happily.

"Lisa, I am getting cards from your mother."

"Are you?" That seemed a bit surprising as her mother didn't do much writing to anyone.

"Yes, she's sending them quite regularly. She writes little notes in them about you."

"Oh."

"They are really nasty. She's writing really horrible things about you. She says things like, you can't be trusted. That I have to watch you. They are really nasty."

"Oh. I didn't know." Lisa was thinking, 'What a bitch. Who would write nasty things to her daughter's mother-in-law? For no reason.'

After a while Lisa took Jim home and put him in the cot for a nap. Lisa then rang her mother.

"Mum, it's Lisa."

"Oh, it's nice to hear from you."

"Mum, I have just seen Mary. She told me that you are sending her cards."

"Oh yes, I want to keep in touch with her."

"Mum, can you please stop sending her notes about me? Why would you write nasty things about me to her? They aren't even true." Lisa was struggling to understand why her mother would do something like this.

"Did she show them to you?"

"Yes. Can you please stop?"

"I will have to be more careful in the future", Mum said in a loud, angry voice. She then slammed the phone down.

Lisa sat looking at the phone, thinking, 'Why, why would you do that?' Her mother in law didn't exactly approve of her. Lisa wasn't what she wanted as a daughter-in-law. She wanted a daughter-in-law who was on the play centre committee, the plunket committee, and a member of the local national party. She didn't want a daughter-in-law who worked on the farm. That was not the expected role.

Lisa carried on with everything she had to do in her day. She kept wondering why her mother would do that. Why would a mother write nasty things about her daughter? Lisa knew she didn't like her. Over the years she had told Lisa repeatedly how she had a nasty streak in her. All Lisa had ever done was try and do what was right.

Lisa remember one time when she was living at home and working on the farm.

They were in the kitchen having a discussion about the meaning of a word. Lisa went and got her dictionary. It had been on the school list of books her mother had to buy for her. After Lisa had found the word and handed the dictionary over to her, she had closed the book and turned it over in her hands.

"You have looked after this book," Mum said in a quiet voice.

She put it on the table and opened it to a random page. She then put a finger at the top of the page in the middle, and with the other hand, she lifted up the corner. Mum then watched Lisa intently as she ripped the page in half. Lisa just stood there watching in shock. Lisa reached over, took the dictionary, closed the book and walked back to her room. Why would her mother do that? What a destructive thing to do with absolutely no benefit to her.

Her mother was still trying to make her life difficult.

Chapter Twenty-Eight

The Farm

The farm had been run as a fattening breeding block. Robert had fertilised the block and maintained the existing fences. He hadn't done anything else. The farm had big paddocks, fenced to allow for natural water at one end of the paddock. This meant that when it came to fencing, they were limited, due to the lack of water.

Lisa and Simon needed a water system. The whole area struggled with water supply. Being limestone, the water just disappeared down holes and would reappear somewhere else. They had creeks that disappeared into hills or just popped out. Most places used bores for water. The trouble with drilling a bore is the unknown. There may be water, or maybe not. If there was water, would it remain there?

The creeks and dams were a long way from the power source and down gullies. To get power to the site, the cost was heinous. If they had water at the front of the property then they had power and gravity on their side.

They drilled bores and more bores. It was like standing by a hole and throwing money down it. They eventually found water. Not brilliant, but enough. They then got the local farm water company out.

A system was designed, and they bought troughs, pipe and fittings. It was expensive.

Robert did not approve. "Stock don't need water. They get enough water from the grass. You don't need to put in a water system. It's a waste of money."

Lisa and Simon wanted to subdivide the paddocks and then split the paddocks up with tape to run bulls and fattening steers.

"Robert, stock need water. They can't be fattened without a good water system," Lisa explained. He wasn't convinced.

They carried on putting in the water system against a backdrop of disapproval. Robert and Mary went round to some friends who farmed locally and complained to them about their son putting in a water system.

The father said, "You can't fatten stock without good water. You need water."

After their visit, Robert was happier about them putting in the water system. Once they had the water system in, they employed a local fencer to put up five-wire electric fences. Things were happening. They had better control over the stock and the ability to control the feed.

They had one paddock which didn't grow any grass. Lisa decided that if they applied some nitrogen, it might kick it to life. They needed the feed. The nitrogen went on and nothing grew except some Dandelions. Lisa went and had a closer look at the paddock. There was nothing there to grow. They talked it over and decided to re-grass.

Lisa rang up the local stock company and asked to talk to the rep about grass seed. He rang back that night, and Lisa answered the phone. She had never met him before. Lisa started talking to him about what seed they wanted.

"I want to speak to Simon."

"You can talk to me. I have had a look at the brochures of the pasture mixtures."

"I want to talk to Simon. Is Simon there?"

"Yeah, he's here, but you can talk to me. I'm organising this."

"No, I will talk to Simon." The rep said in a very firm voice.

"OK."

"Simon, it's the rep about the grass seed. He wants to talk to you."

Simon got on the phone. "You need to talk to my wife. She's organising the seed. I will put her back on."

Simon handed the phone back to Lisa and gave her a roll of the eyes. "Hi."

"Oh, um, you, well, um, I talk to you?"

"Yes."

"Oh, about the grass seed? You are making the decision about the seed?"

"Yes", Lisa was thinking 'Will this guy ever get over himself.'

"Um, well, Um we have this mixture of seed you could use."

"Does it have red clover and cocksfoot in it?"

"Um, no, you don't need to add those."

"I want them added to the mixture; they give good autumn feed." After further discussion, an agreement was reached.

He wasn't happy about dealing with Lisa at all. He just didn't think women should make any decisions regarding the farm. Lisa's place was in the house. If he saw Simon in the distance, that's where he headed.

Lisa and Simon did a soil test, expecting the fertility to be reasonable. The sulphur levels were off the chart, but the alkaline and the phosphate were very low. It should have been a lot higher, which explained why they had low fertility grass species. They needed fertiliser and lime.

They sprayed out the paddock, which was growing weeds, and applied four tonnes of lime and a massive amount of super. They then direct drilled the paddock with a new grass species. It grew. They had feed.

They decided to soil test most of the farm to see what the rest of the fertility was like. It wasn't good. Fertiliser is one of the most expensive things to add to a farm system, but without the fertility, it is very difficult to grow good quality feed of ryegrass and clover.

They put together a program of winter crops followed by a summer crop and then into a new grass. Large amounts of fertiliser were applied to the cropped paddocks, and they slowly worked their way around the farm.

They started to buy in lambs and cattle to fatten over the summer. It gave them more options and spread their income. The farm performance improved, and the farm returns improved.

All spare funds were ploughed back into the farm. Lisa was still living on a very limited budget. She was supportive of the farm policy as she could see that in the future, it would give them a good living and provide a future for her son.

The agents from the stock firms and seed companies would turn up at the house. The new reps seemed quite happy to talk to a woman, so it was easier for Lisa to work with them.

They bought out experts in the different fields. The look of shock on their faces when they came to the house indicated just how bad the house looked. They would then go reluctantly with Simon around the farm to come back all smiles and very positive.

Chapter Twenty-Nine

Swimming

Lisa lived on a farm with water troughs, dams, creeks, ponds, a river and bogs. Lisa was really scared about Jim drowning. It only takes a few seconds for a kid to drown, and one of the district's children had recently drowned in a pond by the house. The mother was cooking for the shearers and had only turned her back for a few minutes.

Lisa knew that she couldn't stop her children from being around water, but she could give them swimming lessons. Lisa told her in-laws that she was going to take Jim to swimming lessons. They did not approve. It was a waste of money and time. No need for her to take Jim swimming, and it was just stupid to take a child less than a year old.

Lisa persisted and took Jim to the heated undercover swimming pool. Jim wasn't too sure about it at the start. The parents held their children in the water and moved them slowly around the pool. It was wonderful, especially for Lisa. In the cold winter months in a damp house, it was a little piece of sunshine and warmth.

Jim slowly got more confident and started looking forward to going. Before long, he could float on his back, blow bubbles and kick his legs.

Lisa was pregnant with her second child. As she got bigger, it was pure heaven lying on her back in the warm water. Totally pressure-less. She never wanted to get out.

Chapter Thirty

Holidays

Robert and Mary went on holiday every year over seas. They had been all over the world, China, America, and Europe but mostly to England and Scotland. They never really discussed their plans. Lisa and Simon just found out when they were leaving or after they had gone.

When Jim was about 11 months old, mid-winter, they headed off on another trip. This time, they wanted Simon and Lisa to move into their house to keep it safe. The house was located at the far corner of the farm, completely away from the sheds, dogs, in fact everything.

It was a far bigger and warmer house than theirs, with a log burner in the kitchen, which warmed the whole house. It had been built and decorated in the 1970s and hadn't been touched since. It had the 1970s wallpaper, which would give you nightmares. Big plates in some rooms, triffid-looking flowers in others and a well-worn kitchen. It also had Chinese silk rugs, a leather sofa, antique carved Kauri furniture and expensive china. Lisa was terrified that Jim would damage some of the antiques, so she shut some rooms off. Jim was walking now on unsteady little legs, and he spent a lot of time hanging onto chairs.

The section had a mature garden, so the house was well-screened from the road.

Mary didn't garden, so the ivy was overrunning everything to the point it was fighting to come in through the windows. Some windows Lisa couldn't open due to the ivy covering it. The trees along the driveway were forming a dark corridor. It was a bit like driving through a jungle. The car would get whacked as Lisa drove along it. She spent some time outside cutting it all back.

Lisa hated it. Jim and her rattled around the house and all of Mary's stuff on their own. Being so far away from the woolshed and yards, she couldn't hear what was going on or walk up to the shed with Jim. The house was situated behind a ridge and trees, so the rest of the farm was hidden. All she could only see were two paddocks and she couldn't hear anything.

Simon would go out in the morning and have lunch at the other house. Lisa didn't see him till the evening.

Simon had some family friends staying from Sweden, who spent all day with him. Lisa just did all of the cooking and cleaning. They were a nice couple, but Lisa had no real connection with them.

Simon and Lisa had been guests at the neighbours, who lived just across the road, on a number of occasions. It was their time to return the favour and invite them for dinner. Mary had a large dining table, so space was going to be fine. Lisa was cooking for six adults, three children and Jim. She decided a roast lamb dinner was her best option.

Lisa had everything organised and set the table, and Jim's food sorted. With any dinner, it requires attention just before serving.

Simon had come home from the farm and was sitting in a chair by the fireplace. It was about half an hour before the guests were due to arrive. Lisa was shifting pots around on the stove.

"Simon, go and have a shower."

"Yeah, I will in a little bit."

"Simon, if you have a shower now, you will be ready to greet everyone."

Simon just carried on sitting in the chair. The Swedish couple had come back earlier and were all ready for dinner. They were sitting at the table, watching and listening. Simon carried on sitting in the chair. Lisa wanted Simon to get ready so that he could help with Jim and serving the food.

Lisa carried on making gravy and checking if everything was cooked. Their guests arrived, and Simon leapt to his feet and answered the door.

"Here you are, come in, come in, to where it's warm. Just leave your coats over there. Have a seat. Lisa has some wine for you. Sorry, I am in such a mess. Just came in from the farm. Haven't had a chance to change yet. I must go and clean up now". With that, Simon left.

Lisa was not happy and sent Simon a dirty look. All that crap about how he had just come in pissed her off. The Swedish couple intercepted the look and then exchanged glances.

It was at this point that Jim decided to have a screaming match. Lisa was right in the middle of serving the food and making the gravy. She needed to look after Jim, but she couldn't leave the food. The mother came over to her and said, "I will finish this off; you go and sort Jim out."

"Thank you. I'm so sorry about this."

Lisa grabbed Jim and headed to the bedroom to change his nappy. She whipped through the nappy changing and got Jim back into his high chair.

She went back to help with the food. All of the plates were on the table, and the father carved the roast as Simon still hadn't come back. Everyone was sitting at the table with a glass of wine and orange juice for the kids. Jim was happy with his baby food, which Lisa was spooning into him.

"I don't know when Simon is coming back. We might as well start, as the food will get cold," Lisa said.

They all started eating, and about halfway through the dinner, Simon appeared. Washed, clean clothes and relaxed. Lisa was not happy. He had just walked out on her and left her to cope by herself. He had taken ages to change. Now, he was the life and soul of the party with stories and anecdotes.

Lisa collected the plates, served dessert and made sure everyone was enjoying themselves. The guests left happy, and Lisa cleaned up the kitchen while Simon and the Swedish couple relaxed by the fire.

The Swedish couple left a couple of days later. The day before they left, they got Simon and Lisa to sit down at the table to have a discussion. They were both psychologists. They started the conversation about the couple's expectations of each other and the importance of communication. They started to explain that if couples didn't recognise what was important to each other, then a rift would develop. Simon shut them down.

"We are good. There is nothing wrong with our relationship. Lisa and I get on just fine."

They exchanged looks, and the conversation ended. Lisa got up from the table and went back to organising the lunch. Lisa thought about the conversation for the following days.

It was a good experience staying in the house. It made Lisa realise that being more centrally located on the farm was important to her. Lisa didn't like the isolated feeling and not knowing what was happening.

Chapter Thirty-One

Apartment

Robert and Mary came back from their holiday and caught up with everyone. Lisa and Simon were invited for dinner one night. The discussion turned to the subject of Auckland and buildings. Robert had decided they should have an apartment in Auckland.

They had spent some time looking at plans and locations for the apartment. A block was going to be built in an upmarket area. It was close to the museum and a block of shops. Robert was buying it off the plans. He was very happy with the plans and the cost. Lisa wasn't sure what the final cost was, but it was over a million.

Consequently, Robert and Mary travelled back and forth to Auckland to inspect progress. The building of the apartment block got delayed, which stressed Robert out. Once the apartment was finished, Robert and Mary had three houses. The apartment, the house on the farm where Lisa and Simon were and the house on the farm further south. Between overseas trips, they flitted between the house on the farm and staying in Auckland.

Chapter Thirty-Two

Scanning

The ewes were mated, and when the foetus had developed to the right stage, the ewes were scanned. The scanner uses exactly the same equipment that is used in the hospital to scan pregnant women. The sheep scanner uses warm water, and there's no sound. They sit in a small canvas tent attached to the side of the pen. This eliminates the issue of light on the screen or rain damaging the equipment. They watch the screen and yell, dry, single, etc. The ewe is then spray-marked with a colour so that she can be identified later. The drys are normally drafted out at the time and sold as soon as possible. The scanner only takes seconds to scan each ewe. They can do up to 5000 ewes a day.

A lot of scanners travel around the world scanning. Those in England will come to NZ in their off-season and vice a versa.

Simon and Lisa started scanning in their second year of farming, and they had a high rate of drys. Many of them would be big ewes, which had never had a lamb.

Robert came down and watched the scanning. "That's a good ewe, you can't sell her. You are selling good breeding stock."

Simon replied, "She is not in lamb, why would we keep her? She probably has never had a lamb."

"That's a big healthy ewe. Next year, she might have a lamb. She may have missed being with the ram."

"Dad, she has been marked as being serviced by the ram, so there's no reason why she should not be in lamb."

Robert stomped off back to his house grumbling about how 'no one listened to him and they didn't know what they were doing. He had been farming for years and knew a good ewe when he saw one'.

Scanning the ewes two months before lambing meant the drys could be sold and not be on the farm eating up feed. The twin and triplet-carrying ewes could be fed better and put into more sheltered paddocks. The single ewes would be put on a tighter feeding regime, reducing the lambing problems.

Lisa and Simon's lamb survival rate jumped in the first year, and in the following years, the scanned lambing percentage continued to jump. They could select their replacements from the twin-bearing mobs so higher fertility. The national lambing percentage increased as well.

Chapter Thirty-Three

Docking

Lisa worked on the farm most days and was in charge of all the sheep planning and budgeting. In October, they did the docking. That's when all of the ewes and lambs are bought into the yards, or temporary pens are set up in the paddocks. The lambs get drafted off, and then each lamb is picked up and put in a cradle, which hangs on the side of the pen.

It holds the lamb while it is ear marked. This is done so that they can tell a ewe lamb from a ram lamb and it distinguishes their stock from the neighbors. The earmark is registered, and it is checked that no one else has the same earmark in the area.

The lambs get dosed and vaccinated against pulpy kidney, blackleg and scabby. The tail is then chopped off and spray is applied to stop the fly and to help it heal.

Lisa was picking up the lambs, dosing and ear marking. Simon was doing everything else.

They lambed in August, so the lambs should have been docked in September/ October.

They only really started docking in late October, and it normally took them about two weeks to get all the mobs done. The lambs Lisa and Simon were docking on this day in November were a mob of singles running on a hilly block. They had been docking for a week and Lisa had been struggling with picking up the big lambs.

Simon was laughing. "These are big lambs. Look at that one. Boy, they are doing well. We should get our first pick from these."

Simon had a great big grin on his face. "They are too big to sit in the cradle. Watch it; you will have to hold him in it". The big lamb was rolling sidewards and about to fall out.

Lisa had stopped Simon from chopping off the tails, as they really were too big for that. After struggling to pick up these 22kg plus lambs for some hours, Lisa decided that something had to give. She had been nagging Simon to start docking sooner, which she had been doing for the last two years. Simon just kept putting it off and delaying.

"Simon, you can pick up the lambs, and I will dock."

"Really, you won't know what to do." Simon looked a bit surprised.

"I've docked before. These lambs are too big for me to pick up. You can pick them up." With that, she climbed out of the pen and stood by the cradle.

Simon climbed reluctantly into the pen and started picking up the lambs. He stopped laughing. Lisa's day got a lot easier.

"Wow, look at that lamb. He's a beauty", Lisa exclaimed to Simon, who was holding him in the cradle. Lisa had decided that two could play the game. Simon didn't say anything. In fact, he got quite quiet. Lisa was quite happy as Simon had to pick up all of the remaining lambs.

One day, they were docking on a warm spring day when they had run out of a vaccine. Lisa went back on the bike to get some more. When she got back to the yard, Lisa couldn't see Simon anywhere. Lisa walked over to the docking pen. Here was Simon, completely naked, lying in the lamb pen on his back.

"Simon, what are you doing?"

"Getting some sun."

"Really, in the lamb pen?"

"Why not? It's sunny and warm here."

"I suppose ... whatever does it for you."

Simon got up, dressed and they went back to drafting and docking lambs for the rest of the day.

Lisa went up to her in-laws to collect Jim. He had been with them while she was working on the farm. Robert wanted to talk about the farm and what was happening. Lisa sat down at the table and Mary got her a cold drink. Robert talked about the outlook for the farm and what was happening with the world markets.

Lisa was about ready to leave when Mary said, "I am still getting little cards from your mother."

"Oh."

"She is still saying nasty things about you. She hasn't stopped."

"Oh, I rang her up and asked her to stop. I thought she had."

"No, she's still writing them, and they are really nasty."

"I will contact her again."

With that, Lisa took Jim home, thinking, 'What the hell? Why would she do that?' Lisa got tea started, wondering what to do. She had to make her stop. Why would she want to keep doing it, especially as Lisa knew what she had done.

After sleeping on it Lisa decided to write her a letter.

Lisa sat down and wrote a two-page letter asking her to stop writing nasty things about her. Lisa pointed out that quite often, parents and children did not get on. There was no law that said parents had to like their children. But it was no reason for her to write nasty letters about her to other people. Lisa read it through and wondered if she should post it. Lisa then thought about the trouble she was causing with my mother-in-law. She posted it.

Lisa had given her mother what she wanted. She wanted a reason to go round the local district telling everyone what a terrible daughter she had. Poor, poor her, what parent deserved a child like Lisa; after everything she had done for her? The letter gave her proof of what a terrible person Lisa was. She must have been delighted with the letter.

Lisa's mother liked drama and could turn a performance on and off at will. She would have done the tears as she read sections out of the letter. Lisa was bloody certain, she would not have allowed anyone to read the whole letter. She would have done the 'pathetic me'. She didn't deserve this. And, of course, it would have given her another reason to empower her son's position as being the caring, grateful child.

Lisa should never have sent the letter. It was the worst thing she could have done. Lisa just wanted her to stop sending nasty notes about her to her mother-in-law.

Chapter Thirty-Four

Friends

J essie and Matt, who were very smug about arranging the blind
date, came and stayed. They knew Simon's parents, so they
stayed in their sleep out. They would eat with Lisa and Simon, or they
would go up and have dinner with them and Simon's parents. On this
night they were at Lisa's and Simon's home. Simon and Matt were
talking about past times, drinking parties, nightclubbing, etc. It was
before Lisa met Simon so Lisa was just listening. They got onto one
night in Palmy, and Matt started laughing. They were out at a bar when
a group of girls walked in.

There was some discussion about whether one of them was
wearing underpants or not. Apparently, she had on a very tight, body-
hugging dress. Simon decided to find out. He took his beer and
wandered over to her. He then bent down and looked up her skirt.

Matt said "He then stood up, looked over to me and shook his
head as he smiled." They were laughing about it. Lisa was shocked he
would do that.

"Simon, you didn't really do that, did you?"

"Yeah, what of it?"

"It's wrong, that's, that's wrong."

"If she didn't want anyone to look, then she should have worn something else."

"But for you to look, in a crowded bar. That's rude. It's not right. How could you?"

"She was asking for it wearing a dress like that. All I did was look. Stop being a prude."

My God, what a thing to do. How rude and arrogant could he get? Lisa couldn't believe that he would do something so blatantly wrong. She was disappointed and shocked that her husband had done that. The conversation turned to other subjects.

Chapter Thirty-Five

Lisa's Second Pregnancy

When Jim was 15 months old, Lisa conceived her second child. Lisa was a bit wiser with her second baby and wasn't as sick as she was with her first. Lisa had the same midwife, Sue, which was great and the pregnancy went along with no issues.

As Lisa got bigger, it became harder for her to do things, and at times, it was a risk to the baby. Like when she was in the cattle or sheep yards. It only needed a cow to kick her or a sheep to run into her.

Lisa did all of the drafting of the stock. She would be standing at the gates, watching the sheep run up the race. When they didn't run, she tried to encourage them to move up the race by stepping away from the gates. Lisa then had to get back to the gates before they got there. It made for a long day when she was heavily pregnant.

Simon organised for them to go to Auckland and stay with his parents for a night. Lisa was a bit surprised about the trip.

'Where are we going, Simon?"

"Just wait and see. It's a surprise."

Lisa was at a complete loss as to what was happening. Jim was asleep in the back of the car, so he was quite happy.

They arrived at this building, and Simon said, "It's in there. Just go through those doors. I will be back in two hours to get you," Whereupon he left. 'What the hell.' Lisa went inside, and there were all these women of all ages getting seated. The conversation had an excited vibe to it. Lisa sat down, wondering what the hell she was at.

'Wow, bloody hell'. Out walks Diane Gabaldon, who wrote Outlander. Her favorite author. Lisa was delighted. It was wonderful listening to her speak about writing the books.

Simon came and collected Lisa.

"Thank you so much, Simon, that was wonderful."

"So you enjoyed it then?"

"Oh yeah, it was brilliant" Lisa was so impressed that Simon had thought to do that for her. Lisa hugged the experience to herself.

*

Lisa hadn't seen the apartment before, so she was given a tour of it. It was lovely, with three levels, large living areas and a top wet bar lounge with a tiny view of the sea. Therefore, it had a sea view. The fact you had to stand in a certain spot and stretch to see it was irrelevant. It had a water view! The roof was flat and was designed to be walked on.

"Oh, it's a Spanish bungalow." Lisa said.

Robert looked at her and said, "No, it's not."

"Yes, it is. It has a flat roof. They leak, they are really bad for it."

"No, it most certainly is not, and it will not leak. They have modern products now, which stop the leaks." Robert stated in a defensive voice.

Lisa looked at him, wondering why he was getting worked up about it. It had been shown over and over again that flat roofs in New Zealand's climate were high risk.

"There's nothing wrong with this build." Robert stated in a firm voice as he escorted them back down the stairs.

The conversation turned to other topics like the farm.

When Lisa was 7 months pregnant, all of the ewes had to be dagged for shearing in June. All of the ewes were in one mob, and they were going to be put through the Racewell clamp. They had a family friend's son, Liam, staying with them, who was helping. Simon wanted Lisa to dag as she was faster than either of them.

It was the last thing she wanted to do, but Lisa went up. Simon and Liam chased the sheep up the race for her to dag. So in two and a half days, Lisa dagged 2,500 ewes while Jim spent time with his grandparents. Lisa would take Jim up to Mary and then start dagging. Afterwards, she would collect Jim, go home, cook tea and start it all again the next day.

By the third day, Lisa was tired and sore from the standing and bending over. Simon started talking about where the ewes were going before shearing and what Lisa could do to help.

Lisa up and said "I am going home, do what you like." She walked out and down to the house. She went and got Jim.

Robert started talking about child rearing and the importance of the environment that children are raised in. Robert then started in on Lisa.

"There's something wrong with Jim. You are not bringing him up, right. He shouldn't be behaving like this."

Lisa had heard him on the subject before. He had regularly criticised her about how she was raising Jim. Every time Jim did something Robert did not approve of, he blamed Lisa. With her first child, Lisa wanted to do what was right and tried to give Jim a loving environment. She also wanted to raise a lad who could make decisions and was independent.

She was a new mother, living in poor conditions and working on the farm. Sometimes she was so tired she fell over her own feet, while she was doing things. Lisa went home wondering what was wrong, questioning herself.

The baby and Lisa met all of their milestones, and the baby kicked and jumped up and down on Lisa's bladder, as per normal. Lisa had cramps and trouble getting comfortable while sleeping.

Lisa was taking Jim swimming each week, and she wanted the lessons to continue. Lisa talked to Mary about taking Jim to swimming when she had the second baby. After some discussion, Mary finally agreed to take him.

Chapter Thirty-Six

Lisa's Second Birth

L isa rolled out of bed one morning in her 9th month and said, "Simon do whatever you have to now."

Lisa spent the rest of the day feeling miserable as the nagging, irritable pain kept coming over her in waves. She just hung over the chest in their room, feeling sick. That evening, they went up to the birthing unit an hour away. The closer one had closed. Lisa went into labour. The labour was very intense as she took a long time to dilate, and the contractions were strong.

When Lisa started pushing, she didn't just push once but pushed three or four times before the rest. While she was trying to rest, the baby would kick very forcibly. Her first child did not kick during birth, but this one did, and it came as a real surprise. Lisa was trying to breath and relax when she would have this massive kick completely out of the blue.

Lisa was more aware of her body the second time and felt the head move through the cervix. Lisa kept moving and twisting on her knees and the baby was born as she kneeled. Lisa could see the top of its head as it slowly came out.

They talk about the ring of fire and it's a good way to describe it. It happens when the head is partially out, and the mother's outside skin is stretched to an impossible size. At this point they ask the mother to stop pushing, so it has time to stretch and she doesn't rip. Lisa was just at this point when the baby let go with another massive kick. She was knocked sideways with the shock of it. This baby, quite clearly, was not going to lie back and go with the flow; it was going to take an active part in life. Lisa did not have any pain killers at all, for which she was quite proud of. It was another boy. She had been convinced that it would be a girl.

Lisa refused to be told at the scanning if it was a boy or a girl. She reasoned that after all that work, she wanted a surprise at the end of it. It upset some friends, who wanted to know so that they could choose the present. So, one healthy baby boy was born on 1st September at 10:30 pm, 8lb 11 oz and 51cm long. They named him Andrew.

Lisa was enjoying her baby and relaxing, when Sue gave her the jab in the leg to contract the uterus. All seemed well. Lisa wasn't expecting the acute pains which ripped through her when the uterus was contracting. Lisa hadn't had them with Jim. They were really painful, and after all of that effort, it seemed quite unfair.

The baby was healthy, fair-haired and feeding well. He was perfect with his tiny little feet and fingers.

A problem developed. The after-birth wouldn't come away. Sue tried everything. Breast feeding, sending Lisa to the toilet (with the after-birth partially hanging down between her legs), massaging her stomach. Nothing.

An ambulance was called, and the baby and Lisa were loaded into it and driven to the hospital an hour away. Lisa was feeling like an absolute failure. She had wanted to have a normal birth and have everything go smoothly. Lisa was not living up to her expectations, of being a capable woman, able to deliver and carry on with life.

She was admitted to the theatre later that night. They gave her an epidural in the back, then rolled her back onto her back. Her legs were in stirrups, and they proceeded to scrape the inside of her uterus out. It didn't hurt, but Lisa could feel the pushing around inside of her. The baby was positioned so that she could see him.

Andrew was very good and just slept through the whole drama. All that kicking during the birth must have worn him out. Simon sat beside her, determinedly, not looking at what they were doing. He really didn't want to see anything.

100 years ago, Lisa would have died from septicaemia, so she was lucky, they had this technology. They then wheeled her back to recovery and then to the ward.

In the morning, Lisa woke up in bed feeling good. The bed was very high. If you stood next to it, it would be above your waist. She was in a private bedroom with the baby beside her. Simon was asleep in the chair on the other side of the bed. Lisa was busting to go wees.

She flung back the bed covers, swung her legs around and, slid off the side of the bed and promptly hit the floor in a heap. Her legs didn't work. It came as a bit of a surprise, but they felt quite numb. Lisa hauled herself up the side of the bed and leaned against it for a while, testing her legs. She really needed to go. It was a wonder she hadn't had an accident already. Time was of the essence.

After a little bit, Lisa seemed to get some feeling back into her legs and proceeded to struggle out of the room and down the hall to the toilet. Simon was still asleep.

The relief to sit on the toilet, was incredible. Lisa just relaxed and started to take a bit of interest in her surroundings.

She noticed that there was blood on her knees and down her legs, and it reached all the way to the floor and over to the toilet door. It came as a surprise. It hadn't occurred to her that she was bleeding; she just wanted to use the toilet.

There was no pain. In fact, Lisa didn't feel a thing. Those drugs must have been gooood. She tried cleaning herself up. She folded toilet paper over into a pad and wiped her legs down. The toilet paper just fell apart and she ended up with bits of paper all over her and the floor. The same thing happened when she tried to wipe up the floor by the toilet. It was a complete waste of time. Lisa gave it up.

Lisa started the slow trip back to her room. They say that when one is out tramping and hunting, one should always mark their back trail so that they can find their way back and not get lost. Well, she had no issues with that. In this spotless, clean ward hallway, there was a trail of blood about a foot wide, leading all the way back to her room. It was a well-marked trail, and there was no chance of getting lost.

As Lisa climbed back into bed, she noticed the pad they had put under her to collect the drainage. Lisa was just lying slowly back when the nurse came in.

"You country girls are far too independent for your own good. You are impossible to deal with. You never ask for help. You cause more trouble by not asking than if you had just asked. Why didn't you use the buzzer? It's by your pillow." The nurse fished around by Lisa's pillow and produced the buzzer.

"We have to lock the toilets down now and wait for the specialised cleaners to come. No one can use the toilet. Your actions have completely disrupted the ward, and now the other patients have to use the toilet at the other end of the hall!"

She was really angry as she bustled around the bed and checked under Lisa to change the pad. Apparently, Lisa had caused massive disruption to the whole ward. All she wanted to do was use the toilet.

Lisa didn't know that there was a buzzer. On American TV hospital shows, buzzers are being pushed, but it never occurred to Lisa that she had one. If Lisa had known, she probably still wouldn't have used it. It's one of those things other people use, and she just wanted to do a simple thing like go to the toilet.

Simon had woken up by this stage and was just listening to the tirade the nurse let fly. Not long after that, Lisa got a tray of food, fed the baby and went back to sleep.

Lisa was in a ward with other mothers and nurses, and the La Leche women were very visible. Funny thing. They would come to

Lisa's bedroom and be about to launch into a lecture about breast feeding and being a good mother. At the same time, they would be checking her chart and once they saw it was her second baby, they would make some comment about her knowing what to do and leave. It was like they knew that if they started the same drama with a second-time mother, they would get a short shift. They were right, too. They obviously preyed on the new insecure mothers, who were scared of doing the wrong thing.

They let Lisa go back to the small hospital closer to home that afternoon. Quite clearly, she was a liability to the smooth running of the ward. Simon loaded them into the car to drive them back. By this stage, the drugs had worn off, and Lisa was sore. Just bending to get into the car hurt.

Andrew and Lisa settled into their new bed and went to sleep. Andrew was a much easier baby and hardly cried.

Jim had been staying with Mary. Lisa wanted Jim to come in and see her and his new baby brother. Lisa kept ringing and asking for her to bring him in. She refused. Point blank refused.

Lisa was really worried about Jim, as it was the first time she had been away from him for anytime length of time. Lisa's friend Linda, who lived locally, offered to have him and bring him in, but again Mary refused.

Mary got a phone call about attending a meeting in Wellington, and suddenly everything changed. Jim was dropped off at Linda's place with practically no notice. In fact, one could say he was dumped. Mary didn't see Lisa but headed to the airport and took off. Mary, apart from that one time when the hospital rang her, had never come anywhere near the hospital to see Lisa or to meet her new grandsons.

Linda brought Jim in to see Lisa and met his baby brother. Lisa was able to give him a huge hug. He was really pleased to see his Mum and a bit upset that his mother hadn't been around for a bit. He was quite clingy. It was so good to see him and reassure herself that he was OK.

Lisa went home on the fourth day after Andrew had been born, which was a Friday. Mary, by this time, had come back from Wellington and had collected Jim, from Linda's place.

Simon drove his new family home, and Lisa settled into a routine with the new baby for the weekend. This included all the cooking and washing for the household. Linda had been out and cleaned the house from top to bottom. It was wonderful as Lisa walked into a spotless house with all the washing, up to date. She had been expecting to walk into a messy place with piles of farm washing everywhere and heaps of dishes. They did have a dishwasher. Again, it was spring, so Simon was really busy on the farm.

On the Monday, Lisa went shopping with the new baby, which is always a bit stressful. It's like moving house, with everything one is required to take. Lisa did the grocery shopping, drove back to the in-laws' house and collected Jim.

Chapter Thirty-Seven

Settling In

Andrew was in the same cot Jim had been. Jim was in a single bunk bed in the other room. After the initial battle with getting Jim to stay in the bed he had settled down in his new room just fine.

After Lisa's checkered history with breastfeeding and Jim, she was leaning towards formula. On the other hand, she could see the benefits of breastfeeding. Much cheaper. Jim had been breastfed for three weeks. Andrew was breastfed for two weeks. Lisa expressed milk with the little pump they had given her and fed Andrew from a bottle. It made her feel like a cow, with the clear plastic suction cup on, which pulled the nipple right out. The little motor just pulsates away.

Lisa had bottles of breast milk in the fridge, so Simon had to be careful that he didn't put the wrong milk in his tea. The only real regret Lisa had about formula was the cost. For her sanity, it was worth it.

Bottle feeding gave her more freedom, as it allowed her to leave the boys with their grandparents. After two weeks, Lisa worked on drying off. That was the end of breastfeeding for Andrew.

Once Andrew was a month old, Lisa went back to taking Jim to swimming lessons, and Andrew was happy watching or sleeping. When Andrew was 6 months old, he started his own lessons. They had a ball; it was the highlight of the week for them.

Andrew had a set of shelves opposite his cot. Lisa had done some sewing and had made a boy cat. It had a tail, trousers and a cute little green shirt. It sat on the top shelf. One day, she was getting four-month-old Andrew out of the cot when he struggled in her arms. He started climbing up her to reach for the cat. She was surprised but gave it to him. Andrew grabbed the cat and hugged it to himself. From then on, Cat went everywhere with Andrew. Same as Bear did with Jim.

Andrew must have been lying in the cot looking at the cat for months and wanting him. Since Andrew was too young to talk he had no way of saying. On this day, he was going to have cat one way or another.

Sarah

Sarah came and stayed with her parents for a few days. Lisa was feeding Andrew, and Jim was playing on the floor. Sarah got down on the floor with Jim.

"I think I will have a baby." Sarah suddenly said.

Lisa looked at Sarah in complete surprise, wondering if she had heard right.

"Why?"

"Oh, I was talking to some friends, and they said that if you breastfeed, you lose all of your puppy fat. I want to lose this fat." She explained as she prodded her stomach.

Lisa looked at Sarah's very skinny, attractive figure and wondered what in God's name was her problem. Here she was with two babies and a figure which was overweight, and she had stretch marks.

"Why do you think having a baby will do that?"

"Well, the breastfeeding causes you to lose weight because it uses up so much energy."

"Having a baby will give you stretch marks." Lisa replied.

"That only happened cause you didn't take care of yourself. If you rub oil onto your skin, you don't get the marks." Sarah replied with a knowledgeable air.

Quite clearly, it was Lisa's fault that she had stretch marks. Bugger me!

Lisa seriously toiled with the thought of leaving Sarah in her blessed world. She had no boyfriend that they knew of and lived a migratory life, fluttering from social event to social event. It would be fun seeing how she coped with a baby. It would probably be left with the grandparents or them.

"Sarah, breastfeeding a baby doesn't remove fat. The body needs nutrients to feed the baby, so it works at keeping the weight on."

"Oh, so I won't lose this fat."

"No. Having a baby seems a bit extreme to lose weight and very unlikely to work."

"It might be better if I don't have a baby then. It could be quite time-consuming to look after a baby."

"Yeah, they do take a lot of time and involve carrying a lot of stuff with you. How long are you staying for?"

"I might head back today; not much happening down here."

Sarah left, and Lisa spent the rest of the day wondering about just how obsessed some people are about their figures. Having a baby seemed to be taking things a bit far.

Chapter Thirty-Eight

Second Chance

Lisa was visiting Mary and Robert one day after the play centre. Jim was playing on the floor by Robert's chair, and Andrew was kicking his little legs on the floor.

Robert was watching Jim and said, "You have children and they grow up. I didn't see much of mine when they were young, as I was working all the time. I missed out, and you think that you will never have that time again."

Lisa looked at him.

"But it isn't true. You get a second chance with the grandchildren. You have another chance of raising more children."

Lisa looked at him and thought, "These are my children, not yours.'

Lisa thought it was time to go home, so she said her goodbyes, gathered up the children and left.

Robert had given Lisa a hard time about Jim and why he was the way he was. Jim was a good child and had met all of his milestones correctly. But Robert felt his personality was not as it should be. It was Lisa's fault.

Andrew, being older now, had his own personality. He was totally different from Jim. Lisa looked at Andrew and Jim. They had the same parents, lived in the same house and were being brought up the same way. It was nothing that Lisa had done. They were different children.

Once Lisa realised that, it was such a relief. Next time Robert started in on Lisa about not bringing Jim up correctly, she ignored him. He just had a different personality.

Chapter Thirty-Nine

Toilet Training

Lisa found that when the boys were about two years old, she would let them run around with only their tops on outside in the sun. The wonder on their faces when they saw where the wees came from. It was a revelation for them.

When Jim was about 24 months old, Lisa really started in on toilet training. Jim did wees and poos in the potty and would start to ask for the potty. That was a big breakthrough. Lisa then tried him on the toilet and they had success. For little boys, aiming isn't always that good. Lisa was advised that putting a ping pong ball in the toilet bowl gives them something to aim for. Sounded good to her.

Jim stood on the stool and aimed for the ball and laughed when he hit it. A bit later, Lisa was in the kitchen organising tea when Jim came out to show her what he had. Jim was very proud of himself cause he had got the sopping wet ball out of the toilet and was dripping water??? Everywhere.

Jim was of the opinion that it was a toy to be played with. Lisa rescued the ball and put it back. She then showed Jim the rest of the balls, which came in the packet. They reached an arrangement whereby the ball in the toilet stayed there.

Jim went into underpants during the day when he was 27 months old. Success. Massive savings on nappies.

Jim kept wetting his bed. During the day, they were good with the toilet, but at night, everything sopping wet. Lisa heard about dry nights, which worked like pants. They pulled down when the child needed to go, but if they had an accident, they would absorb the wees like a nappy. Sounded good to Lisa. Would save the bedding. After Jim's bath, they put on the pull-ups.

"Why are we putting these on Mum?" Jim asked.

"These are special pants, so you can pull them down to go wees, but if you have an accident, they will be like a nappy."

"So I can go wees in them?"

"Well, no, you go to the toilet, but if you don't wake up, then these will keep the bed dry." Lisa explained to Jim.

Jim seemed quite happy about the pull-ups. He went and sat on the sofa to watch some TV with the rest of them. Lisa happened to look at Jim, and he had a very blank, relaxed look on his face.

"Jim, you're not going wees, are you?"

"Yeah, I have."

"Why? The toilets right there." Let's face it: their house was so small, it would be a short walk and he could still hear the TV.

"You said I could do wees in these."

"But you are wide awake, and these are only if you don't wake up in the night."

"Why would I go to the toilet when I can go in these?" Jim asked in his childish voice.

Lisa was at a loss. The whole point was so that he could go to the toilet. Jim couldn't see the point of making the effort of going to the toilet, when he had another option. It was so frustrating.

Lisa gave up. Pull-ups were just a pipe dream. Lisa was back to wet beds with Jim. Andrew was two years younger, so he was still in nappies.

Chapter Forty

Grandparents

Lisa was up visiting the in-laws after the play centre. It's not that she wanted to see them; it was that she felt she needed to keep communications open. Jim was about three and Andrew one.

Robert was sitting in his chair after being to town to get the paper. Mary was in the kitchen and Jim was sitting on the floor in front of Robert's chair with a small juice box. It had a straw in plastic and the little sealed hole to put the straw through. Jim was having problems getting the straw into the hole.

Robert put down the paper and was watching, "What's wrong with that kid? Why can't he get it in? What's wrong with him? Why can't he do it? There's something wrong with him. He should be able to do that?"

Jim was having trouble with his little stubby baby fingers to get the straw into the hole. He could hear everything his grandfather was saying and was getting more and more frustrated. Lisa went over to help him, but he pushed her away.

Robert continued with, "What's wrong with him? There's something wrong with him? Why can't he do that? It's easy to do. Why can't he do it?" On and on he went.

Jim was getting really angry with himself but finally managed it.

Robert then gave his paper a good shake and went back to reading it. Lisa felt so sorry for Jim and pissed off with his grandfather.

Mary, who had been quiet the entire time, then said, "Did you hear about Robert getting the ticket?"

"No, what ticket?"

Mary started laughing. "Robert went into town to get the paper and then went home with it. Today, the ticket arrived in the mail. Robert got caught speeding in the 50-km zone. He was doing 70-km, and then he got caught on the same day 10 minutes later speeding in the 50-km zone again. He was doing 60-km. Two tickets 10 minutes apart.

"That was an expensive paper.' Lisa replied.

Mary laughed as Robert gave his paper another shake and said, "He shouldn't have been there. No one has an accident there. It's just revenue gathering" He then went back to reading the paper.

Lisa took the boys home and went about her chores. She had to smile about him getting the ticket.

The next time Lisa saw Mary, she asked that she stop Robert from criticising Jim in front of Jim. Lisa explained that she didn't think it was healthy or helpful for Jim. Mary nodded and agreed she would have a word with Robert.

Chapter Forty-One

Hunt

Simon had owned a hunting horse from the time Lisa knew him. It had run around the paddock on the farm down south and he had bought it up to this farm. Robert had bought the horse for Simon, so he could go hunting with the hounds. They chased hares as there are no foxes in NZ.

Robert thought Simon would start to associate with the 'right' people. Lisa thought Simon enjoyed hunting with all of the colours, the horses, the drinks and the hounds. Lisa didn't ride, so it wasn't anything they could share.

Simon had all the gear: hat, boots, jodhpurs, jacket, stock and pin. Each year in early winter, the farm hosted the opening hunt, and Simon would go off with them. Lisa had small babies, so she was limited.

Lisa had noticed the pins that they wore in the stocks. Some of them were very attractive. Simon's pin was quite plain. Lisa decided for Simon's birthday she would get him a good pin. Each time she went to town, Lisa would cruise through secondhand shops looking. It took a long time, but finally she found one. It was sterling silver designed with a hat and whip. She got it wrapped in an attractive box. Simon opened the box on his birthday and said, "Oh, a pin," shut the box and ate tea. Lisa was disappointed, as it had taken her a long time to find it. Quite clearly, it wasn't something Simon wanted.

One day, Simon disappeared to go hunting, all dressed up, and then he came home again.

"I am never going hunting again."

"Oh." Lisa was a bit surprised as he had friends who hunted.

"It takes too much time and energy to get ready." Simon stated and then headed to the bedroom to change.

Lisa was at a loss as to why, but whatever.

Simon always went up and enjoyed socialising with the guys. The farmer always got shouted, and Simon enjoyed that and always came home in a jolly mood.

At the opening hunt, the hounds are auctioned off as a fundraiser. When Lisa looked over the rails, it would be to see a sea of dog faces with floppy ears. It was a very attractive sight, watching them push their noses through the wooden rails. They are stocky in shape with short legs and are mainly tan and white with long ears. The club had 30 odd hounds.

Each hound would be bought onto the floor and auctioned. At the end of the season, whoever owned the best-performing hound would then win a prize.

Lisa sometimes went up and chatted with the group. Most of them were farming friends of Robert's, Mary's and Simon's. Lisa slowly got to know them but never forgot that they were Simon's family friends, not hers. Lisa had to be careful what she said as it would go straight back to them.

Simon was home with the hunt while Lisa and the boys went shopping. "How did the hunt go, Simon?"

"They had a good turnout and caught a hare. It was a very successful day." Simon replied as he headed to the computer.

Lisa sorted out the boys and started tea.

About two weeks later, Lisa got an account in the mail for $700 from the Hunt Club.

"Simon, what's this account for?"

"What account?"

"It's from the hunt club for $700."

"Oh, it's just something for the club. Just pay it."

"What's it for?"

"I just purchased something. Just pay it. We have to pay it?"

"What is it for?"

"Oh, at the opening hunt, I purchased two hounds."

"What? For $700." Lisa had seen the auctions and most of the hounds went between $50 to $200. This was excessive.

"They are the top hounds, and I wanted to do it for the club. Pay it!" Simon said in an angry voice.

Lisa was pissed off. What had possessed him to bid in the auction, let alone to that level? They didn't have any spare money. All the money was being spent on the farm for fertiliser, fencing, regrassing and water. $700 on two hounds. Lisa could have purchased something for the house with that money.

Lisa had to pay it so she did.

The hunt master was also their fencer. Lisa happened to see him a bit later and asked about the auction.

"Yeah, I wondered how you felt about that."

"How come it was so much?"

"It became a bit of a competition between Simon and the other guy. They just kept bidding."

"I'm not happy about it."

"No, I didn't think you would be." he replied in a sympathetic voice. The conversation then turned back to the farm.

They had the hunt on the farm every year. Simon always went out in the Ute and followed the hunt. Jim and Andrew found it exciting to watch. Lisa got growled at for calling the hounds dogs. Apparently, that was a major insult. Who knew?

Chapter Forty-Two

The Hot Water

The hot water system did not cope with two adults and two children. They were forever running out. To replace the cylinder was expensive, and a bigger one would not fit into the small cupboard. The electrician pointed out to Lisa that the current hot water cylinder was probably on its last legs. The bottom was close to falling out. Something had to happen.

Simon and Lisa went to the field days, and in their travels, they found a hot water cylinder attached to a firebox which impressed Lisa. It had two systems. One was a closed system which could run water heaters. It just circulated water around via a pump, and the other would supply the household with hot water. The idea of not having to pay for the heating of the hot water was appealing. It meant they could use hot water for washing and have heaters in the house. They bought it and installed it in the carport.

Once the fire was light it took only half an hour to heat the water to boiling. Just burning the house hold waste would boil the water. In winter, Lisa had to chop wood for the fire anyway, so the only difference was lighting it in summer.

The house dried out with the water heaters, and it was a lot warmer. Lisa stopped using the log burner, which made it safer for the children. Lisa also gained some cupboard space, which made a huge difference to her storage.

Lisa was very happy, and then Simon got angry about getting the firewood. With a toddler and a baby, it was quite hard for Lisa to get wood off the farm. She would walk up to the trees below the woolshed and collect dead branches so that she could start the fire. Lisa didn't need much, but Simon refused point blank to collect wood. It just seemed so mean to her to not go out and get a small load of firewood. It wouldn't have taken him long, and it would have made a big difference to her. She was reduced to collecting branches, which she could carry home.

When Lisa had the chance, she took the chainsaw out and collected wood from around the farm using the motor bike and trailer. Lisa had a chopping block at the house, which she used to split the wood. Even when Simon got wood for the fireplace, Lisa still had to split it. She didn't mind, as she would go and split wood when she got angry or frustrated. A great way to relieve tension.

Chapter Forty-Three

Vehicles

The Hilux Ute they bought with the farm failed its warrant. Not surprising considering the age, the rust, the life it had led and the miles it had done. To fix it was going to cost a lot of money. It was decided they needed a new Ute.

"I have never bought a vehicle. Dad has just given me his old vehicles. He bought me a car when I was at varsity." Simon said in an apprehensive voice.

"You have never bought a car?" Lisa was shocked.

"Nope."

"I bought my first car when I was 19. It was a Datsun 120Y. It was a good little car. It cost $5000, and I had to borrow $2000 from Mum. I had to give her a cheque every month to pay it back. I had to leave it on the table in the hall outside her bedroom door in the morning." Lisa smiled as she thought of her first car. It had been blue with four doors. When she first got in it, Lisa couldn't believe how much space was her's. Lisa had all this space, which was all hers.

"Well, we will need to look for another Ute." Lisa said.

"It's probably best if it's a new one since second-hand ones come with problems. It has to be a Hilux." Simon said.

They made enquires and found a Ute. It had to be a flat deck, so they got just the chassis. Simon wanted to buy it cause it would be his very first vehicle that he would have paid for. Simon talked a lot about buying the Ute and how it would be his first vehicle that he paid for.

The old Ute, Simon sold it to his duck shooting mate. He paid $2000 for it and took it home very happily. He was going to work on it himself.

The dealership would bring the new Ute out to the farm. A time was made, and Simon was going to be present.

"I want to write the cheque to pay for it." Simon said.

The Ute arrived. It was bright red and looked very clean and shiny. It was a King cab, so the kids could sit in the back, but the deck was still big enough to fit a quad bike.

Lisa invited the guys in for a cup of tea, saying, "Simon shouldn't be far away. He knows you're coming."

No sign of Simon. Lisa made small talk. No sign of Simon. "He knows you're coming, so he should be here soon."

No sign of Simon. The guys started to get restless. They had to get back. After waiting a bit more, Lisa got the chequebook and, wrote out the cheque and signed the paper work. The guys left, and within 10 minutes, Simon arrived.

He sat in the Ute and promptly said, "I'll take it down to the engineering shop so that he can measure it up for the deck." With that, he drove it away.

Lisa was left wondering about all the drama, about how he wanted to pay for it, had never bought a vehicle and how Lisa had waited and waited for him to come home. He must have been up the hill watching until the guys left.

They got the deck put on the Ute. It was longer than normal, so that the crate Simon helped to design with the engineer could fit as many calves as possible. It slid onto the deck and had clips which held it in place. The door on the back was genius. It slid open and shut, but it also folded down so that it made a ramp for the stock to jump off, eliminating the need for a loading ramp. Simon was very clever designing it. Lisa was very impressed.

They had an old trailer on the farm, which they got a crate made for so that they could cart calves. With the Ute crate and the trailer Simon went to the sales and picked up calves for them to rear. Simon would come home with 60 to 80 calves. Any more, and it made for a long night convincing them to feed. It saved them a lot in freight costs.

Chapter Forty-Four

Food

Jim stayed quite a bit with his grandparents while Lisa worked on the farm. Jim had always been a good eater but quite clear about what he didn't like. Jim did not like meat but loved the gravy. Didn't like porridge or certain fruits, but otherwise ate up everything else.

Mary told Lisa that "Jim always ate all his porridge up when he was with them. He ate the whole bowl of porridge and never left anything. Porridge is the best food and sets you up for the day. You can't get a better food then porridge."

"Jim doesn't like porridge; he refuses to eat it."

"You can't be cooking it right or feeding it to him correctly. Jim likes brown sugar on his porridge." Mary explained to Lisa.

Lisa tried feeding porridge to Jim again, but no luck. Jim really didn't want it, and neither did Simon.

Jim started becoming very fussy about eating his meals when he was about three.

He would sit in the high chair and fuss over his food. It was too hot, too cold, wrong flavor or he wanted something else instead. This changed happened in a very short space of time. Lisa couldn't understand why and she was finding it frustrating and worrying. Lisa tried everything to ensure that he ate a good dinner.

One day, Lisa was up at the grandparents' to collect Jim. Mary was running around the house with a cherry tomato on a toothpick. She was chasing Jim around the house, saying, "Eat this for Granny, Jim, pleaseee eat this for Granny. Granny will be very upset if you don't eat this, Jim. Granny might cry if you don't eat this." Granny started to sniff and rub her eye like she was going to cry. Jim ate the cherry tomato she was holding out. "Good boy, Jim, you are such a clever boy eating that for Granny."

Off Mary ran for the kitchen, where she put another cherry tomato on a toothpick and off she raced to find Jim. Mary promptly repeated the whole drama again, pleading with Jim to eat the tomato.

Lisa was fascinated and revolted all at the same time. It just seemed so bizarre. Mary rushed over to Lisa and said. "Jim has been so good today. He has eaten 8 tomatoes and all his porridge."

"Well, that's good." Lisa was still in shock over Mary's behaviour. At this point, Robert said, "We heard from Sarah today. She's doing fine in Auckland."

"Oh, that's nice."

"Yeah, I gave her $20,000 today. It was lying around in an account, not doing anything. I decided Sarah could have it."

"That was nice of you." Lisa replied, thinking bloody hell. There's no way Lisa's parents would have given her anything like that. But then again Lisa's mother did give her brother $20,000 to buy a Ute with.

Lisa didn't get a penny.

"Well, thanks for having the children, Robert and Mary. I'll take them home now."

She headed home, trying to get her head around Mary's behaviour with Jim, 'My God, what a drama'. Jim was really happy. And what a spoilt girl Sarah was.

That night, Jim wouldn't eat dinner. Lisa tried everything. Lisa cooked different food, she tried spooning it into him. Nothing. It is heartbreaking when the child won't eat. Jim would nibble a bit of this or that and only wanted the dessert. Lisa felt like she wasn't caring for her child. She had failed as a mother, and the child would starve.

Lisa cooked porridge for breakfast. Jim flatly refused to eat it. She opened a tin of baby food.

Andrew needed to have his check with the Plunket nurse in town. He was doing just fine and growing well. Lisa asked her about Jim's refusal to eat, and she just started crying as she explained. She told the plunket nurse about Mary and what she said, how he ate everything at her place. Mary had really got into her about Jim not eating and how he must eat a good dinner. Lisa even told her about the cherry tomato on a toothpick. The plunket nurse got a bit concerned.

"That's how eating disorders are created. If you make such a big thing out of eating then the child plays up to it. It becomes a power game. You have to stop it."

Lisa was surprised about her statement as Mary had really convinced her that it was her fault.

"This is what you do. At dinner time, you serve Jim's meal up and give him a good chance to eat it. If he doesn't eat it, put it in the rubbish bin and put him to bed."

This seemed a bit rough to Lisa. "So he will be alright? If he doesn't have dinner."

"He will be fine. If he wants to eat something later on, tell him that he refused dinner and there's nothing else. I guarantee you he will eat a good breakfast."

Lisa took the boys home and got dinner ready. Andrew had his bottled milk and Jim refused his dinner. She did exactly what the Plunket nurse said and put Jim to bed with no dinner.

My God, he ate a good breakfast. They repeated it for two nights and after that no more issues. Lisa was so relieved.

Lisa thought Mary was still chasing Jim around with a toothpick, but Jim knew at home he ate the dinner, as there was nothing else.

Lisa discovered months later Jim did eat all of his porridge at Mary's, but there was more to the story. Lisa was up there at 11.30 one morning to find Mary still feeding Jim his porridge. Apparently, at 8 am, she started spooning the porridge into Jim. The porridge was covered in brown sugar about a cm thick. More brown sugar was added as they worked their way down the bowl. Jim was basically eating brown sugar with a bit of porridge. No wonder he didn't eat her's.

Two and half hours of feeding Jim his breakfast. Lisa couldn't spend that amount of time feeding Jim, and the porridge was stone cold by the end. Lisa took the boys home feeling much better about the whole situation. She was concerned about Jim's teeth. Two hours of constant sugar. There can always be more to a story then what is portrayed.

Lisa went up to collect the children in the afternoon from the grandparents. Jim was sitting at the breakfast bar in the kitchen, and Andrew was playing in the lounge. Jim was laughing, and she sat down opposite him to say hi.

Jim reached across and slapped Lisa hard on her cheek and then laughed again. Lisa grabbed Jim by his arm and dragged him through the lounge and outside onto the deck chair. Lisa then explained to him that you don't slap people and he could stay out there and think about it.

Lisa then went back inside and shut the door. It was all glass, so they could see him quite clearly. Mary stared at Lisa and muttered. Robert muttered something about, 'That wasn't necessary, that's not the way to handle it.'

Lisa sat down next to Andrew and played with him, keeping an eye on Jim. Mary went and talked to Jim through the window. Lisa couldn't hear everything she said, but it involved flowers.

Jim then got off the deck chair and picked flowers. He bought them round to the door where Mary greeted him. She then schooled him up on what to say and bought Jim over to Lisa.

Jim said, "I picked these flowers for you," and gave his mother the flowers. Then, with prompting from Mary, he said, "You hurt my feelings."

Mary then turned to Lisa and said, "Now, you apologize to your son for hurting his feelings."

Lisa thought ' No bloody way am I going to do that. He slapped me.' Lisa stared at Jim, wondering what to say.

Lisa said, "Thank you for the flowers, Jim. It's time we went home. Go get in the car." Lisa collected up Andrew and left thinking, *you manipulative bitch.*

Jim and Andrew stayed at Robert and Mary's when Lisa and Simon were busy on the farm. Once they got over Jim's fussy food issues, things settled down. Then Andrew started to have issues when he was six months old. Andrew was a good eater and was eating solids plus having a bottle of formula at meals. When Andrew came back from his grandparents, he would be constipated. Lisa couldn't understand why, cause he wasn't when she dropped him off. The first time it happened, Lisa thought it might just be a one-off. It wasn't.

When she collected the boys one day in February, she mentioned to Mary that Andrew was constipated when he came home. It was almost like he was dehydrated.

"Oh no, he drinks when he is here."

"Well, what do you give him to drink?" Lisa asked.

"Milk. Milk is a complete food. It supplies all of your needs. You don't need anything else, just milk."

"Don't you give him water?"

"No. He just needs milk."

"Mary, it's a hot 30-degree summer day. Andrew needs water to drink. He is dehydrated from not having enough fluid."

"No, milk is all he needs."

"Mary, he needs water as well. You try only having milk all day and see how you feel. He needs more liquid." Good God, this woman was away with the fairies. Even lambs need water when they are young.

"Mary, you need to give Andrew water to drink as well."

"If you insist, I suppose we can."

"Thank you."

Lisa took the boys home, wondering why the hell, in temperatures of over 30 degrees, they wouldn't give a child water to drink.

Andrew stopped being constipated and dehydrated.

Andrew began eating solids, and he loved them. Quite often, he would refuse the milk. He put on weight and seemed quite happy but didn't like the milk. Some days he would have it and other days totally refused it. Lisa didn't force it, as he seemed quite happy.

When Andrew was old enough to stop having baby formula, he went onto cow's milk. They made the transition slowly, so he had time to adjust. Then Andrew started to vomit on occasions, or he would have acute diarrhoea, but only randomly. Then he would be OK for a while. He started to refuse to have his bottle. Lisa felt he still needed his milk, so she persisted with giving him a bottle.

Andrew vomited some more and just seemed to be unwell. After some tests, it was discovered that Andrew was allergic to lactose. He wasn't a chronic case, but Andrew definitely had a reaction.

The doctor said "Don't stop him having all milk products. Yoghurt is good as the bacteria changes the format of the lactose, so it is safe for him to have. Let him have a little bit of milk, like in baking. Just don't give him a whole bottle of milk. If you allow him to have some milk, he will develop a tolerance to the lactose over time." Lisa bought Andrew expensive goat's milk. Andrew didn't like the taste, and quite frankly, neither did Lisa. Strawberry flavouring stirred in helped.

Andrew and Jim were staying with Robert and Mary when Lisa was busy. "Mary, you can't give Andrew any cow's milk. He is allergic to it."

"Andrew must have his milk. It's the best food."

"I have goat's milk for Andrew to have. It's in these containers."

"Really, you expect him to have goat's milk. There's nothing wrong with cow's milk!"

"Mary, he's allergic to it. Give him lots of liquid like water and some of the goat's milk. Don't give him all of the goat's milk."

Mary muttered things as Lisa went out the door. From the little she overheard, it was along the lines of 'Doesn't know what she's talking about, nothing wrong with milk, depriving her child.'

Lisa left to do farm work and collected Andrew and Jim up in the evening. Andrew once home had acute diarrhoea and vomited.

The next day, once again, Lisa asked them not to give Andrew cow's milk. That night was a repeat of vomiting and diarrhoea. Then Andrew didn't stay with them for a bit as Lisa could take him with her.

Andrew and Jim were going to stay the night with their grandparents as Lisa was going to be home late from work. Lisa went up to collect Andrew and Jim up in the afternoon of the following day. Robert greeted Lisa at the door and said, "We had a terrible night."

"Oh, why?"

"Andrew. He vomited and had acute diarrhoea all night. It went everywhere. He can't drink the milk. He has a really bad reaction to it."

"You gave him milk?" Lisa asked in a shocked voice.

"We gave him ice cream and milk. Milk is the best food, we didn't understand how Andrew reacted to it. We thought you had just made it up about the milk."

Lisa just looked at him. Of all the things to make up, why the hell would someone make that up.

Andrew and Jim were happy to see their Mum and gave her big hugs.

After their experience with Andrew's reaction to the cow's milk, Mary actually went out and bought goat's milk for him. There were no more issues with them forcing cow's milk on Andrew.

Lisa couldn't understand why they constantly question her decisions regarding her children. Whenever Lisa explained something to them they immediately assumed she was wrong and was just trying to cause trouble. It made it very difficult for Lisa and the children.

Andrew, when he was older, would go out to birthday parties. Lisa would say to him, "Don't eat the cream or ice cream. It will make you ill." Course, a five-year-old lad at a birthday party would eat the cream. He would then vomit that night. This was repeated a few times before Andrew stopped doing it.

The hardest thing for Andrew was not being able to eat ice cream. At the time there were very few options in the ice cream department. One time the family was on holiday and Lisa's sister took Andrew to a homemade ice cream shop. They had gelato. A whole range of flavors laid out in the display fridge. Raspberry, banana, vanilla and chocolate all looking appetizing. Andrew's eyes got large in wonder, as he asked Judith in an awed voice "I can have any of these?"

"Yep, you can choose any of these flavours, and you will be fine." Andrew thought he was in heaven as he had a three-scoop cone

Chapter Forty-Five

Clothes

Simon and Lisa went to one of Simon's friend's party. Lisa had organized for the two boys to spend the night at their grandparents. Lisa was home, changed and waiting for Simon to arrive. She was wearing her work uniform. It didn't have any insignia on it, but it was black and work-like.

Lisa didn't want to wear it, so she started going through her suitcase of older clothes from before she married Simon. She was hoping to find something, which would be quite attractive to wear. She was trying clothes on when Simon came home. He walked into the bedroom to see Lisa taking a top off.

"What are you doing? We are running late, and here you are playing at dressing up." Simon was annoyed with her.

"I was just trying some clothes on, that's all."

"We don't have time for this shit." Simon was pulling clothes out of the wardrobe. Lisa put her work uniform back on and went and sat on the bright orange sofa to wait for Simon. She fiddled with the pleats in the skirt. She pulled them together and then let them fall apart.

'Bloody hell, it can't be'. Lisa rubbed the inside of the pleat, and yep, it came off. There was mould growing on her skirt. On the inside of the pleat. Everywhere she looked, there was mould. Lisa stood up to see if it would be noticed when she stood. Lisa didn't think anyone would notice it, but then, who would be looking for mould on a skirt? The outfit had been hanging in the wardrobe in their bedroom and it had mold. Perhaps the fabric attracted mould. Lisa couldn't remember seeing mould on the other clothes.

Lisa spent the trip in the car marvelling over the fact her clothes had mould on them from hanging in the wardrobe. Lisa couldn't see any mould on Simon's clothes, but then she could only see the exposed fabric. The house was so bad for dampness that the clothes grew mould. Lisa didn't say anything to Simon as he wouldn't have been interested.

The next day, Lisa collected the boys from Robert's and Mary's. The conversation then turned to some of their farming friends. One of their friend's son had committed suicide. They were shocked that it had happened.

Robert said, "Apparently, he didn't want to farm. The family forced him into it. It's really sad. He left two young children behind and a loving wife. Not sure what they are going to do. It's such a shame."

Lisa just looked at them, thinking, you have done the same to your son. He didn't want to farm.

"I can't understand it. He had everything. A farm, a wife and a family. Why would he do that?" Robert said in a shocked voice. "It doesn't make any sense. He must have been unbalanced."

With that, he went back to reading his paper. Lisa took the boys home.

Chapter Forty-Six

Cousin's Wedding

Lisa's family lived on the south island. Consequently, they didn't visit them very often. It was February so everything was a bit quieter on the farm. Simon's Cousin was getting married just out of Havelock. The last time Lisa had seen Donna, was at her wedding, when she left in tears. Donna and her mother didn't get on, and Donna didn't come to any of the family gatherings. She had two brothers, one of which was married, but they didn't see much of each other either.

They travelled down in the car, with the two boys strapped into car seats in the back. They were going along the National Park straights with Simon driving.

"Slow down, you are going too fast." Lisa said in a worried voice.

"It's fine."

A bit later, "Simon, you need to slow down."

"It's fine, stop nagging me. I will drive at whatever speed I want to."

"Simon, you could get caught by the cops."

"No, I won't, it's the wrong time of day. Will you just shut up?" Simon was starting to get angry. "I don't need you telling me what to do. I can drive, and it's perfectly safe."

Lisa gave up. She refused to make any more comments. She was at the point of accepting whatever was going to happen, would happen. There was nothing she could do.

The National Park road rises up and dips down as it crosses the plain. As the vehicle rose up a rise, Lisa briefly saw the top of a police car ahead. Lisa kept her mouth shut. Simon carried on hoofing the car along. The flashing lights came on, the siren going, as the police car pulled in behind them. Lisa didn't say a word.

Simon swore as he pulled over.

"Sir, do you know what speed you were doing?"

"Was I over the speed limit, officer?" asked Simon in a very pleasant voice.

"I clocked you at 122 kms per hour. That is very dangerous, and you have a young family with you." The officer was not impressed. He checked the car, WOF, etc and went back to his car to write the ticket.

Simon got given the ticket and was told to slow down.

There was silence in the car as the kids had gone to sleep. Lisa refrained from saying, 'I told you so.' Simon wasn't happy.

About fifteen minutes later, there was another cop. He pulled them over. Simon got out of the car and asked, "Did the last officer radio ahead about us?"

"I have no idea what you are talking about. I am just checking WOF and registrations."

Simon didn't say anything else; just got back in the car and drove off. Simon stayed within the speed limit, including the road works sections. About a half hour later, there was another cop sitting on the side of the road. Simon went past him very slowly and kept checking his rear mirror. Another hour down the road, there was another cop.

By this stage, Simon was getting paranoid. Lisa took great delight in pointing out other cops parked alongside of the road. Simon was not amused. In total, they went past 7 cops and got stopped twice. It got to the point that Simon was expecting to be stopped every time they went past one. Lisa just sat beside him and smiled.

Once they got to the south island, they caught up with Lisa's family for a few days. Judith had travelled up from further south to see them, and they stayed in a motel in Nelson. They organized to visit an elderly aunt who was in her 90s. There was a good chance that they mightn't be able to see Florrie again. She had only ever seen Jim when he was 6 months old, so she was really looking forward to seeing them. Judith and Lisa had the kids all organized and were about to leave.

Simon lay down on the sofa and said, "I'll see you when you get back."

Lisa was very surprised, as she had expected him to come. "Aren't you coming to visit?"

"No, I don't know them. I can stay here and catch up on my sleep."

Lisa walked out to the kitchen area to collect the snack pack for the kids. Judith walked over to Simon and said, "What are you doing?"

"I'm going to stay here. You don't need me. They aren't my family."

Judith was quite shocked, about Simon's attitude. In her firm school-teacher voice, she said, "Lisa visits your family, doesn't she? You can come and meet her family. You are not going to spend the afternoon lying on the sofa. Get off it now and go with your wife. It's the least you can do."

Simon, looking a bit shocked, sat up and collected himself to come. Lisa was a bit surprised that he had come. By this stage, Lisa had resigned herself to going on her own. Judith came up to Lisa as they walked out the door and asked, "You visit Simons's family, don't you?"

"Yeah, all the time, sometimes without Simon."

"I thought so."

The aunt was delighted to see the children. She was grazing a little pony in her backyard, so the kids got to sit on the pony as Simon held them. They thought it was wonderful.

Lisa enjoyed being back in Nelson. They went down to the beach after the visit with the boys, and they paddled in the sea. It was a lovely, warm day.

Lisa caught up with her parents in town. Her brother had made it clear to Judith and Lisa that they were not welcome at the farm. It was a bit hard on Lisa's father, who always liked social occasions and children. Their mother seemed quite happy with the situation. She supported her son in everything he did.

Simon's cousin's wedding was on their way back to the ferry. It was arranged that they would collect Sarah on the way. She was being dropped off by a friend at a small town so she could travel with them to the wedding.

Sarah was wearing a beautiful black dress, with deep white lace at the sleeves and neck. With her blond hair and lovely figure, she really stood out. The guy who had driven her was totally enamoured with her. He seemed like a really nice guy who had just gone out of his way to drive her miles.

It was a garden wedding and Donna was being married under some very old trees. Lisa was pleased to be able to go to the wedding in support. She had been shocked, by the stance taken by Donna's parents. They refused to attend the wedding, as they did not approve.

Donna, years earlier, had left Auckland to move to a house with a bit of land in a small town out of Havelock. She was very happy with her horses and dogs. It seemed that part of the reason for moving was to escape her family. Donna's mother, Barbara, was the main planner of her family and organized everyone. They had done very well due to Barbara's planning. They lived in a very good house, owned farms and had a catering business. Barbara's two sons were fulfilling their mother's expectations. Donna didn't do what her mother wanted and lived a life that she was not happy about. Hence the constant friction.

Donna had a good job and used Havelock as her main center, where she met Tom as he owned a business in the town. After a while, they got together. Tom was 10 years older and had been married previously with two daughters, who were teenagers. Not wanting any more children, he had got a vasectomy.

Donna made it quite clear she didn't want any children. She got on well with his children when they weren't with their mother and was very happy to be involved in their lives. Donna's passions were her horses and dogs.

Barbara had very strong opinions about the fact there would be no children and refused point blank to attend the wedding. Donna's older brother and wife did attend the wedding, and only one of her uncles, Robert's brother attended. He had been ostracized by the family and was quite negative about them.

Simon and Lisa were walking on the family's dark side with all of the black sheep. It was a lovely wedding on a lovely summer day, with the sea breeze from the sounds keeping the air moving. Lisa's boys played between the trees and throughly enjoyed themselves. It was a good chance for them to stretch their legs before the long trip in the car.

Donna had organized the wedding on her own. You could tell that she was hurt about her parents' decision, but was putting on a brave face. Her mother was a florist and had done the flowers for Lisa's wedding.

Donna had done her own flowers, and they were very effective, long-stemmed Campanula Blue Bells. They looked lovely and she commented that "some of my mother's skill must have rubbed off on me" as she fingered the petals of the flowers. She then pulled herself together and put on a bright face to greet the rest of the guests.

Lisa couldn't understand why a mother would shun her daughter on her wedding day. After all, Lisa's mother had attended her wedding. She hadn't expected her to, as their relationship wasn't cordial. Barbara was missing out on the day and she had hurt Donna, her only daughter.

Sarah

Sarah was being the socialite of the gathering and complaining about her stomach.

Apparently, she had eaten a banana. This was bad because the banana was sitting in her stomach, causing a small bulge. This was upsetting the line of the dress. Sarah kept going on about the banana and the problems it was causing. Lisa was having a hard time being sympathetic about it. Thank God she was travelling with someone else after the wedding.

As the wedding wound down Simon and Lisa ended up sitting next to Sarah and having a chat. Simon asked about the guy who dropped her off.

"He seems really nice. Why don't you go out with him?" Simon asked.

"Oh, I couldn't go out with him. He's fat."

Simon and Lisa exchanged looks.

"Sarah, he's not that fat; that can be changed. He is really nice. What does he do?"

"He has an engineering degree or something in boat building. His father builds super yachts in Auckland."

"Well, that sounds like a good job. Do they sail them?"

"Oh yes, they hired our superyachts for the America's Cup to the BMW contingent."

At this point, Simon was even more enthusiastic about his sister spending time with the guy. "You really should give him a chance. He really likes you. He went out of his way by three hours to drop you off."

"No, he's too fat for me."

Simon and Lisa exchanged looks again. It was time for them to leave. After they said goodbye to Donna and her husband, they headed to the car with the boys.

Simon and Lisa visited Donna's parents a month later. Simon showed Barbara some photos of the wedding. Barbara seemed a bit wistful as she looked at them. Then made a cutting comment about the dress and handed the photos back. Barbara, Lisa had discovered, over the years, had no filter. Whatever she was thinking came straight out of her mouth, unedited. It made for some awkward moments.

Chapter Forty-Seven

Funeral

Lisa's aunt Florrie had a growth growing in her bowel. It was now blocking the bowel. It wasn't cancer, and she'd had it before. She needed an operation, but the risk was her age, being 96. They didn't expect her to survive the operation. On the other hand, they couldn't leave her as she was, or she would get gangrene.

The operation was scheduled, and the family waited. She died on the operating table. Simon and Lisa, with their two lads, travelled down for the funeral. Judith came up from down south, and they all arrived in Nelson the day before the funeral.

Lisa and Judith's father had been rushed to hospital a couple of days before they arrived. Dad had a blood clot in his left leg. The doctors were quite worried about his leg and the operation. Being aged 91, he was high risk for surgery, especially as Dad had suffered from two massive heart attacks in the past. The leg wasn't getting any blood flow, and it was quite white and cold. Dad was quite practical and clinical about it, but it was clear he was worried.

Dad loved seeing his grandchildren. Jim and Andrew sat on his bed, and Dad talked and laughed with them. Dad loved Andrew and thought he was a 'real corker'. Dad had missed out on seeing the children.

The surgeon wasn't sure if they would have to amputate above or below the knee. They were all hoping it would be below the knee as he would be able to keep some mobility. Dad was worried about the operation and being able to move around afterwards. Being a farmer, Dad had always been active.

The time for his operation was exactly the same time as Florrie's funeral. The family all sat through the sermon, wondering if Dad was OK. Once the service ended, phone calls were made to find out if Dad had survived the operation.

It had been a long operation as they had first removed the leg below the knee, but when there still wasn't any blood flow, they had then taken off the leg above the knee. It was disappointing. Dad was devastated.

Florrie had been cremated, and her final wish was to have her ashes interned by her mother's headstone. The family gathered at the headstone to intern her ashes and to cover it over. Jim was very happy to have his turn with the trowel. Trouble was, it was far more interesting to throw the soil elsewhere and then laugh. Lisa managed to convince him to put the second trowel load on the box.

The cemetery had a wonderful view over the coast and out to the mountain range. It was very peaceful, with sheep grazing amongst the headstones. The whole cemetery was on the side of a hill, which made it quite steep and difficult for Mum to get down to the site. Once it was all done, Lisa showed Simon where her other relatives were buried, further up the hill.

Afterwards, Lisa and Simon went up to the hospital and saw her Dad. He was upset about losing his leg. It hurt, and Simon went and leaned on the bed right on his sore leg. Dad wasn't impressed. The boys sat on the other side of the bed and cheered their Granddad up, as only little children can do.

Dad asked how the funeral went. It was the burial of his last sibling. He had, had 7 brothers and sisters.

That afternoon, Lisa's mother asked her to accompany her to see Marie. Marie had been living and looking after Florrie. Lisa had never been sure where she had come from, but she had appeared and moved in. Mum didn't exactly like her, but she took good care of Florrie, and they seemed to get on alright. Mum certainly didn't want to take care of Florrie.

Mum was worried about being sued by Marie for wages, for looking after Florrie. Mum kept going on about how much it would cost if she sued for wages and how she didn't want to pay it. Mum got herself quite worked up about it. The other concern Mum had was that Marie mightn't move out of the house. Mum wanted Marie gone and the house empty. Florrie had left all of her assets to Mum except for a few specific items. Florrie was quite wealthy when she died, as all of her siblings had left all of their assets to her, being the second youngest.

Lisa went along as requested, not sure why she was there. So it was just her and her mother who sat down with Marie to say thank you for looking after Florrie. Mum was very chatty and thanked her repeatedly.

Mum then enquired as to what she was going to do now. Her plan was to leave in a couple of months and travel down to stay with her son. Lisa didn't even know she had a son. Mum then produced a large diamond ring to give to her to say thank you. Lisa didn't know where she had got it from as she had never seen it before that day. Mum had shown it to her earlier and asked if she thought it was suitable to give to Marie.

Lisa wasn't too invested in any of this, so she just went along with what she wanted. It had nothing to do with her. Marie accepted the ring, and they parted.

Since Lisa lived so far away, it was agreed that she could collect what Florrie had left her in her will, even though probate hadn't been granted. She had been left a chest. The public trust lady who was overseeing everything pointed out that there were three chests. Lisa had to choose which one, unopened and then sign that she had received her inheritance. Lisa stood there looking at the three chests.

Finally, she decided on the chest which she remembered being in the hall. They took it back to the motel room and opened it. It was the right one. It contained a ring, china, old coins, letters and some linen. It was quite exciting going through it to see what it contained. Simon and, Lisa and the family had to leave for home the next day on the ferry. They said their goodbyes and set off.

Dad was admitted to a rest home once he was released from the hospital. Mum wouldn't have coped with him at home, and the house wasn't set up for a wheelchair. Dad hated it with a passion.

Lisa and Judith arranged to meet and stay in Nelson to see their father. He was in a room on the cold, dark side of the unit. They had a common sitting room where all of the residents gathered. Dad hated it, and the residents hated Dad. The nurses would wheel him out to the sitting room and leave him there.

Dad would then sit and talk to himself non-stop, about what he hated, the other residents, the idiotic nurses, in a loud monotone voice. Lisa walked around the unit looking for him and found him in the sitting room in a wheelchair. As soon as he saw her, he wanted her to wheel him back to the room.

"I can't stand it here. I can't stand being around these idiots." Dad said in a loud voice. The other residents were pleased to see him go.

Dad wanted to go home. Mum had made it quite clear he wasn't to go anywhere near the farm. It had been his obsession for 67 years. He had taken a very run-down farm and developed it. He'd been to hell and back to keep it, which included fighting his family in court, surviving a major financial depression, a world war, and he had raised a family on it.

It was his whole life, and now he couldn't be on it. He was like a fish out of water. Lisa thought they could organize a van or something so that Dad could see the place one last time. She was blocked at every turn as no one wanted to support it.

Lisa really felt for him. One of the guys who used to be out on the farm and lived in Nelson took Dad out occasionally in his truck around town. It gave him something else to see, other than the four walls of his room.

Mum was difficult and quite nasty. The rest home asked if she would buy him some track pants as they would be easier for him to change. She refused. Judith bought them for him.

The food didn't do anything for Dad either. Judith organized with a local fish and chip shop to deliver some oysters and fish n chips to Dad on a Friday night. Dad loved oysters.

Lisa and Judith went home to their families and jobs. Just before Lisa left, Mum contacted her and said she wanted to see her. They arranged a meeting at the motel. Mum arrived, got out of the car, threw a bag at Lisa and said, "You are meant to have these."

Lisa caught the small bag wondering what the hell. "What is it?"

"It's the family jewelry that Florrie had. I wore it to bed one night and woke up strangling. I was being strangled. I had to get your brother to take it off. I am not meant to have it, you are." Mum said in a very angry voice.

With that said, she got back in the car and drove away. Lisa was left standing there with the bag as Mum's car disappeared into the traffic. Lisa took the bag inside and opened it. In it were gold necklaces, pendants, bracelets and brooches. Lisa discovered that the diamond ring Mum had given to Marie was part of the collection. It should have come to her.

That was why Mum was insistent that Lisa went with her when she gave the ring to Marie. In her head, she had justified giving the ring away, because Lisa was present, therefore she had agreed. Lisa had no idea where the ring had come from. Mum could have purchased it for all she knew, but it explained why she kept asking her if she approved. Lisa, by that stage, was just going through the motions and not asking questions. Mum had been very difficult.

At home, Lisa got a phone call from Mum: "Donald (Donald was a local hunter who had hunted on the property for years) was out on Saturday. He said he had gone and seen Dad on Friday. Dad was having fish n chips for tea. I said it must be something the rest home did. He said no, he was pretty certain it had been organized by the family. I know nothing about it. What do you know?"

"Oh. That's nice that Dad is getting Fish n chips."

"I want to know where they are coming from and who did it?" Mum sounded really angry. Quite clearly, she wasn't happy about it.

"I don't know where they are coming from."

"Well, I want to know. I have to put a stop to it."

"Why do you have to stop it?" Lisa asked in a concerned voice.

"I can't have someone sending him fish n chips and people knowing he's getting them. It's not from us. It makes us look bad. I want to know who it is."

"Well, I don't know." Thinking, what a miserable bitch. What harm is it doing that he is getting some oysters on a Friday? It's not causing any harm to Mum. She had not done anything to make his life easier.

Lisa didn't know which shop Judith had set it up with, so she was being quite honest.

Mum rang around every fish n chip shop until she found out who it was. She put a stop to it. She then sent David around with a hug feed of fish n chips. Dad ate them and was sick. Because he was sick he didn't get anymore. Mum had successfully removed his little highlight for the week. It made no difference to her, but she had done it. Her whole focus was making David, her son, look like the big boy and in charge. He had to be the one making the gesture.

Judith had organized with the rest home to contact her if Dad deteriorated. There was no information from Mum and they had serious doubts if she would tell them if anything happened to Dad.

Lisa's nephew Paul had visited Dad, and they had, had a good discussion about the freezing works, hunting and life. At the end, Paul said, "Mum and Aunty are coming in a couple of days to see you."

"Why? I won't be here. There's nothing they can do." Dad replied.

"Don't be daft. You will see them when they get here."

"No, I have lived my life. I don't want to see in the new century. I was born in the 1900s, and I will die in the 1900s."

Lisa got a phone call from her mother just before she left. Mum said in a very reasonable, caring, calm voice, "Your father is deteriorating, dear, but there's no need for you to come down. Don't waste your money by coming down. You don't need to be here for the funeral. It will be better if you stay up there. There's nothing you can do. I know you were close to him, but he wouldn't have wanted you to come."

"Mum, I am booked to come down. I am flying in tomorrow."

"Why would you do that?" Mum sounded surprised and put out.

"The nurse contacted Judith and told her Dad was going downhill, and she rang me. So I organized to come."

"Why would the nurse do that? She had no right to do that." Mum started to get worked up.

"Cause Judith asked her to."

"Well, cancel, you don't have to be here." Mum said in an angry voice.

"I am booked, and I am coming. Why wouldn't I want to see my father before he died?" At that point, Mum hung up the phone. Lisa looked at the phone, wondering why she didn't want her to come. What mother tries to ensure her daughter doesn't attend her father's funeral? It wasn't right.

Judith drove up, and Lisa flew in. Her plane got in at 4 pm, 10 minutes after Dad died. He had been in a coma for the last 12 hours, so Lisa couldn't have talked to him anyway. Judith met Lisa at the airport and told her. They went around and saw his body. He was lying in the rest home bed in his red-striped pyjamas. No one else was there. Judith had walked into the room earlier in the day to find Mum was at Dad's bedside.

When she saw Judith, she had said, "Oh, you came then," in an angry voice. She then grabbed her bag and walked out.

Dad's breathing was laboured, and he died about half an hour later. Judith tried to get a message to her mother. She contacted an acquaintance who lived on the route Mum would be driving and asked him to stop her on the road and tell her.

Once they told her, they expected her to go back to the rest home. Mum said, "I have to get home to cook David's tea." She then drove off.

Lisa sat by her father's bed and thought of everything that hadn't been said. Judith watched her.

"I need to walk." Lisa said. Judith put her in the car and they went round to the local park. Lisa walked. Dad had died on the 31st December 1999.

Neither Judith nor Lisa were welcomed by the immediate family, which consisted of their mother and brother. They booked a hotel in the middle of Nelson City and stayed the night there. The celebrations to welcome in the new century were in full swing in town. They went for a walk around the streets and looked at all the people sitting in the bars. It was loud and wet. They spent two nights in the hotel.

Judith and Lisa's families arrived three days later. Simon had booked the ferry and arrived with the two boys. It was good to see them. Adjoining motel units were booked, and they all moved in.

They all had a meeting with the undertaker. Dad wanted a full burial, and Florrie had bought him a plot in the cemetery that the family used. It wasn't far from where Florrie's ashes had been buried.

Both Judith and Lisa wanted to speak at his funeral. Mum was determined that no one would speak. She didn't approve of people speaking at funerals. Only the minister should speak. They asked her to bring in a suit for Dad to wear. She refused. The lid was to be screwed down, so there was no need for him to have a suit. The question of pallbearers came up. Judith and Lisa expected that the family members would fill the role. Dad had two older grandsons, two sons-in-law and a son. That made five, so they only needed another one.

Judith asked Mum what she thought. "We have already organized the pallbearers."

"Oh, so who are they?" Judith asked in a surprised voice.

"They are people your father wanted. There is no need for any of you to be pallbearers." Mum answered in a very angry voice.

The rest of the family exchanged looks. Lisa thought they would be the Masonic Lodge members cause Dad had always said that they would organize his funeral and would provide pallbearers. That was fine with Lisa.

Mum was so rude to the undertakers and so determined to have her way that they felt sorry for the rest of the family. After Mum and David had walked out, they said to the remaining family that they would set it up so that there could be a viewing before the funeral for those who wanted to.

They had put a red rose in Dad's crossed arms, still in his pyjamas. Lisa felt so sorry for Dad cause he had always been a proud man and took pains with his appearance.

At the next meeting with the minister, hymns were discussed, the order of the service and what photo was to be used. Mum produced a photo someone had given her of the valley. It wasn't even a very good photo, but she insisted that it be used.

Lisa had a brief moment alone with her mother. "Mum, did Dad say anything to you before he died?"

"Nothing of concern for you. It was what a husband and wife would say to each other. Nothing to do with you at all." Mum replied in a really angry voice.

"I just wondered if he said anything about me. That's all." Mum just glared at Lisa and then walked away.

Once the funeral discussion was finished Mum said she wanted to have a meeting with Lisa. Judith had to leave.

She pulled out a chequebook and said, "I will pay you the money that is owed to you as listed in the accounts". It was money dating back 10 or so years from when Dad had bought rams from Lisa.

The cheque was in Dad's name, and Lisa knew Mum had signing authority. She did all of the bookwork. Mum was sitting in the chair, and David was standing behind her, with his hand on her shoulder, glaring at Lisa.

"You can't write out a cheque, Mum." Lisa said.

"Why not? I have the authority to do it."

"Mum, Dad's dead, and any cheque written out now will not be valid."

"Why not?"

"Cause Dad is dead. The bank will freeze the accounts."

"They have no right to do that."

"Yes, they do. You will have to wait until probate."

"How would they know that he's dead?"

"Well, they could read it in the paper."

"They have no right to read it. It's private."

"Mum, you cannot write out cheques, now that Dad is dead, on his account."

"They can't stop me. I can do what I want."

"No, you cannot do it."

At this point, she shut the chequebook angrily while David continued to glare at Lisa. Lisa walked out to Judith, who was waiting for her.

Lisa had organized for Simon to bring down her old photo albums, which had photos of Dad in them. Since Lisa and Judith couldn't speak, they got the photos copied and set them up on some cards with writing about the photos. They put them up on the wall at the funeral home. They also picked some wild flowers to put on the coffin from his grandchildren. Mum was still being really difficult and quite nasty.

They all turned up on the day to say farewell to their father/grandfather. The family pews had been filled with random people invited by Mum. So Lisa and Judith, with their families, sat together further back.

The minister spoke, and then David got up and spoke. All along when Mum had refused to let the sisters speak, she had organized for David to speak. It was a poor speech. Lisa thought, 'What a bitch', This has been organized to make David look big. The minister looked at Judith and Lisa pointedly and asked if anyone else wanted to speak. They didn't. Judith was too angry, and Lisa was really pissed off. The rest of the mourners must have wondered about the whole funeral.

Mum had ensured that it was a battle, and in reality, it made her and David look bad. The exact opposite of what she wanted. People aren't stupid. They would have wondered why they were sitting in the family seats while the rest of the family were sitting elsewhere. Many of the pallbearers had worked alongside Lisa and Judith in the woolshed and on the farm. They knew that they had contributed to the farm. They had also seen David and knew what he was like. They must have wondered about Mum's actions. On the day of the funeral, she couldn't bring herself to be gracious or considerate.

Lisa sat in the pew, watching her two young sons playing at the front of the pulpit, thinking, 'Well, that's in your face, David.' He didn't have any children or was married. Then, the pallbearers arrived. They were not Masonic Lodge as Lisa expected (They did put flowers on his coffin). They were a motley bunch who had been asked to be pallbearers when they turned up at the farm to give their condolences.

Mum and David had made the request of them because they didn't have anyone else to ask. A complete lie about Dad wanting them.

They weren't best mates of Dad's. They had worked for him over the years. So the pallbearers were David and this random bunch of guys. Lisa was pissed off. Really pissed off that her mother had gone out of her way to make sure that Dad's family were cut out, except for her son.

Part of the reason would have been the fact that Bryce, Judith's other son, was gay. David was homophobic to the point he wouldn't even shake hands with him. Even so, for Mum to do as she did, it was a real slap in the face and, quite frankly, made it look really bad for the family.

After the service, they all got ready to leave for the cemetery. "I'm not going." Mum said very firmly

"Mum, you should come." Judith said.

"No, I don't need to see them put my husband in the ground. I am going into town to have coffee with Jean." Mum said in a tearful but on the verge of a full-on drama voice.

Mum used to be an actress and could turn it on and off at will. After her behaviour leading up to this point, Lisa thought it was more an act than anything else. Lisa really thought she was quite happy he had died.

"Alright." replied Lisa, who didn't really care at this stage what she did. Lisa asked Judith, "Who's Jean?"

"Oh, she's Dad's old girlfriend. Apparently, he went out with her before he met Mum."

That would have been at least 37 years ago. "When did she meet her?"

"Oh, she discovered about her when Dad went into the rest home. She's been going around and talking to her."

"Oh. Seems a bit strange."

Judith just nodded.

They went round to the cemetery and buried Dad. His plot was just down below his mother's grave. It was a nice summer day, and a Puhutukawa tree was in full flower beside Dad's grave. The red petals drifted down onto the grave.

Lisa held her son Jim in her arms as she convinced him to take a handful of soil in his hand and then throw it onto his grandfather's coffin. She then did the same with a red rose. Simon repeated it with little Andrew. A few words were spoken, and they went back for the wake.

Lisa talked to neighbours and guys who had worked for Dad. David was there trying to be the big boy in charge. Mum turned up towards the end to do the grieving widow and accept all the condolences.

At the end of the wake, Lisa and Judith and their families went back to the motel room and prepared to go home. There were no goodbyes with their mother or brother.

Lisa was sorry Dad had gone, but she understood that it was his time. On the way home, Lisa thought about Mum's behaviour. She had caused a lot of hurt just for the sake of causing the hurt. There was no benefit to her.

Her whole focus was to make her son the big guy and eliminate her daughters. Funny thing was, her daughters had produced four grandsons' and her son had no children. David just played her for his own benefit, and he didn't want his sisters around cause they might show him up or gain some inheritance.

David spoke about his mother in very derogative language. He called her a 'Paranoid slut', but to her face, he was polite and looked the doting son. He gave her expensive china ornaments and soppy cards for her birthdays and Xmas. Mum just lapped it up while all the time he was just using her.

In their mother's head, he was going to provide and care for her in her old age. He was going to be the hero and continue the family's legacy.

David saw himself as the 'big frog' in the pond due to the size of the farm. In reality, he was poorly educated, had limited experience, was emotionally unstable, drank heavily and had no social skills. Their mother had helped create him by her emotional blackmail and by supporting his ego. He could do no wrong. She even stood up in court when he was sued and lied for him. The pair of them altered the truth to suit their narrative. This was what she had tried to do with the funeral. The son would be the hero, and the daughters the evil sisters.

271

Chapter Forty-Eight

Lisa's Third Pregnancy

L isa's first two sons were exactly two years and ten days apart; right in the middle of spring, a busy time. Lisa wanted a third child and before they were married, Simon had said that he wanted four children. Lisa hadn't committed to four and her reply had been. "Let's see how things go."

They tried to have an autumn-born baby. Nothing happened. Lisa felt great, but in amongst the wanting a third child were the thoughts about all the issues of having a new baby involved. Cramps, being uncomfortable, sleepless and then all that comes with caring for a newborn.

Lisa conceived at the same time as the other two babies. So, a spring child. No idea why. One theory was Simon would be putting the bull out and feel left out, so he would come home to prove a point!

Another theory was that some women are seasonal, and Lisa was one of them. Whatever the reason, one more spring baby coming up.

Lisa went up one afternoon, after coming back from the doctor to collect the two boys and told Mary.

"I am pregnant. We are going to have another baby." In a pleased voice.

"Is it a mistake?"

"No, we want a third child." Lisa was wondering why she thought it was a 'mistake.'

"You don't need to have another baby. You have the heir and the spare. Why have another?" Mary was really angry about it.

Lisa began backing out of the room, with the youngest in her arms, as Mary advanced on her, demanding to know, "What possessed you to have another child? Does Simon know, or did you just get pregnant and not tell him?"

"No, we talked about it. Simon wants the baby as well."

Mary turned around and stormed back into the kitchen, muttering.

My God, Lisa didn't expect that reaction. She drove home wondering what her problem was. Most grandparents are happy about another grandchild, and she had three children. And what the hell was this about, the heir and the spare? Talk about an old-world attitude.

Chapter Forty-Nine

Aussie Holiday

Lisa and Simon decided to go and see their friends in Australia while they could. Once the third baby was born, it was going to be difficult to go anywhere for a while. Their friends lived on a farm in NSW with their three children, who were a lot older than theirs. They would spend time with them on the farm and see some of the local sights.

The plan was to fly to Melbourne and then travel by train up to NSW. The train would allow the boys to move around and use the toilet when they wanted. Lisa was excited to catch up with their friends and see what they had done to the farm. The boys' bed-wetting wouldn't be a problem, as Rose's two boys had bed wet as well. Rose had it all covered. It would be a good break for them to get away for a while.

At dinner one night at the in-laws, they explained about the trip to Australia.

"You won't be talking the boys with you. They will be staying here with us." Mary said.

"No, it's a family holiday. The boys are coming." Lisa explained.

"No, you don't take children on holiday with you."

"Yes, we are. The boys are coming."

"We never took the children with us. It was our holiday, not the children's."

"Yeah, we always stayed with the neighbours while Mum and Dad were away." Simon explained. "Each of us would stay with a different neighbour."

"So you never took the kids with you on holiday? Not even when you travelled in NZ?"

"Course not. They would have just got in the way. We went on overseas holidays every year, and we never took the children." Mary explained.

"So when you were first married you went on overseas holidays?" Lisa asked, thinking about all of the lectures they had given her, about how hard it had been for them, when they started out farming. No money and debt.

"That's right, we haven't missed a year away." Mary replied.

Well, that was a turn-up for the books. So much for them having it tough when they started out.

"We are taking the children with us. We are hoping that you can feed the dogs and keep an eye on things while we are away."

Robert agreed to do that. Mary still wasn't happy about the children going. Simon was beginning to think it might be better if the children stayed with them. Lisa was sticking to her guns; it was a family holiday, and the children were coming.

Lisa tried to get seats on the plane so they were all sitting together. Once Lisa was on the plane and realized who was sitting where, she tried to change it. The hostess insisted they sit in the seats allocated for them. Lisa was on the aisle with Jim beside her and Simon by the window. Andrew was across the aisle from her. They got the boys strapped in. They were really excited about the trip.

The plane taxied down the runway, ready for take off. The plane then started gathering speed and lifted off. The floor tilted sharply as it reached for the sky. Andrew's eyes got really big, his hand clasped the armrest with a talon-like grip, and his face took on a look of terror.

Lisa reached across the aisle as far as her seatbelt would allow and grasped his hand. His whole body was rigid. Once they levelled out, they allowed her to kneel beside Andrew and give him a hug. Andrew calmed down once the plane levelled out. Lisa will never forget the look on his face when the plane lifted off.

Lisa explained to Andrew what would happen when they landed. Andrew freaked out again, but not as badly.

The train trip was great. The boys could move around, eat, use the toilet and watch the scenery.

They had a great holiday. They went to a petting zoo and the boys got to feed kangaroos and pat kolas. Jim latched onto Rose's big boys and chased around after them. He completely ditched Andrew.

Rose's boys were teenagers, but they looked after Jim and seemed quite happy to take him on trips. They went yabby hunting, saw black snakes and discovered fire ants. Andrew was upset about that and became very clingy to Lisa. Lisa had to carry him everywhere.

Ross came and got him one day. He said, "He can come with me so you get a break." Andrew screamed as Ross peeled him off Lisa and carried him away. Being a father of three kids, he wasn't fazed. Rose and Lisa settled down to a peaceful afternoon, drinking wine and talking.

When they came back, Ross said, "He had a ball. Once, he was out of sight of you. He's a very tired lad."

Rose took Lisa's lads round the farm with her, as she did jobs. Lisa was up the hill one afternoon with Simon and Rose's oldest, shooting. She looked down to see Rose walking along with her daughter and Lisa's two boys, all trailing along behind her, as she lit fires. It looked like mother duck and all of her ducklings.

They went to the local reservoir, where they all went swimming. The boys loved it, especially when the big boys put them on their shoulders and then tossed them into the water. Lots of yelling and screaming.

All too soon, the holiday ended, and they repeated the trip back to NZ. The plan was to break the trip in Auckland and stay the night at Robert and Mary's apartment before the four-hour drive home. It seemed like a good plan as they would have two very tired boys.

When they arrived at the apartment, they discovered that Robert and Mary had organized a dinner party. They had invited distant family members plus Sarah. Lisa couldn't believe it. They had two tired and scratchy boys and were now expected to play ladies and gentlemen at the dinner table with the boys.

The boys mucked around, screamed and complained just like two over-tired kids would do. In what world was this a good idea? Lisa wasn't impressed. Once the boys had eaten, she took them away for bedtime, leaving the rest of the guests to continue the dinner party.

Lisa had a bad night as Andrew was beside himself and wouldn't settle for the night. He screamed and screamed all night. He literally climbed the wall as Lisa tried to cuddy-hold him in bed. In the morning, Mary had the grace to recognize that the dinner party hadn't been a good idea.

They got home and adjusted to being back on the farm. The boys settled down to playing with their toys. Simon and Lisa caught up on the farm work.

Chapter Fifty

Genetics

Lisa was in the bedroom doing the accounts. It was a hot, late summer afternoon. The heat was just sapping with high humidity. Simon and Jim were sprawled across the sofa in the lounge resting.

"Lisa, come quick." There was a note in Simon's voice, which caused Lisa to drop everything and rush out to the lounge.

Simon was sitting on the sofa, looking at Jim worriedly and trying to get a response. Lisa looked at Jim in complete disbelief. Jim was completely limp. No response at all. Lisa picked up one of his hands and lifted it up. When she let it go, it just fell, no resistance at all. Lisa opened one of his eyes and all she could see was the whites of his eyes. It was like he was dead. Just seeing the whites of her son's eyes was like something out of a horror movie. It's really freaky.

Lisa couldn't understand it. How could a perfectly healthy child suddenly go completely limp, inert, comatose?

Simon rang the 111 number. Lisa collected Jim and, took him outside to lay him on the grass, by the carport, in the shade. She had his shoulders lying across her knees, trying to see what was wrong.

"Please, please don't let him die. Oh God, why would this happen?" Lisa rocked him in her arms, crying and pleading for him to be alright. He was pale in colour, but he was breathing. She pried open his mouth, which was clamped shut, trying to see if his tongue was blocking his throat. Lisa couldn't get a good look cause his mouth was like a steel trap.

Lisa kept rocking him and crying in a complete state of shock and disbelief. Jim started to have some response. Jim's eyes were coming into focus instead of just being rolled back. His body wasn't quite so limp. Lisa couldn't believe it and was so relieved. She had thought he was dying.

The ambulance turned up, and they rushed over to Lisa. They took Jim from her, saying, "We got him now. It's OK. We will just put him on the stretcher and check him out."

Lisa was just in a state of shock, wondering what had happened. She got in the ambulance with Jim and sat by him while they asked her questions and checked him over.

Jim was starting to take some interest in his surroundings but was still very groggy. They took Jim's temperature, which was slightly above normal. They then took his clothes off and started bathing him in cool water.

"We will take him to the hospital and get him checked out, but it's most likely to be convulsions."

"What causes it? What is it?"

"We don't normally see it fully cause by the time we arrive, the child has started to come out of it. It's reasonably common, and children grow out of it by the time they are 7."

"They get a high temperature, and the body just shuts down. You need to reduce their temperature, slowly, so no cold water, as the shock would be too much. Just gently sponge them down; see, he's getting more alert all the time. Once he comes out of it, he will start to shake, and you will need to wrap him up warmly as the body re-adjusts. The main issue to be aware of is not to cause a big shock to the body with extreme temperature movements. Slowly reduce the temperature."

Lisa just sat by Jim, watching as he slowly came back to being his normal self.

They were half an hour away from the hospital, and Lisa started to feel sick. Lisa was pregnant with their third child. The swaying of the ambulance around the corners, was having a very negative effect on her.

Simon had to stay home and organize Andrew to come in with the car. Andrew was having an afternoon nap.

Jim was looking a lot better and by the time they got to the hospital, he was sitting up and asking questions.

The doctor checked him over. Simon arrived with Andrew, in time to see the doctor. Jim wanted to get down and play.

"Convulsions are quite common and have no ill effect on the child. It can happen when they have a temperature or overheat. Very common in Ireland, so if you have Irish ancestry, then you are more likely to experience it. We don't know what brings it on, and most children grow out of it by the time they are 7. They become less severe as the child gets older." The doctor explained to them, "If it happens again, just bring his temperature down slowly by sponging with tepid water. Avoid major extremes in temperature variations.

"Thank you for that." Lisa said.

Simon headed over to the ambulance staff, who were in the hospital lounge. He gave them $200 and a gift basket to say thank you for everything. They had a chin wag about the trip and their experience with tending other children who had the same thing. Simon kept thanking them.

Lisa collected Jim and Andrew up and they all headed to the car and home. Once the children were fed and put to bed. Lisa rang her sister Judith and told her what had happened. Judith completely understood everything Lisa told her. To Lisa's complete surprise and shock, her nephew had had the same thing. Judith had been home alone when Paul had convulsed. Only the whites of his eyes showing, and no response.

Judith had put him in the car on the floor, convinced he was dying and rushed him to the local doctors. Exactly the same thing, as what Jim had. Lisa got off the phone, a bit pissed off that she hadn't told her about it. If Lisa had known, at least she would have known what to do.

Quite clearly, it was something in their family. Paul hadn't had another attack. Here's hoping for them.

Chapter Fifty-One

Gold Fish

Jim loved fish. He was completely fascinated by them. They got him two goldfish and a small goldfish bowl. It sat on his window sill, and Jim would be entertained for hours, watching the fish swim in and out of the little castle and through the water weed they had in the bowl. One day, Lisa was in the bedroom doing the accounts. Jim was being really quiet. That's when Lisa got worried. Silence was a sure indication the boys were getting into trouble. A general background noise generally meant everything was OK.

Lisa went into Jim's room to find Jim on his window ledge. He had got the fish out of the bowl and had them lying on the windowsill beside each other. The fish were gasping and wiggling their tails. Jim was intently watching them as he poked them. Lisa wasn't sure what he was expecting them to do.

Lisa rushed over to Jim. "Jim, you have to put them in the water." She hastily scooped the fish up and put them back in the bowl. They were a bit wobbly but were swimming.

"They can't survive out of the water. Jim, you have to leave them in the water." Jim was watching the fish.

"Why can't they be out of the water?"

"They have gills, which allows them to breathe in the water. They can't breathe in the air. They don't have lungs like us."

"I wanted to see if they could move, like they do in the water." Jim was concerned that they couldn't move on the window sill.

"Jim, fish swim, they can't walk. You have to leave them in the water."

"Ooh." Jim was staring at the fish intently.

"Jim, you have to leave them in the water."

Lisa went back to the accounts, wondering how a small mind works. Quite clearly, Jim felt that those fish should be able to wander around the house on their own.

Sarah

Sarah was home visiting her parents when Lisa went up to see them with the children. They were all sitting at the table when she walked in and looked to be having an intense discussion.

Sarah was explaining to her parents about her social inadequacy.

"All of the other girls have diamond rings, and I don't. I don't fit into the group because I don't have one. They treat me differently 'cause they have diamond rings, and I don't."

Lisa was sitting at the table, unable to believe this bullshit. Robert was frowning and Mary was nodding her head at Sarah.

"I am not invited to special parties 'cause I don't have one, and they all do. I don't fit in with the right people. You need to buy me a diamond ring so I am part of the group." Sarah explained in a pathetic voice.

Lisa looked around the table and said, "Well, perhaps you have to wait to get married like the rest of us."

Robert got up from his chair and moved to the lounge. Mary went back to the kitchen, and Sarah threw her a look, which would have killed her on the spot if looks could kill.

Lisa hid a smile.

Chapter Fifty-Two

Pregnancy Complications

Lisa was feeling great. She wasn't sick or bloated, and then she had a scan. The nurse scanning her kept going over one area in her lower abdomen.

After a while, she finished and said, "I will send these through to a specialist. You may have a small problem."

"What? Is the baby alright?"

"The baby is fine. It's healthy, moving well, a good size."

"Well, what?"

"It's best you wait until the specialist sees the scan; it could be nothing." They sent her off to a specialist, who carried out more scans.

Lisa had a placenta previa, which is high risk. Apparently, 1 in 100 women have it. A hundred years ago, both the baby and mother would have died by haemorrhaging. They were scanned monthly to assess how things were looking. The specialist was located two hours away, so with the boys and the farm, it was a pain. It wasn't looking good. In the last month the scans became weekly.

A placenta previa is when the placenta covers the cervix. The placenta transfers all of the blood from the baby to the mother and back again, so it is a major blood vessel. If you go into labour, in this situation, then both the mother and the baby will bleed to death. Both lives are lost in a very short space of time. Normally, the placenta is attached further up the uterus, so it is quite safe during labour. Once the baby is born, the blood vessels contract and all is good. Nature is quite amazing, how it all works.

Sue, Lisa's midwife, said, "It is a very high-risk pregnancy. If you see any spotting or feel any pain, don't hesitate; ring the helicopter. Even then, you may not make it to the hospital in time. You could bleed out. Don't take any risks, and make sure you stay close to the phone or with someone."

Great. Just great.

Lisa had two kids to look after anyway, so not much changed. The normal daily routines of washing, cooking, shopping, and chasing after the runaways all had to happen anyway. Simon was out on the farm most of the day and was unable to be contacted, so Lisa was on her own.

They went round to Simon's cousins, dairy farm for a visit. They gave them a tour of the farm on a quad. It was a nice sunny day, and the tracks were pretty good. Lisa got so far around on the bike, and things didn't feel so good. Simon and Lisa stopped and took their time. Everything settled down. In early evening, they came home and got the kids organized for tea and bed.

That night, Lisa had some spotting. She felt good, though. She went to bed and just lay there, hoping that all would be good. Please,

God, let it be alright. Please let it be alright, Lisa kept asking as she lay on her back. Lisa spent most of the night worrying and staying still. In the morning, she felt good and the spotting seemed to have stopped.

Lisa told Sue on her next visit, and she said, "You have been very lucky."

Lisa drove herself back to the doctor for another scan. The boys spent the day, at their grandparents. The specialist, who was also a private surgeon, took a long time to complete the scan. Lisa had been holding onto the hope that she wouldn't need a cesarean. They had discussions about how it was looking and if it would be OK. This time he said that it was looking like a classic case and he would book her in for surgery. They really didn't want to risk her going into labour.

Chapter Fifty-Three

Surgery

For the last two nights, the TV news had a story about how all the junior doctors and nurses were going on strike. Surgeries were being cancelled, and patients sent home. This was right at the time Lisa's surgery was booked.

Lisa rang Sue and asked if it was all still happening. "Your surgery will still take place as you are too high a risk to leave."

Two weeks before the due date, they found themselves on the way to the hospital to have the baby at an appointed time, in the middle of the afternoon. It was a bit weird.

Sue met Lisa at the hospital and sat with her, waiting after she had been prepped. Simon wasn't allowed in pre-surgery. They took him away and gowned him up so he was ready to enter at the appointed time.

It was really nice of her, as Lisa was very apprehensive about it all. Sue just talked to her about other things. She put the catheter in.

One of the nurses came in and asked if Lisa would donate the placenta. The cytogenetic lab wanted the placenta to help grow bone marrow for a cancer patient. It's very high in nutrition and provides an excellent median to grow cells. It can help burn victims as well. Not sure how exactly, but apparently, it can save a lot of lives. In this case, they urgently needed one to help with a case. Sue said it was a worthy cause and Lisa was quite happy to donate it.

They then came in, in gowns and masks, to wheel Lisa to the surgery room. Lisa didn't want to be knocked out, so they gave her an epidural in the back. Lisa was hidden behind a green screen, and they went to work. All of the surgeon's team were heads of departments, as everyone else was out on strike. Not sure about the nurses, but none of them were young, so again, must be the senior staff.

Simon was sitting by Lisa's head, determinedly not looking. He really didn't want to see anything they were doing. Lisa even asked him to look at one point. A look of horror crossed his face just at the thought. This time, they didn't ask him to cut the cord.

When they cut Lisa open, she didn't feel any pain. All she felt was the pushing and pulling. Lisa could hear them talking, and apparently, she was a classic placenta previa. Lisa would have died if she had gone into labour. Lisa felt it when they pulled the baby out. They brought him around to her so she could see her new baby. He was covered in globs of white fat, which is a sure indication that he was early. The fat is reabsorbed into the skin just prior to birth. Two weeks early, and, he was a big baby. The doctors said that if he had been full-term, Daniel would have been over 9 pounds.

Another boy. Lisa had waited until the birth to find out the sex. She really wanted to have that surprise, as to whether it was a girl or a boy.

The doctors were talking about how much blood Lisa had lost. She had lost between 3 to 4 pints of blood. The specialist was ordering a blood transfusion when Lisa interrupted and said, "No, I don't want one."

"You really need one. You have lost a lot of blood. It will aid your recovery from surgery."

"No, I don't want the transfusion."

They gave in to Lisa's wishes. They weren't happy about it. Lisa figured if she was awake and speaking, then it wasn't so bad. Lisa wasn't against blood transfusion, but Sue had contracted hepatitis B when she had a transfusion. Lisa didn't want to run the risk.

As they started to prepare Lisa to be wheeled out to the recovery room, they removed the screen. She caught a brief glimpse of the room and bed. The nurses were busy wiping her legs down, and there was blood all over the floor. Lisa really had lost a lot of blood.

Lisa was left alone in the recovery room with her baby. The drugs were good. No pain. It was the best time for Lisa as she was left alone with her baby. She was on a high, narrow bed with her son right beside her. He was in a hospital bassinet, glass sides and wrapped up. Lisa ran her finger gently over his soft, round cheek.

Her sleeping, soft, gorgeous baby boy. In the surgery room, once they had slapped his bottom, he had screamed in outrage while they cleaned him up. They had run all of the post-birth tests, which he had passed with high scores. Lisa touched his soft black hair and watched his chest rise and fall as he twitched. It was lovely and peaceful to just connect with her son. Normally, once someone gives birth, they have all these people around them asking questions, demanding that things are done, watching; constantly watching. This was just Lisa and her baby.

After a while, a nurse came back in and said she needed to put some needles into her legs for the morphine. By this stage, Lisa was beginning to have some more feeling in her legs. They then wheeled Lisa out to the ward, where Simon was waiting.

Lisa had her own room and settled down for the night. Simon went home.

A cesarean is not something Lisa would recommend to anyone. They wanted Lisa out of bed as soon as possible. Apparently, moving around helps the healing. They still gave Lisa painkillers, so no pain. It's just that as Lisa moved down the corridor to the toilet, it felt as if her guts were going to fall out. Stomach muscles are taken for granted. Lisa went past all of these other mothers who were in the same boat. All holding their hands against their stomach, like they are trying to hold everything in.

They had stapled the wound closed. Lisa had these large industrial-looking staples right across her front, just above her pubic hair. It's a bit freaky looking at the skin with staples in it like it is a bunch of pages.

It just seems wrong to be stapled. The staples being spaced out pull the skin, and it gets red around them.

The specialist came round in the morning and asked how she was.

"I'm tired."

"That will be due to the loss of blood. A blood transfusion would have given you more energy and faster healing. You were a classic case of placenta previa and very high risk." He wasn't happy that Lisa had refused the blood transfusion.

"Thank you for what you did. I have a lovely baby boy." The specialist nodded and headed out the door.

Lisa settled into breastfeeding and getting to know her son. He had the biggest feet. They were like paddles on the end of these tiny little baby legs. Anyone who came and saw her got shown his feet. Lisa couldn't get over how big they were.

Breastfeeding still wasn't a great arrangement. Daniel got enough milk for the time Lisa was in the hospital.

The nurses kept pushing for Lisa to use the common room, the toilet and do anything to keep moving. They slowly reduced the painkillers, as they wanted Lisa off them as soon as possible due to risk of addiction.

Sue came round and saw her. She checked the baby over and settled down to complete the paperwork. After going through the normal questions like, 'Was it a live birth?' Yes, it is a question. When Lisa went to have her baby, the paperwork asks questions like, 'What birth number is this?' and 'How many live births.' For any mother who has lost a baby, it must be quite traumatic.

They then got down to the question about the type of birth. Sue started to tick the box 'requested caesarean,' At which point Lisa objected. Lisa had not requested a caesarian. It was the last thing she wanted.

Sue looked surprised and said, "No, it wasn't. I will put it down as a medical requirement".

At the time, the news kept going on about more women requesting cesareans for convenience and how they wanted them reduced. Lisa wasn't surprised since they just automatically ticked the requested option. In Lisa's case, she would have died without it, so if that wasn't a medical reason, Lisa has no idea what it would be.

After six days, Lisa was sent home with the following instructions from the nurse. "Do not lift anything heavier than your baby."

"Do not lift your arms above your head."

Thinking about home, Lisa asked, "Can I hang the washing out?"

"No, do not do anything which will stretch your stomach muscles. Walking is good, but do not carry the washing basket and lift anything which is heavy. You will run the risk of a hernia".

Simon drove them home. After a day at home, Lisa drove up and got her other sons from the grandparents. It was the first time they had seen their brother. They had not visited Lisa in hospital at all. Lisa had reached the point where she knew they would not be bought to see her. At least they had each other to play with this time.

Lisa had a new baby, a two-year-old and a four-year-old. Telling a mother that she is not to lift anything or raise her arms with two small children and a baby is next to impossible. Just getting the boys in and out of the bath and the cot was hard enough. Lisa was always bending down to pick things up off the floor, talk to her children and to rescue things. Bending over hurt and standing up was harder. Her guts still felt like they were going to fall out. Lisa decided that anyone who has a cesarean voluntarily is nuts.

Lisa was home all day on her own, with all of the normal household chores to do. She had to do the cooking, the bookwork, the cleaning and the washing with two bed-wetting boys. Lisa now had disposable nappies, thank God. They just went down the rubbish hole. Only downside was the cost of them, but for her sanity, they were worth it. The baby had less nappy rash than Jim due to the disposable nappies, so he was quite happy.

After a morning at home, Lisa realized this was going to be hard. The floor seemed like the best option, so she just crawled around the floor with the boys. They thought it was great. Mum down on the floor with them. When it came to bathing the boys, Lisa would kneel beside the bath, and they half crawl up her and she heaved them in. For the washing line, Lisa took a chair out and put the washing basket on it. She hoped like hell nothing would happen and just hung it out. No other option.

Sue came out and checked the baby and Lisa. Daniel was doing well. Gaining weight, 4 kgs and 400g by the third week. A happy baby who loved being held. Put him down, and he screams; pick him up, and he settles. Daniel got carried around a lot. He started sleeping through the night, 7 hours straight, by the third week. Early morning feeds, but oh, the joy of an unbroken sleep.

Lisa had breastfed him in hospital but had come home with newborn formula, and that was the end of breastfeeding. He was breastfed for one week.

Lisa's staples were still in, but the skin was pulling. It was quite red around the staples. One staple was weeping, as she had an infection. Sue gave her some antibacterial cream and that seemed to clear it up. It took a long time to heal.

The Results of Lisa's Breast Feeding Efforts.

Lisa's first child was breast feed for three weeks, her second son for two weeks and her last for a week. Lisa has three well-grown young men who have done well.

Lisa's oldest was in the top class, below the accelerate learning program, played for the first XV, was a senior prefect and well-liked.

Lisa's middle child did not like school. Andrew had a good time. He left as soon as he could, which was at the end of year 12, cause Mum insisted he pass level 2!

Lisa's last child, who had the least breast milk, was in the accelerate learning program, played for the first XV, was a senior prefect and won many school prizes.

Lisa sat in his last assembly, clapping as Daniel was awarded prizes. Lisa thought about those nasty, bullying La leche women. 'Well fuck you, her sons have done just fine for all of the emotional blackmail and shit you put me through. None of them needed braces either, and I used a dummy'. A baby needs love, care and good food in whatever form it comes in. Do what is right for the baby and the mother. Not everyone is a great cow.

Chapter Fifty-Four

Washing Machines

Lisa was washing large loads of clothes each day. Between the farm clothes, the toddlers, the baby's washing and the bed linen, she did at least two loads a day. Lisa had a top-loading machine, 8kg. It had been going along OK since they had been married.

It stopped working, and they were told it would be best to buy a new one. They bought the same brand, which had a good reputation. They had it for about six months when it stopped working. The repair guy said it wasn't worth fixing; they needed to get another. Lisa couldn't survive without a washing machine. They bought a new one. Same brand.

About three months later Lisa had the electrician out to fix the plug in the washhouse. Lisa was in the kitchen when he called out to her. The washing machine had thick, smelly black smoke rising from it. He said it needed to be turned off, as it could burst into flames. The circuit board had fired itself. Lisa would need to get a new washing machine. Lisa couldn't believe it. She had just replaced it. Lisa needed a washing machine.

Simon came home to find Lisa worked up about the washing.

"I have had enough. We are going to town today to get a washing machine."

"Now?"

"Yes, now in the Ute, so we can bring it home."

Lisa packed the kids up into the Ute and they headed to the main center two hours away. Lisa went into the shop and found a salesman.

'I want a good washing machine, which takes at least 8kg or more."

The salesman started showing her washing machines like she already had. Simon was wandering along with the kids.

"No, I want one which will not break down." Lisa stated in a firm voice.

The salesman replied, "We have these. They are very good but quite pricey. They will see you out your lifetime."

Lisa looked at the machine. It was solid, large and had a good reputation. "I will take it."

It was loaded on the Ute, taken home and installed. It worked just fine. 10 kg loads, and it didn't miss a beat.

Chapter Fifty-Five

Manipulative Mother-in-Laws

Lisa got a phone call from Mary. They were staying in the apartment in Auckland. "All our friends have their grandchildren come and stay. It makes us look bad that we don't have our grandchildren come and visit. When can you bring Jim up to stay?" "Oh well." 'Why the hell should I drive my son to Auckland' Lisa thought. " I am not able to take Jim to Auckland."

Lisa had three sons, a load of work and driving to Auckland was the last thing she wanted to do. Especially as she was still recovering from the surgery.

"That's alright. We can come and get him. Next week?"

"How long will he be staying, and will you bring him back?"

"Oh yes, he can stay for three days, and then we will bring him back."

"Oh...I suppose that will be alright."

Robert and Mary came and collected Jim up with his bag. Jim was excited to go and stay with them after Mary told Jim all about the goldfish they had in their pond.

In the morning of the third day, Lisa rang Mary up and asked, "What time are you bringing Jim back today?"

"Oh, I can't bring Jim back. Robert is far too ill."

"Ill?"

"Oh yes, Robert is so ill. He's in bed all day."

"What's wrong with him?"

"Oh, he has the flu. He's so ill."

"Jim needs to come home. It's been three days."

"I can't bring Jim down. I can't leave Robert. Why don't you come and get Jim?" Oh God, to pack up a new baby and a two-year-old for an 8-hour round trip to Auckland. That came under the heading of nightmares. "I am unable to come to Auckland. You said you would bring Jim back."

"Robert is far too ill for me to leave him." Mary said in an angry voice. The telephone conversation ended.

The next day, Lisa rang Mary, "When are you bringing Jim home?"

"Jim is fine here, and I can't leave Robert; he's far too ill. You want me to leave my ill husband alone to drive your child home?" Mary's voice was getting frustrated and angry.

"Jim needs to come home."

"Well, you can come and get him." The conversation ended. Lisa wanted her child home. If Lisa didn't have a baby and a toddler and still getting over a cesarean, she would have gone and got him. Trying to negotiate the Auckland traffic with the boys was going to be difficult.

Lisa rang the next day and had the same conversation. Except this time Jim came on the phone "Mummy, I want to come home. Why won't you come and get me?"

"Jim, I want you to come home, but it is really difficult for me to come to Auckland. Granny said she would bring you home."

"Ooh, I want to come home." Jim was quite tearful down the phone. It tore Lisa's heart. Lisa wanted to just get in the car and get him.

"You will come home soon, Jim. I love you very much."

After three days of this, Mary and Robert bought Jim home. They arrived at the house, got Jim and his bag out of the car. They seemed quite angry about it, didn't say much and drove away. Jim had been with them for a total of six days.

Lisa gave Jim a big hug and got him inside with his bag.

"Mummy, why didn't you come and get me? Granny said you were going to get me." Lisa was kneeling on the floor, giving Jim a hug. Jim was crying as he ran his little hands over Lisa's face.

"Jim, I wanted to get you, but with your brothers, it was quite hard."

"Granny said you wouldn't come and get me 'cause you didn't love me."

"No, Jim, that's not why. I love you very much" She gave Jim a big hug, thinking, 'You miserable bitch. How could you do that to a child, telling him his mother didn't love him.'

"Jim, what did Pa do while you were in Auckland?"

"He went and got the paper every day."

"So he did that every day?"

"Yeah."

"Was he in bed all day?"

"No, he got the paper each day, then read it."

"So he wasn't in bed?"

"No, he sat in the room downstairs."

Lisa gave Jim another hug. "I love you, Jim, and I wanted you home. It was just really hard for me to come and get you."

"I asked and asked Granny to take me home." Jim said.

"Did you?"

"Yes, and she started to get angry with me, but I kept asking."

"Well done, Jim." Lisa said as Jim went off to play with his brother.

That lying, manipulative bitch. Robert quite clearly had not been sick, and she had lied to Lisa's child. What a nasty, shitty thing to do. Lisa couldn't trust her with anything. The whole point of them wanting Jim in Auckland was so Mary could be part of the scene with her grandchild. It wasn't even about Jim. Lisa decided that Jim was not going to stay with them in Auckland again.

Jim settled back into being at home and playing with his brothers. Lisa slowly got better and was able to do more and more around the house and farm.

She still had to be careful for months later. Lisa was drafting the ewes and lambs in November, three months after surgery. In December, four months later, Lisa was back dagging again for shearing. The boys stayed with their grandparents while she dagged. It took about six months for Lisa's stomach muscles to get back to normal.

Lisa took Jim and Andrew to the play centre. Daniel had spent the morning with Robert and Mary. Lisa went back to their place to collect Daniel and head home.

Lisa had a word with Jim before they got into the house. Jim was being criticized regularly by Robert and he would get upset. This led to more criticism and Jim would get more upset.

Lisa said to Jim, "When I say get in the car, just go and do that. Don't argue. Just go and get in the car. OK"

Jim said, "OK."

They arrived, and Robert and Mary wanted to talk. Jim was given a tennis ball to play with. He was bouncing it in front of Robert's chair and trying to catch it again. Jim was tired from spending all morning at the play centre. He was getting frustrated.

Robert started, "What's wrong with him? He should be able to do that. Why can't he catch the ball? There's something wrong with him. It should be easy to catch the ball. What's wrong with him?"

Jim could hear everything Robert was saying and was getting really upset. Lisa went over to Jim and said, "Go and get in the car. I will be right out."

Jim dumped the ball and went outside. Lisa told Andrew to get in the car and went to collect Daniel and all of his blankets. By the time she got outside, Mary had the door open on Jim's side and was talking to him. Robert was standing in the doorway. Lisa got Daniel strapped into his car seat and then strapped Andrew in. In that time Mary had given the ball to Jim and told him to give it to Robert.

One very tired, frustrated boy promptly threw it into the bushes behind Mary. Mary got angry with Jim and told him he had to find it. She pulled Jim out of the car and started looking around the bushes for the ball.

Saying, "I think it's over here, Jim. You need to look here, Jim. Can you see it?" Jim was just standing there. Lisa thought, 'Bloody hell, what a drama over nothing'. She just wanted to drive away, but she thought she had better sort it out. Lisa went and helped to look for the ball.

Mary found the ball and gave it to Jim to give to Robert. Jim promptly threw it again. Lisa thought, how stupid could Mary get? Lisa felt she had to do something to admonish Jim, but this wasn't his fault. She gently slapped the back of Jim's hand for throwing the ball again and then grabbed his arm and took him over to the car.

"Go and get in the car, Jim." She then went and got the ball, gave it to Robert and said, "Here's your bloody ball." went back to the car, checked that Jim was strapped in, got in the driver's seat and started the car.

By this stage, Mary had her head nearly in her car door window and was saying things like, "You don't speak to my husband like that. How dare you speak to him like that. He is a far better person than you. I won't put up with your behaviour. You are abusing your children; we will report you to child welfare for assault. You hit your child; we won't stand by while you assault your children."

Lisa revved the engine, thinking if she drove off Mary's head would be wracked. She got the message and stepped back. The car wheels spun as she drove away. Lisa drove home. When she arrived home,

Simon greeted her at the door and said, "My parents rang about you hitting Jim."

"Really? in that time. All I did was slap the back of his hand like this," and Lisa showed Simon what she had done.

Simon said, "I told them to pull their bloody heads in."

"Thanks."

Lisa stopped seeing Simon's parent for quite some time.

When Sarah was down on one of her visits, Lisa asked her about their childhood. "Did you ever get punished when you were kids?"

Sarah said, "Oh yes, all the time. The boys had it worse. Mum used to wash their mouths out with soap if they swore. She would grab the soap bar and force it into their mouths as she held their heads over the basin."

"Really."

"I can remember a time when Simon did something. He got into something he shouldn't have. Mum whacked him around the legs with a stick for that. She was always whacking Simon when he was little. He used to try and do things, and she would hit him with the stick. I think he got it worse than our brother. Simon, in the end, would just stay in his room."

"Oh."

"I was younger, so I didn't get into so much trouble as the boys."

"Thanks for telling me. I appreciate it. Your parents keep telling me they never hit their children."

Sarah laughed.

Well that put a different perspective on things. Robert kept saying they never hit their children. While all the time, Mary was home with the children and physically punishing them. Lisa wondered if Mary thinks about how she used to behave.

Lisa never punished her children using a stick or anything else. They occasionally got a slap on their bottom on the spur of the moment. Generally, Lisa tried to make the punishment fit the crime. Like when Jim didn't eat dinner he didn't get pudding.

Lisa looked at Simon differently as she wondered what effect his mother's punishment had on him. For a kid to stay in his room instead of coming out cause he was whacked all the time would have a large effect on his socializing. So much for Mary being the perfect parent. Lisa wondered if she choked on her lies occasionally. Knowing Mary, she doubted it. She would have made her life a rosy world and rewritten her past to suit her vision.

Chapter Fifty-Six

A Child's Mind

Lisa was putting the washing away. She went into Jim's and Andrew's room with a load, which she promptly dropped. Jim had the fish out of the bowl again. They were on the windowsill with Jim watching them.

"Jim, you have to put the fish in the water." Lisa said as she rushed over to rescue the fish.

"This one has stopped moving, Mummy." Jim said in a concerned voice.

Lisa scooped up the one fish still alive and put it back in the water. It was a bit wobbly. The other fish was dead. "Jim, I told you the fish can't live outside the water. They can't breathe in the air."

"Is that why he won't move now?" Jim asked as he poked the fish.

"Yeah, he died. I will have to get rid of it. Jim, you have to leave the fish in the water" Jim nodded his head as he watched the remaining fish swim around the bowl.

Chapter Fifty-Seven

Swimming

Once Lisa had healed, she took all of the boys swimming again. Lisa took them in the winter months only as she was too busy in the summer months. Daniel was six months old when he started to swim. By this stage, Jim could swim the width of the pool, swim underwater and pick up items off the bottom of the pool. He was very confident in the water.

Andrew was doing well and trying to be as good as Jim. Daniel was a fast learner and was progressing well. Lisa was reasonably confident that all three boys were safe around water.

The teacher, in one block of lessons, would do an emergency drill. The kids had to get in the water in their clothes. They then had to demonstrate how they would get out while being hampered by the clothing. It took a while before the kids got comfortable with it. It's amazing how much the clothing can hamper their ability to move. It tended to cause the kids to panic a bit when their faces were covered by the T-shirt ballooning up. It was easy to see how a kid would panic in water and drown. The instructor kept saying, "Remain calm; you know how to float; kick for the edge."

All of her boys enjoyed the swimming, especially Lisa.

Sarah

Lisa had the stock agent coming to mark lambs. Simon was away, and Sarah was staying with her parents. Somehow, it came up that Lisa would be in the sheep's yards. Sarah decided she would come down and help, which she never did, so Lisa was a bit surprised. The lambs were in the yards, and the agent was marking them when Sarah arrived in her car.

Lisa was drafting the marked lambs out and the agent was moving through the race marking the lambs. Sarah walked along the side of the race and helped to run them up to the drafting gates, after they had been marked.

The agent was having a spot of trouble keeping his eyes on the sheep. He would mark some lambs and then shoot a quick look at Sarah. He would then go back to marking lambs and shoot another quick look at Sarah. Lisa didn't think he could quite believe his eyes. He had to just keep checking that what he was seeing was actually correct.

Sarah, who only ever wears designer labels, had turned up in an outfit which had Lisa doing a double take. It was an eye-opener. They were on a large sheep and beef farm, in a set of sheep yards, miles from anyone else, and Sarah was wearing an outfit. Not sure if she thought she would have a conquest or it was just what she thought would be suitable. The agent was happily married with kids, so Sarah really was wasting her time.

Sarah had on cream-coloured sailor-like pants, which hung on her hips. They were see-through in the right light. They were held in place with a drawstring tied at the front. Above was her pink G-string. The G-string elastic around her waist was visible, and where it dipped down to the cheeks at the back. The top of her buttock cheeks were very visible. Round the front the top of the G string triangle was visible. Above this, she had a loose-fitting crop top, exposing her tummy button. Sarah's pieced tummy button was on full display. The top was low cut, with cap sleeves and her bra was easily seen every time she bent over. It was a halter bra with ties at the back of her neck. More like a bikini.

Lisa couldn't believe that she was wearing creamed-coloured pants in the sheep yards.

Lisa did a double take on the G-string.

Once they had finished marking the lambs, they needed to count them. Sarah left at this point and went home.

The agent and Lisa were setting up the gates to count them when he said, "Who was that?" in a shocked voice. Now, their agent was an ex-shearer, so he had seen a lot in his life.

"That's Simon's sister."

"Really, she's nothing like him" The agent replied, as he threw a look at Sarah, getting into her car.

"No, they are quite different."

"She looks like a real piece of work. You don't want to get involved with girls like that. They are trouble."

"Sarah lives a different life. She is a ski bunny and just flies around the world skiing."

Nothing more was said, but the agent definitely got his shock for the day.

Chapter Fifty-Eight

Convulsions

Jim had another convulsion about two years after his first. This time, Lisa knew what to do. She had Jim, Andrew and Daniel, aged 6 months, all home on her own. It was in the late afternoon when Jim just collapsed.

Lisa ran a tepid bath, stripped him off and managed to get him into the bath. She had to hold his head as he was completely limp. Once he came around, Lisa pulled him out, wrapped him up and put Jim into bed. He got the shakes really badly. Lisa kneeled on the floor and hugged him as he shook in bed. Jim slowly stopped and went to sleep.

Simon came home and asked what was wrong. Lisa explained about Jim having another attack, but he's fine now.

Simon got quite upset. "Why the hell didn't you take him into the hospital?"

"It wasn't as bad as last time, and I knew what to do."

"You should have taken him to see the doctor. You don't know that it was the same; something else could be wrong."

"He's fine and asleep in bed."

"I am going to take him in now. You are just irresponsible, not taking him to see the doctor" Simon stalked into Jim's room, got him up and put him in the car.

Lisa sorted out the other two boys with their nightly routine and had dinner.

Simon came back with Jim about two hours later. Apparently, Jim was fine, and all his signs were normal.

That was the last time Jim had an attack. Neither of the other two boys had convulsions.

Chapter Fifty-Nine

The Climber

The autumn season progressed, all the summer jobs were done, and winter slowly arriving. The three boys were healthy and growing. Daniel was nine months old and crawling. He wasn't just crawling; he was climbing.

He climbed everything. The handles on the chest of draws, the shelves. There wasn't anything he couldn't reach. Daniel couldn't walk but he could push a chair across the room and climb up it. Lisa was forever running around the house trying to rescue him. For the other two boys, Lisa had everything lifted up so they couldn't reach things. Didn't work for Daniel.

One day, Lisa was going into the boy's room to put the washing away. Lisa saw Daniel through the door jam. He was on top of the chest of draws with his face scrunched up. You could almost see him thinking, this is going to hurt. Then he launched himself off the chest onto the floor. Lisa wasn't quick enough to grab him. Daniel never seemed to get injured doing this. He just carried on with whatever he had got.

Lisa had to do the dagging in early May for shearing. She took up the playpen along with old cardboard boxes. Lisa flattened them out in the covered yards and put the playpen on top, next to the dagging plant. Daniel went into the playpen along with his toys. Lisa started dagging. The other boys helped to push the sheep up with Simon. The boys loved chasing the dogs around and catching their tails.

Lisa was dagging away and getting through them when she looked up. Daniel had pushed the playpen over to the rails. He had then climbed up the rails and was standing on the top rail. Lisa stopped what she was doing and rushed over to risk him. Daniel was very happy with himself. It gave Lisa a hell of a fright.

Lisa got Daniel back in his pen, moved the playpen and put some rocks between it and the rails so Daniel couldn't push it. Lisa then went back to dagging.

As the boys got older, they would come up to the woolshed with Lisa and Simon more often. They sometimes helped, and other times, they would be playing around the shed. There were calf feeder bins, which they would slide down the sheep ramp with much delighted screaming. They were where Simon and Lisa could keep an eye on them. Lisa would go and start dagging or drafting and look out to see where the boys were.

Robert would come down to see what they were doing and make some remarks. They would stop to see him and then go back to what they were doing. Lisa would then look out to see where the boys were and wouldn't see them. Lisa would be chasing around, looking and calling for them and asking Simon.

Simon would then say, "Oh, I think Dad took them."

"What? He just took them? With no word, nothing?"

Robert didn't have car seats or anything else in the Ute. He would just take the boys up to his house.

Lisa had to finish dagging to get the mob out and would then go up to get the boys. She was not happy about the situation but wanted to keep the peace.

Mary would greet her at the door. "You didn't ask if the boys could come and stay. I was not organized to have them, and you cannot just leave them here with me like this."

Robert would be sitting in his chair listening and would not say a word. Lisa would look at him, thinking, 'You bastard'.

Mary would be getting distressed and emotional, "I have a life. I am not here to be your on-call babysitter."

"I'm sorry, Mary. I will take them home now."

Lisa collected the children up and took them home. Lisa wasn't happy, as there was no reason for the boys to be at Mary's, and she hadn't asked for them to be there. Robert had caused her stress by taking the boys, and yet he had sat quietly while Mary complained about them being there.

It happened more than once, and Lisa just had to work with the situation. Lisa ignored Mary when she complained and endeavoured to make it hard for Robert to take them. It added to her wish to have them gone from the farm.

Chapter Sixty

Toys

They had many toys in the house for the boys, including marbles. The boys played with them, and Lisa used them in the flower vases.

Daniel was playing with his brothers in the lounge. Lisa happened to look over from the kitchen and saw that Daniel was quite pale.

She rushed over, calling, "Daniel, Daniel, are you OK?" No response. He was sitting up but didn't appear to be breathing. Lisa frantically looked in his mouth but couldn't see anything. She felt down his throat and could feel nothing.

"Get in the car now!" Lisa yelled frantically at his brothers. She carried Daniel, who was going blue in the face, out to the car. Lisa couldn't think what to do. She had to get him to help as soon as possible, and the local small town was half an hour away. Lisa was putting Daniel in the back seat when he suddenly bent over and vomited.

She was never so happy to see a child vomit in her life. Out popped a marble. A small glass marble. Daniel was taking deep breaths and losing his blue colour. Lisa relaxed and took some deep shaky breaths herself. She hugged Daniel and carried her precious son back into the house. Lisa was shaking with relief.

Jim asked, "Are you OK, mummy?"

"Yeah, I'm fine. Just come back into the house."

They all went back inside. Lisa got down on the floor and started collecting the marbles.

"Boys, I want all of the marbles put into this bowl. Can you find all of the marbles for mummy?"

The boys crawled around the floor with her, collecting up the marbles. Once Lisa had all of them, they were put away where no one could get them.

Jim asked, "Why are you taking the marbles?"

"Because they are dangerous. Daniel nearly died 'cause he had one stuck in his throat."

Jim looked a bit surprised at that. Lisa went back to the kitchen. As she organized tea, Lisa kept thinking about what could have happened. It had been a close thing. Every time she thought about it, Lisa got a bit shaky. The boys were back happily playing in the lounge.

Lisa took the boys to the play centre once a week. The parents were on a roster to supervise and had to stay for the full session. Lisa was down there, explaining what had happened to Daniel and how scary it had been.

One of the mothers just looked at her and said, "I would have just squeezed his throat until it came out. That's all you had to do," In a scathing voice.

Lisa didn't say anything. She had felt his throat. Squeezing hard may have worked, but it may not have. Lisa didn't know what would have been the best option. Perhaps she just panicked and did the wrong thing. Lisa went home feeling like she had failed in making the right decision.

Two weeks after this, Mary came down to visit them. She had bought a present for Jim. It was an old denim bag with a drawstring top. It was full of marbles, which had apparently belonged to Simon when he was a boy.

Mary emptied the bag on the table and explained to Jim how he played marbles with them. "Jim you can take these to school with you and play marbles with your friends"

Jim was watching the marbles as Mary moved them around the table. Lisa took the bag, put all of the marbles back in it and gave it back to Mary.

"I need to tell you a story about what happened to Daniel with a marble" Mary looked a bit put out and listened.

When Lisa had finished, she gave Lisa a funny look and gave the bag back to Jim. "These are for you to play with Jim. They belonged to your father. You won't let your brothers play with them, will you?"

Lisa just looked at her. She was expecting a 6-year-old, living in a small house, sharing a bedroom, to keep his marbles away from his brothers.

Once Mary left, Lisa took the bag from Jim and put it out of reach, thinking how stupid can you get? Lisa had just explained that she nearly lost a grandson with a marble and now she wanted to give marbles to Jim.

Lisa was in the kitchen one evening cooking tea. The two older boys were playing in the lounge. They had a toy truck, and there seemed to be an issue over who was playing with it.

"Share the toy; you need to take turns with it." Lisa repeatedly said.

The arguing and screaming continued, "Share. You need to share."

The arguing continued Lisa was tired and didn't need this screaming, as they argued over whose toy it was. They were coming to blows. Lisa had had enough. She went over to them, took the toy away and went outside. Lisa chopped it in half with the axe and brought it back.

She gave Jim and Andrew half each. "Now you each have half, so you can't fight over it."

They both looked at her in complete shock. Their little rosebud mouths fell open as they looked at their toy truck and then back at her.

Lisa went back to the kitchen to finish cooking tea. She looked over at the boys to find them, with their heads together, whispering to each other. Every so often, they threw a look at her of complete dismay and went back to whispering. They had their arms round each other's shoulders. After a while, they headed off to their bedroom, arm in arm, throwing her dirty looks. Nothing else was said.

Some days later, Lisa heard them arguing again. The arguing wasn't the loud screaming like it normally was. But they were quite clearly having an argument. It was low-key and being kept on the quiet side. Every so often, Lisa would hear "shush, shhh, shush, Mum will hear."

This went on for some weeks. They, quite clearly, did not want their Mum to have anything to do with their arguing. Life in the very small house was much pleasanter, as the boys weren't full out arguing and fighting any longer. There were still disputes, but they were kept on the low.

One day, a few months later, when they were arguing over a toy in their bedroom, Lisa sang out. "Do you want me to help?"

"No." came the very clear, loud reply from multiple voices.

"I'm sure I could help."

"No."

"But I am sure I could solve the argument."

"No, we don't want your help."

"Are you sure?"

"Yes"

They were very clear, they did not want their mother, inferring in the argument at all. It became a bit of a family joke. Lisa would sing out, "I want to help. Please let me help," and they would reply, "No, we don't need it. We are fine."

All three boys seemed happy, and they all seemed to be able to take turns with the toys, so they had obviously sorted out a system between them. Lisa left them to it.

Chapter Sixty-One

Queenstown

They all went up and had dinner with Robert and Mary. The table was set with silver cutlery and napkins as per normal. Robert leads the discussion about the economy, investing and farming. Robert was very concerned about the farm and his money on the farm. He always wanted to know what they were spending the money on and if Lisa was wasting any of it on the house.

Lisa felt that their family was living below acceptable living conditions. She had just wiped down the boys' bedroom walls. The mould behind the beds had been thick, and the spores, when disturbed, created a thick yellow cloud as they floated in the bedroom air.

They made Lisa sneeze repeatedly. To clear the room she had opened all of the windows. It couldn't be good for the boys' health. Here, Robert was complaining about her spending too much on personal drawings. Lisa wasn't impressed, but from past experience, she knew it was a waste of time to say anything.

The subject turned to Sarah. Sarah was in Queenstown skiing and had decided she wanted to make Queenstown a home base. Robert and Mary were going down to see her. The plan was to purchase a house for Sarah to live in. She still planned on skiing around the world but would be spending four months or so in Queenstown.

Sarah had been looking at houses and telling them what a great investment they were. They were going to be gone for a couple of weeks. Robert was going to get in some skiing while he was down there, so he was really looking forward to it. Mary didn't ski. After tea, they took their boys home to the damp, mouldy house.

Sarah

Sarah had a new boyfriend. He attended Auckland University, and he was lovely.

Tall, dark-haired and well-spoken. They really enjoyed his company. He was doing an Environmental Engineering degree. He went round the farm with them and talked about water movement and silt management. This was well before the freshwater issues hit the headlines.

A pond they had by the road was apparently just right. It collected the runoff from the sheep yards. The pond allowed the water flow to slow down, allowing the silt to be deposited out. The water then flowed through the culvert and into the freshwater system.

Sarah seemed very happy. They all went back to Auckland.

The boyfriend went to Mexico on a working holiday and Sarah decided to surprise him by visiting him in Mexico. She had arranged with her friends to surprise him at a party. Well, it didn't go as planned.

The boyfriend turned up with another girl on his arm. Sarah was devastated by his two-timing and was inconsolable. The relationship ended.

Chapter Sixty-Two

Drama

Lisa went outside to the carport to get some chops for dinner from the chest freezer. She dropped them in the sink to defrost. As Lisa turned away, there was a grating sound. Lisa looked back to discover that the sink had fallen out of the bench. It was now sitting at a funny angle on the shelf below.

"Simon, the sink has fallen out." Lisa yelled.

Simon came over and looked. Didn't say anything but went outside. Came back with an old staple box and pushed that under the sink. By some amazing chance, it was a perfect fit.

Simon looked quite pleased with himself and said, "Problem solved", and went back to the computer.

Lisa had a look. The sink was firm and didn't wobble. She was still a bit shocked about the sink, but it worked. Every so often, the box would move, and she would have to re-adjust it.

The oven was a stand-alone oven jammed in the corner of the kitchen. It had four electric rings and a good-sized oven with a warming drawer. It was quite old.

Lisa turned on the front hot plate for a pot of soup. There was a massive bang, like a shotgun blast and a cloud of thick black smoke. Lisa shot across the kitchen, to the lounge. She stood there watching the cloud of black smoke rise up to the ceiling. It scared the hell out of her, and she was scared that there would be a fire.

She wasn't sure what had happened, but it didn't look like they were going to have a fire. She couldn't see any flames. The boys came barreling out of their room to see what the noise was. They were very impressed with all of the black smoke and wanted to have a closer look.

Once the smoke had cleared, Lisa went in to have a look at the range. Where the electric ring should be plugged in, there was now a large hole. The plug had blown out. In the process, it had created a hole on the opposite side of the plug. It must have blown out with a lot of force. The actual electric ring now sat at a drunken angle.

Lisa rang the electrician and told him what had happened. He didn't seem too bothered about it. Apparently, she would need to replace the whole unit, and it would probably be best to replace the oven.

It would be fine to keep using the stovetop; just keep the damaged one turned off. Lisa decided just to wait since they were going to upgrade the whole house. Lisa was now down to three hot plates. This made things quite difficult, as the other three hot plates were either against the wall or the back of the oven. It limited the size of the saucepan she could use.

Lisa didn't like handling electricity, and anything to do with it freaked her out.

Sarah

Sarah, after five years of being a ski bunny, decided she would attend university and signed up for a marketing degree. She stayed in her parents apartment in Auckland and went to university.

At the end of the second year, she had to do work experience. Sarah got accepted into 'Mars' in Melbourne for her summer holidays. Lisa didn't know everything that went on, but apparently, Sarah was very unhappy and rang her parents regularly.

Mary told them one night at dinner that; "Sarah is lonely; no one at work will talk to her. They are all useless, and she is the only one who knows what to do. She is actually running the department on her own with no help. She needs us to go over and support her. She is so lonely." Mary sighed about her poor, lonely daughter.

Lisa listened to all of this, thinking, 'Sarah being lonely, that didn't sound like Sarah'.

Sarah has travelled all around the world and hadn't been this lonely before.

"Rose, my bridesmaid, lives four hours away from Melbourne. Sarah knows her, she could go and stay with her at the weekend. I'll ring Rose and see if it's OK." Lisa said.

Mary looked happy about that option. "Oh, that sounds good. It will give Sarah somewhere to go."

Lisa talked to Rose, and she agreed that Sarah could come. Lisa gave Rose Sarah's phone number and left them to organize it.

From what Rose told Lisa, they had organized a weekend when Sarah could come and were all ready to collect Sarah from the train station.

"I got a phone call from Sarah two hours before she was due to arrive." Rose said.

"Sarah said, 'I'm not coming this weekend. I got a better offer,' I replied. I thought you were coming on the train. I was quite bewildered by the change in plans at such short notice. She must have known sooner what she was doing cause the train trip is six hours. Sarah then said in a very happy voice, 'Oh no, I have a better offer. A guy from work is going to take me out to Phillip Island. He has a Jaguar Sports car which has .....' Sarah then listed off all of the luxury items the car had. She seemed more excited about being seen in the car than anything else. We had gone to a lot of trouble to organize things for Sarah. It was really rude of her to cancel like that. I felt used."

"I'm so sorry. From what Sarah had told her parents, she seemed very lonely, so I thought seeing you could be a good idea." Lisa replied.

"We had to cancel things. Sarah just cares about who she is seen with. She is totally self-absorbed. Don't apologize. It's Sarah's behaviour. It was a good idea, and she would have been fine to stay."

"Yeah Sarah has lived a transition social life, so perhaps having to turn up regularly for a job was a bit wearing for her.

They said their goodbyes. Lisa got off the phone and thought, what a rude thing to do.

Apparently, after that, everybody at work started to talk to Sarah, and she started to have a good time.

Robert and Mary didn't have to go over to Australia straight away to entertain their daughter. They seemed quite happy about that. They did go over to Melbourne later on to see Sarah and take her shopping.

As far as Lisa knows, Sarah finished the degree. She didn't have a graduation ceremony, which upset her parents. They would have liked to have gone to it. To Lisa's knowledge she has never worked as a marketer either.

Sarah did do an ad for BMW. She had to ski in a bikini down the snow slope, then get in the BMW sports car and drive away. Sarah had a tape of the ad for them to watch. In the off-takes, she had her fingers over her nipples as they were very visible through the fabric due to the cold. She may have done some other modelling, but not sure what for.

Chapter Sixty-Three

Birthday party

The swimming coach had a graduation ceremony at the end of the class. The kids got a certificate and a little speech about how well they were doing after the lesson. It was Jim's last day as he started school the following week. Lisa and Simon had decided to have a big birthday party for him, with all of his play centre friends and the swimming kids, he had made friends with. It was to be held at McDonalds in the same town as his swimming lessons.

Lisa and Simon invited his grandparents, Robert and Mary, as well as his cousins, to the final swimming lesson. The boys demonstrated their water skills to much applause. Robert and Mary seemed very happy with Jim's progress and made much fuss over him. Lisa was late leaving the swimming area as she had to dress the other two boys and collect all of their things. Jim was first out and went out with his grandparents. When Lisa got out they had Jim in their car, in his car seat and were standing around talking.

"We will take Jim with us." Robert stated firmly.

Lisa wasn't happy about it as she had gone to a lot of trouble organizing the party. Jim had all of his mates arriving in about half an hour at McDonald's. There wasn't much Lisa could do about it, and

Simon seemed quite happy with the arrangement. "We will see you at McDonald's then in half an hour?" Lisa replied

"Yeah, for the party." And off they drove.

Simon and Lisa drove around to the restaurant and sorted out which tables were allocated to them. Lisa set up the cake she had made with all of the candles. The guests started arriving with presents for Jim.

No sign of Jim. They all asked where Jim was. After all, it was his party. The kids all wanted to see Jim and see if he liked the present they had for him.

Lisa felt really let down as she stood there wondering where Jim was. It was like being a loose spanner.

"Jim should be here soon. He's with his grandparents. They said they would bring him." Lisa replied, hoping he would turn up. They couldn't be that mean that they wouldn't bring him.

The other kids started to get hungry. After all, they were in McDonald's with 20 kids and parents.

Lisa made an announcement to everyone "Jim seems to have been delayed, why don't you start to order. It will take a while for the orders to all be done."

Lisa had organized all of this and made the cake to make Jim's birthday an exciting one. No sign of Jim.

Lisa really felt they had done this deliberately. They always seemed to sabotage anything that she had organized for the kids. It was unreal. The guest of honour was not at his own party. The parents and kids gave Lisa the presents they had got for Jim. They kept throwing Lisa glances, and Lisa could see them wondering why Jim wasn't there. Lisa felt really let down and like a complete twit. Who organized a party and did not have the guest of honour present?

"Here we are! Jim, look, all of your friends are here, isn't this wonderful? We were having so much fun we forgot about the time." Mary said as she bustled into the restaurant with Jim. Robert followed in behind them.

A great fuss was made as Jim got a seat and ordered. By this stage, all of the other kids were eating their food. Simon didn't seem to have any issue with what had happened.

He was having a great time talking to the parents and seemed to think that Lisa was overreacting.

Jim got seated, and all of his presents were given to him. He was the centre of attention, and things got back on track.

"Mary, where were you? Everyone had arrived and were asking where Jim was. He wasn't here to greet his guests."

"Oh, we had some time, so we went round to the cousins to see them. They were just up the road and we just forgot about the time. No harm done, look, Jim is having fun." With that, she rushed over to help a kid with their rubbish.

Lisa thought, 'What a bitch'. That was done deliberately. They arrived late to cause her as much hurt as they could. The cousin's children had all grown and were at university, so Jim would have been left to play on his own as they talked.

Lisa lit the candles on the cake, and they all sang Happy Birthday to Jim. Jim had requested a cake in the shape of a Kiwi fruit. Lisa had gone to a lot of effort into making the cake and then ice the top to make it look like a cut Kiwi fruit. Lisa had used little chocolate sprinkles for the kiwi fruit seeds. Lisa thought it looked good, but judging from the comments, apparently, the centre looked like something else. No one seemed to understand it was the centre of the kiwi fruit. The kids didn't care; they all enjoyed the cake.

After the party, which went on for a couple of hours, they paid the bill and went home with all three sons. Lisa made certain that they were all in their car. They had three very tired but happy boys. They all dropped off to sleep in the car within half an hour.

Jim had been really happy with his birthday party, and that was what was important, Lisa consoled herself as Simon drove home.

Chapter Sixty-Four

School

Jim started school

Jim had to go on the school bus. It picked him up a km from their house. On the first day, Simon rode the bus with Jim. Everyone came home happy and relaxed.

After a while Jim refused to go to school. He would start screaming and pleading not to go. Lisa had no idea what the issue was.

"Jim, are you being hurt at school?"

"No," sob, big sigh, more sobbing,

"Jim is another kid bullying you."

"What?" sob, sob.

"Is another kid saying nasty things to you?"

"No." Huge gasps.

"Do I need to see the teacher?"

"No. I just don't want to go to school."

Lisa couldn't see what else to do other than send Jim to school. So, every morning, Lisa got Jim in the car, drove him to the bus stop and literally pushed him up the steps of the bus as he screamed. The bus driver just looked at Lisa and smiled. He had grandchildren, so he had probably seen it all before.

Lisa would see him sit down through the bus window as they drove away. This went on for a week and Lisa was getting more and more concerned. Couldn't figure out what was wrong.

Jim was always happy when he got off the bus. One day, Lisa picked Jim up on his own. Normally, she had his brothers with her.

"What did you do today, Jim?"

"We had fun; we went to the hall and did some singing, and then we drew some pictures."

"That's really cool. So you had fun?"

"Yeah."

"Jim, why don't you want to go to school in the morning?"

"Cause you do things at home without me."

"Oooh, so you are scared you will miss out on stuff at home?"

"Yeah, you do all sorts of things when I'm at school."

Suddenly, Lisa understood. School wasn't the problem at all. Jim's brothers always told Jim what they had done for the day cause they wanted to share it with Jim as soon as they saw him.

From then on, Lisa schooled them up that they were not to say anything about what happened at home, while Jim was at school. They lived very boring lives for about two weeks. Jim, after a couple of days, was very happy about going on the school bus. He was having a much more interesting day than his brothers.

The school had a swimming pool, and the teachers gave swimming lessons. Lisa sent Jim off to school with his swimming togs and towel thinking he must be top of the class. Every day that Jim had swimming lessons, Lisa asked, "How was swimming today?"

"It was good." Jim replied happily.

"You must be doing well at swimming after all those lessons we did?"

"Yeah, it's good."

Lisa didn't get much else out of Jim. She was sure Jim must be doing well. He had four years of swimming lessons and was progressing well before he started school.

Chapter Sixty-Five

Revelations

When they were first married Simon did the bulk of the farm work as Lisa was working or looking after babies. She did the dagging but left the shearing to Simon to organize. He likes being with the blokes and having a beer after work with the gang. Sometimes, Lisa would take the kids up to the woolshed to see how things were going. Simon always greeted her outside the door, looking rushed. Lisa thought he was helping in the shed and keeping things moving along smoothly. They would walk around and look at the sheep in the yards while they talked, or Lisa would take the boys in to see the shearing. Simon would be rushing around picking up wool.

She would then go home and carry on with her day.

As the boys got bigger, Simon wanted Lisa to take over the organization of the shearing. After all, it was part of the sheep work, which she was in charge of. From then on, she took it over and would be up at the shed for six to seven days, making sure the mobs didn't get mixed up, bringing the mobs in, penning the sheep up the night before and taking the mobs away. She also helped on the board and with penning up.

One day, at morning tea, one of the shearers said to the other one, "At least she helps." Lisa thought it a strange thing to say. The next day, she was talking to one of the wool handlers. "You see that couch there?"

"Yeah," Lisa said, thinking this is a bit weird.

"Simon used to spend the day asleep on it. He would say to us, 'If you hear a bike, wake me.' Then, he would lie down and go to sleep. We would hear you coming and wake him. He would then rush out the door to greet you, trying to look busy. God, it was funny." she said, laughing.

"Really." Lisa couldn't believe it. Bloody hell. She had no idea that was what Simon was doing. She thought he was in the shed working, not asleep. Lisa had been so tired from broken sleeps and looking after the boys that she had been falling over her feet, literally.

She had cooked all of the meals, looked after the boys at night and tried to make life easier for Simon cause she thought he was working hard. It had all been a lie. He had been asleep. She didn't say anything to Simon as it would have resulted in a row and nothing would change.

Chapter Sixty-Six

Xmas Eve

Lisa's three sons, aged five, three and one-year-old, were all running around their small house. Lisa had a live Xmas tree up with Xmas decorations. She had made some Xmas stockings, which looked pretty fancy, like the sort seen on Xmas cards. They were doing OK financially, still tight, but OK. A lot of money had been spent on the farm, and it was starting to pay off.

December on the West Coast can be wet, and this December was no different. Simon and Lisa had managed to get the weaning and shearing done, so things were a bit calmer.

The house had just deteriorated further as nothing had been done.

It was Xmas Eve. The boys were excited about tomorrow and checking out the Xmas presents under the tree. Lisa was trying to organize dinner, amongst all of the baking she had done for Xmas day.

Once again they were going to the family Xmas luncheon, an hour away. Lisa just wanted to stay home and have a quiet Xmas with the family. Packing the kids up after they had opened their presents and explaining to them that they couldn't take the presents with them was difficult.

A light drizzle had been going on all day and the kids were in the lounge playing. Well, the two older ones were. The youngest was desperately trying to join in. Something cold and wet landed on the back of Lisa's neck yeek. It made her jump, and she nearly dropped the salad bowl that she was getting out of the fridge.

Lisa looked up and just stared in disbelief. The ceiling's particle board above her was bulging. Lisa looked across the ceiling of the lounge and dining room in shock. All of the ceiling was bulging in the squares between the rafters. Deep bulges to the point they looked like they were about to split and dump their load. They were all starting to drip.

This did not look good. "Simon!" Lisa shouted.

"What?" Simon said from the computer. He never helped with the household chores.

"The roof is leaking; you have to sort it now!"

"What are you talking about?" Simon said in a put-upon voice. He wandered out to the lounge area and looked a bit surprised.

Lisa pointed to the bulging ceiling and said, "The roof must be leaking. It's not heavy rain, and it's not leaked before, so why now? That's a lot of water. Ring the plumber."

"No, we can't ring the plumber. It's Xmas Eve."

"Well, do something. The ceiling is going to fall in!" Sections of soft boards were looking heavier all the time as they bulged downwards. Each section was like a large white pimple, with the head being the drip. They all looked like they were going to split and dump their load.

Simon drilled holes in all of the bulging sections and put a bucket under them. Lisa had buckets in the lounge, hallway, dining room, kitchen, and one balanced precariously on top of the fridge.

The kids thought it was great. Lisa managed to convince them, after many attempts, to leave the buckets alone. The baby just wanted to get his hands in the bucket and play with the water.

It just continued to drip. They had to empty the 15-litre buckets out. All that was heard was the plop, plop, plop of the water hitting the buckets.

"Simon, why don't you get in the ceiling and see where the water is coming from? While it's raining, you might be able to pinpoint the leak."

"Na, waste of time, the whole roof will be leaking." with that Simon went back to the computer.

Lisa carried on organizing tea and getting ready for Xmas. Thank God it wasn't leaking in the bedrooms.

When something is done repeatedly, like a million times, it becomes automatic. Lisa was mashing the potatoes and needed the milk out of the fridge. Lisa headed to the fridge and opened the door. Whoosh. Aaawwa, shit, bloody hell! Ow. The bucket tipped off the fridge and fell on her head. Lisa was saturated and nursing a sore head where the 15-litre bucket had hit her. Lisa lost it and started yelling angrily, "Simon, you have to fix this bloody roof. I can't work in a leaking kitchen with buckets everywhere."

Simon reappeared from the bedroom. "What is your problem?"

"The bucket landed on me when I opened the fridge door, and water has gone everywhere."

"So it's your fault, if you had looked at what you were doing, you would have known you had to hold the bucket to stop it coming down. It was sitting partially on the door. You never think what you are doing! I don't need to put up with this shit. It's not my fault the roof is leaking; get over it. You always overreact, grow up." With that, Simon stalked outside, got on the bike and went out on the farm.

"Mummy, are you OK?" asked Jim as he came over to see what had happened. The other two boys were just watching from the lounge.

"I'm fine; the bucket hit me. Go back to the lounge while I get tea sorted."

In a very bad temper, Lisa started cleaning up the water, which had gone everywhere. Re-adjusted the bucket so it wasn't sitting on the door of the fridge. Who would put a bucket on the door, for God's sake?

While Lisa was doing this, the radio started playing the song 'Coal Miners Daughter' Lisa just stopped and looked. 'Oh my God, oh my God' This is the life she was living. They were living in a substandard house on a farm worth four million. (It had doubled in value from when they had bought it four years ago) No one would expect anyone else to live like this. This is crazy. It is fill of mould, it leaks, the oven doesn't work properly and only three hot plates work.

The house is warm now, thank God, with the wet back heaters Lisa had put in. Enough is enough. She had reached a breaking point. Something had to change. Lisa had spent the last four years having a conversation with herself every time something had frustrated her in the house. 'My ancestors had it worst,' 'the early pioneers had it worst,' Lisa would keep repeating this to herself as the linen cupboard door popped open 'cause too much was stuffed in it, or when the water ran across the floor when it rained, or showering in a bitterly cold bathroom, or wiping mould off the bedroom walls.

Lisa had reached the end of her patience. It was going to change. She couldn't continue to live like this, and it was not healthy for the boys. They had trouble with fitting everything into the house now, what was going to happen as the boys grew and needed more space? The house was quite literally falling down around them. She couldn't continue. Simon, quite clearly, was not going to do anything about it.

The morning broke to scattered clouds and sunshine, and the leaks stopped. This made Lisa think that it might be the roof.

The kids opened their presents to great excitement. They then had to decide which toy they were taking with them in the car to the luncheon. Bear and Cat Jim's and Andrew's companions went everywhere with them. Daniel just took Lion, which he wasn't too bothered about. They arrived to have luncheon with Simon's extended family consisting of grandparents, cousins and their children. About

15 adults and 7 children. On the upside, the food was great, and Lisa didn't have to cook it.

The house had been a standard 1950s house, single storey, which Barbara, the wife of the second oldest brother George had redesigned. It now looked like something out of a European magazine. Exposed beams salvaged from an old bridge, a second story, a dovecote, a swimming pool, and a large concrete deck area with strategically placed large pots and tables. A long covered veranda with drop-down sides to protect from bad weather. A large wooden lined dining area with steps down to a gallery, which had multiple uses. A well-designed and mature garden. Barbara used to be a florist and had a real knack for design.

The kids had fun with their cousins. They ran around the garden and played in the courtyard area. The adults split off into different groups and discussed the weather, farming, children, and the political and economic situation. Mostly, it revolved around investments as the two older brothers, well Robert being the eldest, was in a competition about being the wealthiest. George didn't seem too bothered about who had the most money, and in fact, Lisa thought he had probably already outstripped Robert, being a dairy farmer. He never said.

Carol was there with her daughter and two grandchildren. She never stayed for long. Lisa had realized by this point that she only turned up, when she had something to show off. Once Carol had shown off the latest she would leave.

A Father Xmas was organized for the children. Simon dressed up as Santa Claus and bought out the bag with all of the Xmas presents.

They all received a little present, which was nice and kept them entertained. Once everyone had eaten themselves silly, Lisa and Simon said their goodbyes and travelled home.

Lisa got home and heaved a sigh. Changed out of her good clothes and started thinking about tea. It had been a sunny day and quite warm, so the house ceiling was drying out. The soft board in the ceiling soaks up a lot of water, so it was still quite damp.

Lisa looked around the house and thought about the one they had just left. Things were going to change.

"Simon, we need to get the leaks fixed."

"It's Xmas. We can't ring him today."

"Well, I am sure they have emergency call-out plumbers, and if he comes out tomorrow, that should be OK."

Simon rang the plumber that night. Apologized for ringing him on Xmas evening, but his wife was insisting that he ring. It was organized that he would come out the next day. He lived just down the road.

No more rain and no more leaks. The plumber arrived and climbed up the manhole to have a look.

The roof wasn't leaking at all. Nope, it was the overflow tray under the water tank. It had rusted out, allowing all of the water to flow into the ceiling. Lisa and Simon were very lucky, that none of the electric wiring had got wet. Lisa hadn't even thought about the wiring and the risk of fire. The whole house could have burnt down.

Between the plumber and Simon they found a solution to the problem. A plastic drum was cut up and glued in place over the rusted section. Lisa just kept thinking, 'If Simon had actually climbed up into the ceiling, he may have been able to fix the problem and stop a lot of the water'.

Why the tank had overflowed, no idea. Apparently, they just sometimes do it. The ball cock may have got struck down and then released itself.

Everything settled down and they carried on with the farm work, shifting stock, fixing fences and water leaks. Lisa started planning.

PART TWO

Chapter Sixty-Seven

Speech

The plunket nurse had a room in the local town where she saw the local children. Lisa had taken the boys in regularly to see her. It was just Daniel now, and being two, they didn't visit her very often.

As the other two boys started talking, they would have their own words for things, which would be close to the right word. As a mother, Lisa generally understood what they were trying to say. Sometimes, the word they used would stick and they would all use it. Daniel, not so much. Daniel hardly ever spoke. As a child, he didn't gurgle in the cot or make funny noises. He was really quiet. When Daniel did start to speak at an older age Lisa couldn't understand a word of it. She tried and tried to understand but was completely in the dark. Without really realizing what they were doing, Daniel and Lisa started to develop a sign language. It was working well.

The nurse asked how things were. Daniel got weighed, measured, ears checked and asked to look at some pictures. Daniel did as he was asked and produced the unintelligible speech coupled with the sign language. Lisa explained to the nurse what he was saying. She got really upset. Gave Lisa a lecture about how bad it was for her to be using sign language and how his language would not develop properly and sent them off to a speech therapist.

The speech therapist was located in the next town and it took them a month to get an appointment. There was a shortage of speech therapists; consequently, they only saw the really bad cases. Once they were in her office, she got Daniel to look at pages of pictures. Daniel had to point to a picture of what she had said. Daniel did really well. She then pointed at a picture, and Daniel had to tell her what the picture was. This unintelligible speech came out of Daniel's mouth. She then got Daniel to match the pictures up. Like chair went with chair. Daniel did really well and matched them all up.

After she had finished with Daniel, she talked to Lisa. Daniel went and sat in a chair and started playing with some toys. "Daniel is a very bright lad. He understands what is being said. His vocabulary is well in excess of 1500 words, which is well above the average for his age. Look, he isn't playing with the children's toys. That's a toy for the adults."

Daniel was playing with the expandable ball. He was concentrating closely as it enlarged and shrunk.

"Daniel has so many words that he is trying to get them all out at once. He is running words together and dropping off the first letters. It will correct over time, but you need to slow him down. He just needs to take the time to get his words out. He does have a slight problem with his pronunciation of his r's, but that may correct."

"So, is there anything I can do?"

"Just get him to repeat what he is saying and slow his speech down. Correct his Rs. You really don't have much to worry about."

"OK, well, that's good."

"If I had more time, ideally, it would be best if he came back to be checked. We are short-staffed, so we only see the acute cases. Unfortunately, you don't qualify."

"That's a shame for all of those kids that miss out."

Daniel and Lisa left and did the grocery shopping. At least they knew what the problem was.

When Lisa was a kid, her mother said that Lisa didn't talk until she was four and then no one could understand her. Perhaps it was genetic cause Daniel was very similar. Lisa had managed alright. She still had problems with saying Rs and she preferred the written word to spoken. Perhaps Daniel was the same.

Chapter Sixty-Eight

Driving

Jim was at school so Lisa only had two boys at home full time.
Robert and Mary were keen to have Andrew to stay. He spent
the day with them, and Lisa collected him that night. As Lisa was
driving home, Andrew told her about his day.

"Pa and I went into town today. Pa had to get something from
town."

"Oh, I didn't know you were going to do that."

"On the way home, Pa went to sleep while he was driving. I had
to wake him up."

"Really! Was he hard to wake?" Lisa was having trouble keeping
her voice calm. "No. It was scary. I had to shake his arm. The Ute was
moving across the road."

"Thank God you woke him up, Andrew. You could have had a
massive accident." Thinking 'bloody hell. He went to sleep in the
vehicle with her son.' Lisa could have lost him and she didn't even
know they were going to town. This was not going to happen again'.

They were having dinner with them in a couple of nights, so Lisa
decided to leave it till then. Sarah was visiting.

At the dinner table, Lisa said, "Andrew told me about Robert going to sleep while he was driving. That's really dangerous."

Everyone started laughing. Lisa was looking around at them in surprise, thinking, 'this is not a laughing matter'.

Sarah said, "Dad's always goes to sleep while he's driving. You just have to wake him up."

"It's not safe to have someone go to sleep, especially when there's a kid in the vehicle."

"Oh, stop making a fuss about it; nothing happened." Simon said.

"It's not safe; someone could have been killed. I don't want my kids put in danger." Lisa was getting worked up about it.

"It's fine, don't make it into a drama." Simon replied in a frustrated voice.

"How long has Robert been going to sleep while he's driving?" Lisa asked.

"Oh, for years. I used to drive him when I was younger so he could sleep." Simon explained.

"What?"

"I used to drive Dad from the farm down south up to the property we owned three hours away. I was 14 years old, and I would drive the three hours while Dad slept."

"You wouldn't have had a licence then?"

"Na, we never got stopped. I looked older than I was, so it was all good."

Lisa was shocked that a 14-year-old would drive that road. It was a dangerous road with a lot of traffic on it, being a main highway. "You were OK with doing that?"

"It was fine; we never had an accident. I was so used to driving that when I went for my licence when I was sixteen, we forgot I shouldn't drive."

"What happened?"

"Dad and I went into town and I dropped him off at the club and then went round to the police station to sit my licence. I went in to see the cop, and he asked, 'How did you get here?'. I told him I drove. He replied, 'I saw you getting out of the Ute on your own. It's illegal to drive on your own without a licence.' He wrote fail on my licence application and gave it to me. I started to walk out of the station when the cop said, 'Where are you going?' I told him I was going to drive round to the club to pick up Dad. The cop said, 'No, you are not! Give me the keys. You are walking' The cop wasn't happy. I had to walk over a Km down the road to tell Dad what had happened. We then had to walk back to get the Ute, and then I drove home."

"That must have been a pain."

"Yeah, Dad wasn't happy about having to walk back to get the Ute. When I first told him, he wanted me to walk back and get the Ute. I had to explain that the cop had the keys to it."

"I had to go and sit my licence again. We didn't make the same mistake. Dad was with me when I pulled up outside the police station. It was the same cop, too."

Lisa couldn't believe how blase they were about the driving. She was going to have to manage it, so that Robert never took the kids anywhere. Mary seemed to be Ok with driving.

Chapter Sixty-Nine

Swimming Sports

Swimming sports day rolled around in March, and Lisa went off alone to watch. The younger kids went first. Jim had a young teacher who was very encouraging. The kids had to kick across the width of the pool with a paddleboard. The teacher was telling Jim, how well he was doing. "She was so proud of him."

The kids then had to put their face in the water and kick their way across the pool. Jim didn't; he just used the paddleboard again.

Lisa sat on the side with the other parents watching. The rest of the kids had to float on their backs. Jim didn't; he just had to use the paddleboard again. The teacher praised Jim for being so brave. By this time, Lisa was getting angrier and angrier. All those lessons and she knew what Jim could do. All the other parents were clapping for their children. Lisa was just sitting there watching, thinking, 'You little shit'.

When the demonstration had finished Lisa went up to the teacher. "Hi, I'm Jim's mother."

"So nice to meet you, Jim's done so well today. He's so scared about putting his head underwater. It's a shame he didn't have an opportunity to go swimming before he started school. He was so brave today. I am really pleased with his progress."

"You do know that Jim has had swimming lessons since he was one. He can swim the width of the local town's heated swimming pool. He can swim to the bottom of the deep end and pick things up off the floor."

The teacher looked at Lisa in shock. She then looked at Jim and said, "You mean he's been having me on?"

"Ooh, Yeah, big time. He can swim freestyle and was just getting the hang of breathing."

"Really, we'll see about that!" The teacher said in a determined voice as she looked pointedly at Jim.

Lisa left thinking, 'Things were about to change for Jim. Bugger him after all those swimming lessons'.

The night after Jim went swimming again, Lisa asked, "Jim, how did swimming go today?"

Jim replied, "Alright," in a put-upon voice

Lisa thought the teacher must have had an intense discussion with Jim.

Chapter Seventy

The House

The other house on the farm the in-laws lived in. It was part of the farm which they had purchased. So all of the expenses for the house, rates and insurance, they were paying. Due to family considerations Robert and Mary weren't paying any rent. Robert and Mary didn't even live there full-time. They split their time between the house on the farm, the apartment in Auckland and overseas trips. Lisa didn't want to live in it.

Mary and Robert left on their annual overseas holiday to England and Scotland.

They always went in the winter to enjoy the English spring and summer. They would be gone for six weeks and were excited. They were renting a flat from Lord someone, which appealed to their sense of importance. Robert was really keen on family history and attending his Scottish clan reunion. They wore the kilt, and all of the Clan descendants had a large dinner complete with the haggis piped in. They gave Simon the keys to the house to check on it. They didn't ask them to stay in it again, which suited Lisa.

Lisa had plans to sell the house and use the money to reduce the debt and improve their living conditions. Lisa didn't discuss any of this with them, as it would have opened up a very lively discussion and they would have been very negative about it. Since the trust owned it and they were paying for all of the costs, Lisa figured they had the right to do what they wanted.

Robert had not spent any money on the house, and the latest problem was the hot water cylinder. These two wealthy older people refused to get the leak in the hot water cylinder fixed. They discovered they had a leak (or thought they did) when the power bill was excessive. To reduce the power cost, they would turn on the hot water cylinder when they wanted to have a hot shower and then turn it off. All the other hot water used in the house was from a boiled jug.

Lisa knew she couldn't sell the house with a leaking hot water system. Lisa got the plumber out. The house had a concrete floor, and those built in the 1970s sometimes had a problem, when the copper pipe would touch the reinforcing steel. The plumber then went on to explain that the best hope they had was if he put a high-pressure pump on the line. They might be able to hear the water leaking somewhere. Lisa was a bit concerned cause the alternative was ripping up the floor in random places, and that sounded expensive.

Simon and the plumber walked around the house, listening for water leaks. To Lisa, this seemed too relaxed. She got down on her hands and knees and crawled around the floor with her ear to the ground. She crawled down the hall, into the bathrooms and all the way to the back of the house. They laughed at her. Lisa couldn't hear anything.

Simon thought it was a waste of time. Lisa headed over to the attached sleep-out behind the garage and crawled around the floor over there, with her ear to the ground, hoping for some sound.

Bingo. When Lisa heard it, it was as clear as day. She could hear water running. The vanity unit got pulled out from the wall, and they could see all the watermarks up the wall from where it had leaked. The floor was wet from the effects of the high-pressure pump. That bathroom had always been cold and damp. They now knew why.

The copper pipe had been resting on the reinforcing steel, which had corroded it. It would have been a gradual deterioration until finally, it just gave away altogether. It must have been leaking hot water for some years. No wonder the power bill was so high.

One major problem solved. Yeah. Simon had no interest in doing anything else to the house and left it to Lisa.

The garden Lisa attacked with a chain saw and clippers. She hauled ivy off the house and discovered a fish pond out the side of the lounge. Lisa trimmed trees so that they could see out of the windows, and the driveway became an open highway. The car no longer got scratched as they drove down it.

She then looked at the house with a critical eye and decided to start tidying it up. She didn't want to spend much money, so she did it on the cheap.

She had three sons to look after, and it was the winter holidays, so Jim was home all day. Lisa treated it like a job. She had the boys up at the house at 8 am with food. She painted and sanded all day while they played. Lisa went home at night, about five pm and did the nightly chores. Cooking tea, bath time, story time and getting the food organized for tomorrow. Simon didn't help with the repainting at all. He stayed well away.

The wallpaper where it was ripped, Lisa sanded down the edges. The bits that had lifted she glued down. It was quite hard to get the glue right under it. She chose paint colours and kept reminding herself that it had to be neutral so a buyer would not be offended. Some rooms, Lisa painted in a darker shade to hide the distinctive marks on the wallpaper. Some rooms needed two coats!

The two older boys were quite happy playing together in the homemade forts. Lisa had all of the furniture piled up in rooms, and with a few blankets over the top, it became a fantasy playground.

Mary had boxes and boxes of stuff which had never been unpacked for the 12 years they had lived in the house. Some of it was quite emotional for her, as it belonged to her son. He had died 12 years earlier from an attack. Mary hadn't thrown anything out. She still had the shirt he was wearing when he died. The hospital staff had cut it off him, so it was in shreds.

The baby wanted to be with Lisa. He was crawling and liked to play with all of the covers and hidey holes Lisa had created with the covered furniture. Only problem was sometimes he would sit back against a wall on the wet paint and make marks on it. His jersey was covered in paint.

Lisa washed down walls, window sills, and skirting boards and touched up where she didn't have to paint them.

The kitchen was a problem cause the colour had worn off the Formica bench. Lisa searched through different books and talked to shops and her sister, who had done up a lot of houses. In the end, she painted the bench with a special paint. Lisa didn't know how long it would last, but it looked good. The cupboard's doors she scrubbed down.

The outside eaves needed to be painted. They were a funny dark yellow colour, which made the house look dark. Lisa didn't want to paint them, and it was a long way around the outside of the house.

Lisa's aim was to be finished before Mary and Robert got back. She knew they would be shocked and angry with what she had done. She really wanted to be well gone before they got back. She still had a bit of painting to do when they were due back.

She spoke to them on the phone when they were in Auckland and asked them to stay in Auckland for a few days, as she needed to tidy their house up. After a day, Robert rang and said he couldn't hold Mary any longer. They were coming home.

Lisa just managed to get everything out and the furniture all moved back before they arrived. She didn't get all of the outside painted, but she was very pleased with how the house looked, clean, fresh and more modern.

Mary was furious with what she had done. Mary was shocked and angry with the changes Lisa had made and rung her up. How dare Lisa interfere with her house and make all of these changes? She was so angry that, at times, she had trouble speaking.

Lisa decided that it would be best if she stayed well away until they calmed down. Robert seemed quite happy and relaxed about it. Simon didn't get involved at all, except to say it was Lisa's idea. Mary did have a working hot water cylinder now, which Lisa pointed out. It didn't help.

Lisa and Simon organized a surveyor to come out and survey off the house with some land as a surplus farmhouse. Due to the shape of the farm and the narrow road frontage, they could only put three ha's with the house.

It was an attractive area. It had a small wet gully with a dam and quite a bit of native bush. Simon went up to explain to his parents that the house section was being surveyed off. They were planning on selling the block. The general opinion was that it would not sell.

Robert sat in his chair quite relaxed, reading his financial times, he would give the paper a shake and state, "You are wasting your time as no one will buy the house", and then go back to reading.

Mary got very upset about the men walking around with the survey pegs on the road frontage. Considering she hardly ever went outside Lisa was a bit surprised about that.

Lisa went and saw Robert and Mary and explained that she needed to finish painting the eaves. That was OK, and they were looking forward to spending time with the boys.

Lisa went up and carried on painting. It took her two days to work herself slowly around the house. Lisa then had to paint the veranda poles. Mary kept a close eye on what Lisa was doing through the window.

The house looked a whole lot better. Lisa then went to work on finishing the garden. Thank God they had places on the farm where they could dump all of the trimmings. The trees round the house, Lisa chopped back, weeded the flower garden and pulled out anything she didn't recognize. Lisa got Simon on the chainsaw, and they loped off branches, chopped out trees and really opened it up. Lisa got some river boulders to make an attractive feature by the house and it started to look quite attractive.

By this stage, Mary had reached the point of giving up. There were some intense discussions about selling the house. The opinion that Robert struck to was, 'it would not sell'. They were just wasting their time. He did seem quite happy with what they had done to the garden. He liked a tidy garden but never did any gardening himself.

Robert and Mary headed back to Auckland for a few weeks. Before they went Lisa explained that the real estate agent would want to show people through, so could they leave it tidy. They had bought and sold a lot of houses over the years, so were well aware of what was needed. Mary said that she always made a fresh pot of coffee, as the smell helped.

The house was advertised in the local paper. A couple came and looked at it. It was sold in a week at pretty much the asking price.

Mary and Robert came back happily and asked how they had got on. Simon explained that the house was sold and take over date was yet to be confirmed. The shock on their faces. They looked at each other as it slowly dawned on them that they had to pack. They had lived in this house for 12 years. But the real issue was that for the last 30-odd years, they had spread themselves between two, sometimes three houses. All of their homes were fully furnished.

Mary was very upset and told all of her friends that she had nowhere to live. When she went to town, she told everyone that she no longer had a home. Her wicked daughter-in-law had thrown them out, and they didn't know what they were going to do or where they were going to live.

Lisa would go into town to be greeted by some very concerned locals about her poor mother-in-law, who was losing her home. How could she do this to them? Throwing them out onto the street.

Most of Mary's friends were not too stressed on Mary's behalf, as they were well aware of how many homes they owned. As one of the neighbours said, "How many houses do you need? Most of us are lucky to have one house. Join the real world."

Lisa's name was in the mud. It was all her fault, and she had led their son down the dark path. Simon would never have done this to them. They were probably right.

Lisa pointed out to them that they had been offered the opportunity to purchase the house themselves. She would have sold it to them less the real estate fees. At that stage they were still convinced Lisa didn't know what she was doing and the house would not sell.

Mary cried, complained and wrote letters to all of her friends about how they had to move. It was very emotional and tense. Lisa tried to stay as far away as she could, but living in a small rural community meant everyone had an opinion. After some negotiation, a settlement date was set. Robert and Mary now had a date they had to move out by. They started packing, which for Mary was a very slow process. She was a borderline hoarder. Anything that she had done, or been given, or used, she kept. It reminded her of places and people. They had unopened boxes and boxes piled to ceiling height in some of the rooms. Mary was upset.

Lisa and Simon were invited for tea during the packing. They arrived with all three boys and their friends, who were over from Australia, Rose and Ross. Robert and Mary had met them before on a number of occasions. When they arrived, Mary was not to be seen.

The table was set with silver cutlery and blue china serving bowls. The meal was cooked, but no sign of Mary. They were greeted by Robert, who said Mary was down the hall.

Mary rushed into the sitting room from the hall in tears and very agitated. Tea was set on the table, and then Mary said, "I can't stay and eat with you. I have to sort through the boxes. My whole life is in those boxes, and you are making me throw them out."

"What is in the boxes?" I enquired.

"These boxes contain all the paperwork I kept from when I was secretary of the local Plunket."

"Well, they shouldn't take long to check and then put in the rubbish." Mary hadn't been secretary for at least 12 years.

Mary became agitated and tearful and said, "I have to check each piece of paper as it might contain something I want to keep. It's my whole life." she sobbed.

"If they are that important to you, why don't you take the boxes with you?"

"No, they can't come, there's no room!. They have to go." Robert stated very firmly.

With that, Mary, in tears, rushed back up the hall, throwing over her shoulder, "Enjoy the meal!"

Lisa started to go up the hall after Mary, but Robert stopped her. He was looking very happy. Robert had wanted the boxes cleared out years ago. Now, they were being cleared out, and he wasn't getting the blame.

They sat down at the table and started dinner. Jim asked, "Why is Grannie upset?"

"Oh, she has to tidy up her room, and she doesn't want to. Just like you don't like doing it."

Jim seemed happy with that explanation, as he became quite upset, when Lisa put all his toys away.

They got Daniel strapped into the high chair, got the other two boys seated and served dinner. All the time, with one eye on the hall door.

Rose and Ross looked at them and rolled their eyes. They had experienced Mary's behaviour in the past. She had been quite rude to them and very manipulating.

Rose leaned over and whispered in Lisa's ear, "You do realize that this is all an act. She has organized this tea so that we can witness her performance."

"Really, she looks pretty upset."

"It's an act; it's all been planned out! She wants to make you feel as guilty as possible."

At this point, Mary rushed out, waving an A3, very aged brown piece of paper with some coloured paint spread across it. It looked like a child's painting.

Mary, in tears, explained that. "This is a drawing that Simon did when he was at Play Center; look at it. I would have lost it if I had just thrown the boxes out like you wanted! This is a precious memory of when my boy was little." With tears on her cheeks, she laid it by Simon's hand on the table.

It was a finger painting from when he was about three. Someone had written his name and date on it. Simon rolled his eyes at Lisa and put it on the sideboard behind him.

After a while, Lisa got up and followed Mary down the hall to find her sitting on the floor, going through a box, one sheet of paper at a time. She had papers all around her on the floor and boxes piled up.

"Why don't you come and have tea with us? You haven't eaten, and your tea is getting cold."

"I can't. I have to sort through all of this." More sobs, eye rubbing and tears. "All my life is in these boxes. Once they are gone, I have no life left; you are making me throw out all of my life."

"Mary, you have a lot of other memories, and you have grandchildren now. You have lots of pictures, and most of these papers have nothing to do with your family. Come and have some tea."

At this point, Mary looked a bit calmer and came out to eat dinner. She was still very upset. They settled down at the table and finished the meal. Once the meal was over, they all went home, leaving Mary and Robert behind to carry on packing.

Their friends thought the whole thing was quite funny. Simon threw his finger painting out. The boys were bathed and put to bed, and the adults settled down with beer and wine.

Rose pointed out that Robert looked very happy about the whole situation.

"He's just loving it. You are going to have some more dramas like tonight. Mary is going to be as difficult as possible."

Rose knew about difficult in-laws. She had coped with a very difficult mother-in-law. Rose had married the only son, who was the youngest of six children, and she had been to hell and back. Ross was supposed to stay home, run the farm and look after his parents. When he had married Rose he had wrecked all of his parents and siblings plans. They blamed Rose for manipulating their precious son.

Robert and Mary carried on packing, and Lisa stayed away. It's a small town, so when Lisa went into the shops in the local town, she was told how upset Mary was. It was her home, and how could Lisa force her to leave?

They looked a bit surprised when Lisa pointed out that they had a three-level apartment in Auckland with three double bedrooms, all with en suites, a large lounge with a wet bar on the top floor, plus a large kitchen and lounge on the bottom floor. None of this information fitted with the story Mary was tearfully telling everyone.

Chapter Seventy-One

The New House

L isa got the architect out to look at the house. Lisa wanted to extend it, replace the kitchen and fix all of its issues. The architect, John, came out, listened to her, made a full inspection of the house and made comments like, "You are living in a substandard house. It's a wonder you are not all sick. You do realize that this mould on the walls of the children's bedroom is toxic. It can cause severe breathing issues. This house is not livable."

After John had fully inspected the house, Lisa explained, "We have lived here for 7 years. It's a lot better since the heaters were installed."

He just looked at Lisa in pity and shock. "To fix this house up, you will need to rebuild the entire building, and then you will still have an old house. It would be cheaper to build a new one. Do you have any area where you could build a new one?"

Lisa hadn't considered a new house site.

Building a new house seemed to be a big step. On the other hand, Lisa could see his point about the house they were in. Lisa took him out around the surrounding area, and he had a look. There was a ridge that ran above the airstrip down towards the woolshed. John jumped the fence, stood on the ridge and got really excited about the view and how the house would fit into the landscape. They had power as the power lines went along the ridge to the neighbouring property.

He left to draw up plans for them to look at. It seemed a big expense to build a new house, but continuing where they were was not an option. Lisa had had enough, and with three small boys, it was becoming unbearable.

Lisa thought if they waited another year then they would be in a better position financially. Simon was all for the new house. Funny thing, when it was discussed with Mary and Robert they were quite keen on it as well. That surprised Lisa, considering their feelings about spending money.

The plans were drawn up and discussed. They were then redrawn and discussed. It was to have three levels. A basement with a double garage, a bathroom, a large bedroom and a unity room. The main floor and then the top floor. Lisa had a few demands, which were not negotiable.

One of these demands was that one could drive the car up to the kitchen door to unload the groceries. Lisa did not want to carry bags upstairs. As the house was cut into the bank, this worked out well.

The second condition was that it was easy to access cupboards with good storage. Lisa had been in houses, where you had to open this door, to move this, to reach around that, to get to. None of that. Lisa wanted to open a cupboard, and there it was.

Third condition was a double oven and a bench, which could have hot oven dishes placed directly on it. Lisa also wanted gas hot plates.

They frequently lost the power and Lisa wanted to be able to still cook. Simon didn't want gas. He didn't like gas and argued passionately about not having it. When Lisa questioned him as to why it was such an issue, it came down to his past experience.

When he was cooking a barbecue with his family years ago, things had gone horribly wrong. The gas had built up in the tubbing, so when he lit the barbecue, there had been a massive fireball, which had taken off his eyebrows and singed his hair. Simon really didn't want gas anywhere near the house. Lisa stuck to her guns and got the gas.

It was wonderful. Lisa had a big gas unit, so she could have a large pot on a burner and still be able to use the other gas rings due to the space.

John seemed to think that those requirements could be accommodated. The stairs were an issue. In the original plan, they had a big sweeping staircase. It took up a lot of room and squeezed everything else up. They lost a bedroom and a pantry. Lisa wanted a pantry. After much discussion and moving things around, Simon came up with the idea of putting the stairs on top of each other. It worked well and meant they had three bedrooms on the main floor and the main bedroom on the top floor. The plans were redrawn.

They went up to Mary and Robert's for dinner one night. They were still in the process of packing. Mary was still stressed about the whole move, but she had calmed down.

The conversation centered on Sarah. Sarah was living in America now for a good portion of the year. Not sure why, as she was still skiing all over the world.

Anyway, Sarah wanted to buy a house in America. Apparently, it was a good time to buy. Houses were cheap.

"I want you to pay the stock loan back." Robert stated.

Lisa just looked at Robert in shock. "Robert, you said that it was a long-term loan."

"No, I never said that."

"Yes, you did. I asked you on three separate occasions about that loan. I didn't want any future surprises. I asked you, and each time, you said it would be forgiven on your death."

"It's my money, why would I say something like that? I want the money to buy the house for Sarah in America."

"We are in the process of building a new house. We are not in a position to pay that back to you."

"I want the money to pay for the house for Sarah. The value of the farm has far exceeded what I thought it would be, and it's not fair to Sarah."

"We took the risk with the farm. You can't keep trying to make it even years later. Values change. It could have gone down."

"I want you to pay me the money for the stock loan."

Lisa just looked at him and thought, 'I can't do this. We have committed the money, and I am not cancelling the house. I had asked and asked about that stock loan to make certain.' "No, I will not be paying that money back to you."

Robert looked at Lisa, then huffed and went back to reading his paper. Simon didn't say anything.

That was the end of the conversation.

Sarah got her house in America. The money came from somewhere.

John came back with the plans to be finalized. Lisa was very happy with them. Simon then said, "I don't want the stairs like that."

John just looked at Lisa in complete shock.

"But this is what you suggested, Simon. It was a good idea." Lisa replied.

"No, I want to have the stairs so that you walk in the door, and the staircase goes straight up to the top floor. I want a grand staircase."

This was what the original plan was, but they lost the pantry and the bedroom. He wanted the stairs to be out the front so that they were seen when someone walked in the front door. A grandiose statement.

John, at this point, was heaving some heavy sighs and looking at Lisa with raised eyebrows. They had done what Simon had wanted, and it worked beautifully. Lisa took a deep breath and said, "No, Simon, the stairs work beautifully where they are. It was a good idea of yours; we will stick with the original plan." Simon looked crestfallen, heaved a sigh and lost interest in the rest of the discussion.

It was happening. The house site was levelled. The house fence was put up to keep the stock out. The concrete pad was laid.

As the take-over date drew closer for the house sale. Robert started arriving at Lisa's place with boxes. It was boxes of stuff that was too good to be thrown out, but they weren't taking with them. Lisa dutifully stored them in the shed, knowing that somewhere down the track, Mary would suddenly demand to know where such and such was that somebody had given her about 20 years ago.

Robert and Mary's house sale was finalized. Lisa relaxed as they were no longer living just down the road. The new owners moved in.

Lisa and Simon paid the bulk of the family debt off and refinanced the rest with the bank. They could get an overdraft to ride out the seasonal lows. Apart from the stock loan, which they had said would be forgiven on their deaths, they no longer had family debt.

Being independent from the family was good. They no longer had intense discussions about what they were doing and why. Neither did they demand to see their accounts to make sure that they could pay the interest and that their money was safe. Lisa no longer had to justify her personal expenses. Their personal expenses were below the government's poverty line, but according to the in-laws, Lisa was spending more than they had 30 years ago. Financially, they were in a good position.

Lisa went up to the new house site regularly and just looked at the progress. The view was amazing, but so was the wind. Lisa looked down at the flats below the house. It would be so cool if they had daffodils planted down there in the paddock.

The local stock firm had a special on bulbs that autumn. The manager had bought too many, and they were trying to clear them out. Lisa bought bags and planted them in the paddock. Lisa had grown up with daffodils growing under the trees next to her childhood home. They had always come out in time for her birthday so they held a special place in her heart. Lisa could just imagine a riot of yellow just below the house in spring.

Lisa was out shifting the cattle on the flats below the house site. It is an area of undulating ground with flat areas. Most of the flat area was a drained swamp so some places were very wet with many, many drains. There were so many drains that it was like a maze. All of the drain cleanings were piled up along the side of the drains, and in places, they stopped the surface water from entering the drain. The cattle would be on a small area between drains and would refuse to go back through the maze to get out. Lisa would be chasing them around trying to get them out. It was a nightmare.

The higher ground was ash soil. They ran bulls down there in mobs of 20 to 30 and were rotated around a fixed area on two-day shifts. Bulls just love to fight, and if they got close to another mob, all hell broke out. They would bawl, dig holes, fling dirt over their backs and smash fences. It was a constant game of chess as to which mob went where to ensure they never got close to each other.

The area was very exposed to the westerly wind. They had planted some douglas fur to provide a wind break and as a visual barrier for the bulls. The trees struggled to grow, with the wind constantly buffeting them.

Lisa was off the bike, shutting a gate about a kilometre away, when she heard this horrendous, pain-filled scream. It echoed around the hill.

The builders were on the site, and Lisa couldn't think what the problem might be. She headed up to see if there was an issue. Lisa was expecting to find someone crushed, fallen or near death.

Lisa found all of the builders laughing except one. In fact, they seemed to be having a hard time trying to stop laughing. The other guy didn't seem very happy. Not much was said. They talked about the progress being made, and Lisa left.

Simon, who had been home with the boys, hadn't heard anything. He went up the next day and found out what had happened.

One of the builders had decided to have a quiet wee on the fence. Only problem was that the fence had an electric wire on it, which was doing 8kw. Water conducts electricity; he had produced a constant stream, which conducted the charge straight up his penis and into his bladder. He had felt a burning sensation in his waterworks before it radiated out through the rest of his body. It had left him withering on the ground. It must have seriously hurt, judging by that scream. Lisa had had electric shocks before. Once, she had an 8kw shock. It had made her feel like her heart had stopped and dropped her to the ground.

All the rest of the builders thought it was hilarious. Lisa reckoned it was a story told over and over again at the pub. She bet he never did it again. The very thought of it made her shudder.

Sarah

Sarah came and stayed at the house for a couple of days. She slept on the orange sofa. She was living in Auckland and was attending Auckland varsity doing a marketing degree. Boyfriends came and went.

It was winter, which is always a miserable time. The house was damp and cold. Lisa now had water heaters running in the lounge, so it was better. The kitchen was still being held together on a wing and a prayer. Stable box still in place, only three hot plates working, the cupboard doors marked, a hole in the bathroom floor, leaking windows and mould on the bedroom walls and all of the window frames.

Lisa was in the kitchen peeling spuds when Sarah explained that she had a boyfriend she wanted to bring down to visit.

"Oh, that will be nice. When are you planning on bringing him?"

"In a couple of weeks, he's a really nice guy who comes from a very important family. Mark likes to surf, and we could go down to the west coast and surf, as there are good waves now."

"That sounds nice."

"Can you buy some new clothes before we come? You are not dressed appropriately to meet him."

"Ooh." Lisa just looked at Sarah. Then she looked at her three boys, who were playing on the floor, around the kitchen at the broken lino and the poor insulation, and thought about the issues in the bathroom, the water running under the house and the dampness. Then Lisa looked out the window at the mud and rain. If Sarah's only problem was what she was wearing, then bloody hell.

Lisa looked at the old T-shirt and pants she was wearing. She then looked at Sarah and her fancy clothes. If she didn't like how Lisa dressed, too bloody bad; don't come.

Lisa didn't say anything and went back to peeling spuds.

Two weeks later, Mark turned up, and they stayed for the weekend. Mark didn't seem to be anything special and went off surfing on his own. After the weekend, Mark and Sarah went back to Auckland. Not long after, Lisa heard they had split up. Perhaps she wasn't dressed appropriately.

Lisa was into energy efficiency, so she wanted a wet back on the fire and double glazing to reduce the heat loss. They ordered coloured aluminium windows throughout the house. The open-plan dining room and lounge had two bifold doors, which opened onto a veranda and then a courtyard. These had a spectacular view over the valley. A family-owned company making the windows and doors arrived to install them. As they were unloading one of the large bifold doors, it got dropped onto the concrete.

"That has been damaged; it will have twisted the frame. We will have to take it back and re-make it." The owner said to his employees. They started to load it back onto the trailer.

"No, it will be fine, just put it in." Simon said.

The owner looked a bit surprised and explained that dropping it would have twisted the frame.

"Na, it'll be fine. It looks good; just put it in."

By this stage, Lisa was beginning to get over her surprise about Simon's position. "Simon, are you sure? He said it needs to be redone."

"It'll be fine, just put it in." Simon replied in a frustrated voice.

Other than making a huge fuss, there wasn't much else Lisa could do, so she didn't say anything else. Things between her and Simon were already strained as she had been making all of the decisions regarding the house, and Simon felt like he had not been consulted.

The door was installed and screwed into place. There was about a half cm gap between the middle door and the frame. Lisa kept her mouth shut.

Once all the windows and doors were installed, the house started to look liveable. Lisa was really pleased with how it was all coming together. She walked around it just checking things out. She was so looking forward to moving in. It was already warmer than the house they were living in.

"Simon, why don't you buy the fireplace for the lounge? You could go to town and look at all of the fireplaces and choose one."

"The leaf?"

"Yeah, I don't like how the leaf is shaped." Simon explained again.

"What about the colours? You like the colors?"

"I don't mind the colours, they are fine. It's the leaf shape I don't like." Lisa just looked at him and said, "OK so none of these then?"

"No. You must be able to find something better than this."

This was about the fourth sample of swathes Lisa had brought home. She had trawled through so many shops over weeks and had really thought she had reached the best decision based on price and design.

Simon had turned it down due to the shape of the leaf. Quite clearly nothing Lisa brought home was going to satisfy him.

She went back to town and started looking for curtains with a different mindset.

She made a selection based solely on her choice. It was a deep red fabric with gold vines across it. The fabric cost $3000 about three times the cost of the one which Simon didn't like the leaf shape on. Lisa took the fabric plus lining home and began making the curtains.

Simon never made a comment about the curtains. Lisa had no idea whether he liked them or not. They were very effective hanging up. Every time Lisa thought about them, she remembered the cost and just how stupid Simon had been over the shape of a leaf. To this day he has no idea what the result was from his statements about the leaf.

Lisa had to choose lights and appliances and make decisions about how things were going to be finished off. She had no idea how many choices there were with light fittings. She also had no idea about the prices of lights. Lisa wanted good lighting. She solved the kitchen lights by talking to the electrician. She told him she wanted brass fittings and did not want any shadows anywhere. Lisa left the rest of it up to him. Lisa figured he would have put up enough lights to know what would work.

Lisa loved the lights in the kitchen. It didn't matter where she worked, she had good light. He had done a great job. It always surprised Lisa that clients don't ask the advice of the tradespeople. They work on all sorts of jobs, know the products and see what works and what doesn't.

They had high ceilings, sloping ceilings and low ceilings. Once Lisa got down to the details, the light choices were actually quite limited.

Lisa cruised through all of the appliance shops, looking for an oven. She had no idea how people bake and cook in those small miniature ovens. They were tiny. Didn't people cook any longer? They would have held two chops at the most. Lisa went home and looked at her commercial-sized meat dishes. Lisa needed them 'cause when a hogget (a year-old sheep) was killed for the house, one of its legs completely filled the dish. They were big meat eaters and Lisa cooked big meals. She also did a lot of baking. They went grocery shopping every two or three weeks.

Lisa went back to the appliance shop with her meat dish. She walked over to the ovens while throwing glances at the salespeople, who were all standing talking in one corner. They must have been drawing straws as to who was going to deal with this mad woman. One guy eventually came over. Lisa explained that the oven had to fit this dish.

Well, that narrowed it down to two choices, or Lisa went to a commercial oven. Lisa would have loved a commercial oven. Unfortunately, it wouldn't have fitted in the kitchen. She got a double-wall oven.

Lisa was so happy with her gas hot plates, wall oven, a separate fridge and freezer in the kitchen. She also had plenty of bench space.

The builders, who had a view of the majority of the farm, made comments about how much Lisa did on the farm. She was left with the impression that they didn't think Simon did much.

The builder saw Lisa one day and showed her the boards that were to go up on the eves.

"If you paint them before I put them up, it will make things a lot easier for you later."

Lisa could see that as some of the eves were very high off the ground. "Thanks for that. I will come up and paint them."

She went up in the evenings and painted the boards. Simon refused to help and it took her a few days to get them all done.

The house was warm. A fire combined with insulated walls and double-glazed windows made a huge difference. The curtains didn't flap in the wind any longer, and no mould. Lisa didn't get her wet back, but she had a linen cupboard, with many shelves, where the hot water cylinder was and a large pantry. The boys had separate rooms. In the hall, they had a separate toilet, shower, and bath so that all three could be used at the same time.

Lisa had an office with shelves, drawers and cupboards. Oh, the shelves. Lisa had spaces for all of the files. She had taken up the ring binders when the builder was making the shelves and said they had to fit these. It was wonderful.

In the old house, the files had been pushed under the bed, beside the computer desk, on the floor and spilt out onto the shelves in the dining area. To work on a budget or to find something had been a nightmare.

Downstairs, Lisa had the two chest freezers, a large tub, a washing machine and a dryer all inside. She was no longer standing in the carport, being buffeted by the cold wind as she got the washing. They also had a large room with a spare bed, a bathroom and a double garage.

On the top floor, they had their main bedroom with an en suite. On the other side from the bedroom, facing south, was a space for craft work, which included large bookshelves. The view from this side was even more spectacular. The windows look directly at the lone cone-shaped mountain. In winter, it was covered in snow, which stood out in the cold wintery sky. Sometimes, the view was like a fairy tale. The morning or evening sky would be like a picture postcard as the pinks of the sunrise or the oranges of the evening sky would be reflected on the snow.

They moved into the house in August, just before Jim's seventh birthday. They moved everything into the house from the other house using the Ute. They didn't have much stuff to move. It was really just the beds and kitchen items. They bought a new sofa and a large dining room table.

Lisa had insisted that the builders build her a clothes line. Lisa could see that if they didn't, she wouldn't have one. Hanging the washing on the fence could be a bit risky with the electric wire. She wanted a clothesline, which had four wires stretched between posts. Lisa did a lot of washing with all of the bedding.

Lisa was out talking to the builders, who really wanted to finish up and move on. The boys came rushing out the back door crying, "Mum, come and see what we have done."

They were all excited and proud of themselves. Lisa followed them upstairs to the top floor as they proudly hurried her along. She was speechless when they showed her.

The boys had hung up one of their paintings about child height on the wall where they were hanging the family photos. Simon and Lisa had been so careful to try and not mark the newly painted walls and the boys had done this.

"Look, Mum, we have hung up a picture for you."

"Yeeees.. I can see that. How did you do it?" Lisa was still slowly digesting what they had done. They were so proud, she didn't have the heart to yell at them, but oh God, Lisa wanted to scream.

"We got the drill, and see you put this in the end and hold it against the wall. You push here on the button, and it makes this go round and makes a hole to put the nail in, to put the picture up."

Lisa was impressed with how they had figured it all out and how they had all worked together. They were only 7, 5, and 3.

What they had done was get hold of a large screw their father had left lying on the floor and put it at the end of the drill. They had no idea how to tighten the drill so had held it in place until they had it pushed against the wall. It had wobbled around and made a hole the size of your thumb. They had then left the screw in the wall and pushed the picture over the screw.

Lisa took a deep breath and shared their moment of triumph 'cause she was impressed. Mentally Lisa was quietly killing their father for leaving the portable drill and screws on the floor.

The picture stayed up for a number of weeks, which delighted the children.

When they first moved in, the kids and Lisa would lose each other. The kids would be yelling Mum as they ran up and down the stairs looking for her. They soon figured it out.

The boys also figured out that they could slide down the carpeted stairs from the top floor. The stairs went down to a small landing, and then turned to step into the room. There was just enough space to get furniture around the corner, tight, but it worked. They had great fun sliding on their stomachs. One day, Lisa's youngest slid down the stairs and didn't stop. He went straight into the wall and made a hole the size of his head. Lisa still doesn't know how he came down the stairs so fast, but he did and just missed the stud. If he had hit the stud, it would have been all over. They were so lucky. After that, no more sliding down the stairs.

It was a big hole. It took a while for Lisa to fix it. Lisa discovered through trial and error that polystyrene placed behind the plasterboard will hold it out from the wall and support it. Then, it can be plastered over the top. Sand it back, and no one would be the wiser. She still had matching paint from the painters. Lisa became very good at plastering.

Lisa was so pleased with the house. She had storage, and all of the boys had their own rooms. It was warm, and the kitchen was wonderful. Lisa really wanted to keep it clean and nice. She found herself cleaning the floor at 10 pm at night after spending all day doing farm work, with a 5 am start. Simon was doing less and less on the farm and left it to Lisa. She finally decided she couldn't keep working all hours. The house would just have to get messier.. Simon didn't do any cleaning other than hanging the washing out occasionally.

The garden area was quite large, and Lisa had plans. She had got the digger to landscape some of the area around the house, with limestone rocks positioned and driveways put in. She bought a lot of native plants and flowering trees and shrubs, which she planted down the banks. It was looking quite good. Lisa didn't have a lot of time, and the main issue was the lawn.

She loved wildflowers. At the other house she had planted a small section of wildflowers, which had been very effective. All the different colours, the delicate blooms, and they were easy to care for. The house section had a long flat strip running from the house down to the fertilizer bin and the woolshed. It would be perfect for wildflowers. She got the local contractor to spray and cultivate the ground for her. The area would have been over a hectare. He wasn't happy about it, as it was a busy time of year for him, and this was a stupid job. After many phone conversations, which included Lisa pointing out how much money they had paid him over the years. He finally came and did the job. Lisa hand-planted the wildflowers.

They came up in a riot of colours. Blues, yellows, purples, pinks, whites, reds, oranges and all the colours in between. The delicate little petals waved gently in the wind. It looked spectacular and very effective. Grasses came up amongst the flowers. Lisa figured that the grasses just added to the effect and in the wild, grasses would be present.

The boys would wander amongst the plants and pick flowers for the house. The insects loved it. There were ladybirds, bees and dragonflies, to name a few. The birds would be in constant movement, flicking through the flowers. They had sparrows, goldfinches, redpolls, yellow hammers, silver eyes, fantails and swallows. In the mature native trees around the garden, wood pigeons and tuis could be seen and heard.

The flock of magpies would gurgle in the mornings as they flew around. Swooping over the top were a pair of NZ falcons and hawks as they searched for prey. When they flew below the house, Lisa would be looking down on them and be able to watch their effortless gliding. Lisa left the flowers to seed and that increased the bird population in the autumn.

Chapter Seventy-Two

Calving

They started spring calving not long after they moved into the house. They also had the fencers working, and Rose's son from Australia was staying with them. He was helping Lisa on the farm. Simon was working with the fencers, making sure they had all the materials they needed. Mostly, Lisa and Simon agreed where the fences were going. Sometimes, they had disagreements about the fence lines, which ended up with them yelling at each other. Sometimes, Lisa thought Simon arguing about the fence line was just to prove her wrong. He had to be right, even when the fence was quite clearly in the wrong place.

They were both checking the cows and shifting their breaks depending on who was out there. One of the cows had gone down. Sometimes, they do that if they have calving problems. They need to get up as fast as possible. If they are down for any longer than three days, then they normally won't make it. Sometimes, they just sulk.

Lisa once had a cow which was down and wouldn't get up. She had pulled a calf out of her, which was dead, that morning. She would try to stand and then just flop down again. She wasn't putting much effort into it. Sometimes, they will get up if they are patt them around the head. This cow didn't seem to be bothered about Lisa getting close to her. She was wondering what she was going to do when her dog walked over to the cow and started licking her face. Lisa couldn't decide whether the dog was thinking, 'you are going to be my dinner' or if she was trying to comfort her. Whatever her motives, the cow totally freaked out and leapt to her feet. She stood there shaking. Lisa patted the dog, thinking, 'Thank God for that, well done'.

They had a cow, which had been down for nearly two weeks. Simon had got the fencers to move her closer to the shed below the house with their front-end loader. They didn't have a tractor with a loader.

Lisa repeatedly said to Simon that she needed to be put down. It had been too long, and she wasn't going to get up. Simon disagreed and carted water and hay for her. She was eating and drinking but not moving. After a few days of constantly mentioning her to Simon, she went and had a good look at her. She was in a bad way. Her leg muscles had all deteriorated.

Lisa told Liam to shoot her and cut her up for dog meat. Liam was a keen hunter and more than happy to kill her.

Simon found out and started yelling at Liam for shooting his good cow. He was tearing strips off Liam.

"Simon, I told Liam to shoot her, so if you want to yell at someone, yell at me." Lisa said.

"You, You, you told him to shoot her." Sputtered Simon. "She was coming right. I have been looking after her." Simon was furious.

"She was flyblown; she was not going to get up. She has been down too long!"

"You had no right to shoot her. She was a good cow." Simon yelled at Lisa in the middle of the paddock.

Simon got on his bike and roared up to the house.

Once he left, the fencer, who used to run his own farm, came over to Lisa and said, "If you hadn't shot her, I would have. She was suffering."

"Thanks. Simon seems pretty angry about it."

"Can't think what he was thinking; she needed to be put down."

Lisa went and saw Liam and asked if he was OK. He just grinned and said it was fine. He was used to being yelled at by his parents.

Chapter Seventy-Three

Household

Once they had moved into the new house for a couple of months, Simon decided he wanted to be a house husband.

"I will stay home and look after the house and children; you can run the farm."

"Are you sure?"

"Yep, you are doing most of the work anyway. I don't want to be involved. I will keep running the bull unit below the house."

"OK, if that's what you want."

So Lisa ran all of the farm except where the 150 bulls were run and Simon stayed in the house.

Simon seemed quite happy with that. He made the boys lunches for school, sometimes took them to sports and went to the club on Friday night.

Lisa was busy doing all of the accounts, planning and running the sheep and the breeding cattle. Lisa was busy.

Lisa noticed that Simon got very irritable when the large oven dishes weren't cleaned. They would sit all over the kitchen bench. Once Lisa cleaned the oven dishes, and the kitchen, everything settled down again. So, although Simon was the 'house husband,' he still expected Lisa to do all of the cleaning of the kitchen, the bathrooms etc. He did occasionally push the vacuum cleaner around, load the dishwasher and do the washing, but didn't put anything away.

Lisa schooled the boys up to clean the house on the weekends. Lisa thought it was important that the boys knew how to clean a house. Jim cleaned the showers, Andrew cleaned the toilets, and Daniel pushed the vacuum cleaner around. Simon just spent time on the computer. It was like he wasn't there. Once they were good at their jobs, Lisa decided it would be good if they switched jobs. Variety and learn how to clean the other areas. Well, bloody hell, they had some yelling matches. Jim yelled at Andrew for not cleaning the shower properly. Andrew screamed about having to clean the showers. Daniel complained about the toilets. Lisa gave up, and they all stayed with the same jobs. Lisa came to the conclusion that if they married, the wives would have to have all three lads around if they wanted the whole house cleaned.

They only had a push lawn mover. Lisa had done all of the lawn mowing at the other house. It had a smaller lawn, plus she was home more often with the babies. At the new house, the lawn wasn't too big, but it took a while to mow it, and Lisa often struggled to get it mowed. In spring, the grass bolted while she was busy with the lambing ewes and cows.

The grass would get away on her.

"Simon, could you mow the lawn, please? It means the boys will have somewhere to kick the ball around that's not covered in cow shit."

"You want the lawn mowed, you mow it." He replied in a very firm voice. Simon was sitting in front of the computer and just turned back to the screen. Lisa just looked at him and then walked out, thinking how miserable can you be? When she was home with the babies, she did everything in the house and worked on the farm. Simon was doing the bare minimum and not very well.

She was doing all of the planning and running of the sheep and cattle. Simon did help her when the jobs needed two people, like docking or dagging, but it was always under protest.

Rose rang Lisa one night in a state of shock over Simon. He had sent her an email with pornographic material.

"It's disgusting. Why would he think I would want it?!"

"He did what?"

"It's really bad. I have deleted it. Can you stop him from sending anything else?"

"I had no idea. I didn't know he was looking at it or sending it. I will tell him." Lisa got off the phone, totally gobsmacked that Simon was looking at porn or that he would send it to people.

"Simon, Rose has just rang me. You sent her porn?"

"Yeah, so?"

"She doesn't want it. Why would you think she would? Why are you looking at it?"

"So she's a prude."

"No, she's normal. Don't send her any more." Lisa said in a firm disgusted voice.

Simon huffed and turned back to the computer. "I mean it, Simon. Don't send her anything else."

"Why would I if she doesn't appreciate it?"

Lisa walked away, wondering why Simon thought it was acceptable.

Chapter Seventy-Four

Babysitter

Simon and Lisa planned to go out for an evening to one of Simon's friend's parties. They were all ready to go, and the babysitter was organised. Lisa went into the boy's room to tuck them in and say good night. Jim greeted her at his bedroom door and promptly power vomited down the hall. Lisa couldn't believe it.

"Simon, call the babysitter and cancel her."

"Why?"

"Jim has been sick, and we can't leave her to clean this up. I will stay home. You go and enjoy yourself."

Lisa got Jim into the shower. While he was washing, Lisa changed clothes and started cleaning up the vomit.

Jim seemed fine. Lisa tucked him up into bed and settled down for the evening, watching television.

About two weeks later they had a farming presentation to go to. They were all dressed, the babysitter was organised, and they were ready to leave. Lisa went into the boy's rooms to say goodnight. In Andrew's room, Lisa found him lying in bed covered in vomit. He hadn't made a single sound about it.

"Andrew, what happened?"

"I don't know, I just vomited." Andrew replied in a tired, pathetic voice.

"Simon, you need to cancel the babysitter. You go to the meeting without me."

"Why?"

"Andrew has vomited all through his bed."

Simon left. Lisa got Andrew into the shower and changed her clothes. Lisa stripped the bed. Took the sheets outside to tip the vomit off them in between dry wrenching. Remade his bed and got Andrew tucked in.

Lisa settled down to watch TV with a glass of wine. For the rest of the night, Andrew seemed fine.

A month later, they had organised to go to one of Simon's lodge this evening. They were all dressed and ready to leave. They were just waiting for the babysitter when the phone rang. The babysitter had cancelled.

"Simon, you go, and I will stay home. It's your evening."

Simon left, and Lisa stayed home. She thought about the situation. Quite clearly, they were not meant to go out together to anything. Three times they had tried and three times it had failed. It's not like they went to a lot of things.

It looked like the babysitter had cancelled because they had cancelled her twice. Leaving her to clean up vomit was not fair to her, and Lisa didn't know if the boys were going to vomit again. She didn't have a choice.

She decided that in the future, Simon and her would not try and go to anything together. One of them would always have to stay home with the boys. Don't try and fight against fate.

Thinking about it, Lisa decided that not going out with Simon wasn't any great loss. She remembered the first time they went out locally after they were married. It was to a local party. She was six months pregnant with their first child. They arrived at the house and went to the door together, whereupon Simon had literally pushed her inside, saying, "I will stay out here, you go in."

"But Simon, I don't know anyone."

"You'll be fine. Go in." With that, he had pushed her through the door and shut it behind her. Lisa didn't know anyone. One of the local wives took pity on her when she was standing there. She explained to Lisa who the other people were in the room. Simon didn't reappear until the end of the night. Lisa supposed he was outside smoking.

The other time which came to mine was when they went to one of Lisa's friend's weddings. It was a lovely wedding and it was great catching up with everyone from varsity. Once they were at the reception, Simon sat in the corner and talked to the photographer. He got horribly drunk. All Lisa's friends kept asking her if she was happy as they looked pointedly at Simon. At the end of the reception, Lisa, who was pregnant with their second child, tried to get Simon to go back to the motel.

"The party isn't over yet. It's just starting. You are such a party pooper." With that, Simon had gone inside and tried to find someone to take him home later. He asked an older couple if they would drop him off. "Yeah, that's fine. We are leaving now."

Simon then tried to find someone else. Only to find that everyone was leaving. Simon came back to her, as she waited and said, "They are all leaving, the party is over." Simon got angrily in the car.

Once back at the motel, he wanted Lisa to walk on the beach with him in the moonlight. She refused and went to bed. Lisa had wondered if Simon would be alright as he was dreadfully drunk. In the morning, she discovered that Simon had vomited in the pot plant.

When they went to Simon's friend's parties he was laughing, happy and part of the social scene. All Simon's friends were the 'men about town' who were going places. They saw themselves as the social elite, with overseas holidays, business deals, beach houses and were very critical of the lower social class. All of their wives wore expensive outfits and furnished their homes with select furniture. Lisa talked to the other wives in her dowdy, old, mouldy clothes. They must have wondered who Simon had married.

Simon liked to talk big and be part of the scene. He would be happier going out on his own without a party pooper for a wife present. Lisa went to bed, comfortable with her decision.

Chapter Seventy-Five

Bed-wetting

L isa would be hanging out the washing. Great loads of it, sheets, bedding, towels and quite often, the mattress would have to be sponged down. Waves of frustrated anger would flow over her, and she just wanted to fix it. Why, why couldn't they stop?

The bed-wetting was constant, with no let-up. Why couldn't her sons stop wetting their beds? In winter or summer no difference, except it was harder to get it all dry on the wet, cold days.

In desperation, Lisa went to the doctor to try and stop the bed wetting. Lisa was swamped in wet bedding, pyjamas and mattresses. It was affecting the children. They couldn't stay at friends' houses; going on school camps was stressful and risky. It involved discussions with teachers, providing extra bedding and hoping that their classmates wouldn't find out. It was nearly impossible for them to go away and stay with friends. It was easier if Simon or Lisa stayed home with the boys if they had something they wanted to go to. It was a nightmare.

Lisa was at a point of just screaming with frustrated anger.

She explained to the doctor that all three were bed-wetting and there must be something he could do. The doctor launched into a speech.

"It is quite normal for boys to bed wet, and many up to 15% are still bed wetting when they are 15. It's all quite normal; you just need to let them grow out of it. There's nothing that you can do. Many boys are still bed-wetting into their 20s. Don't worry. Just let nature take its course."

Lisa sat in the chair and just looked at him. It was affecting her life, the boys' lives, and it was becoming impossible. The frustration was overwhelming. The amount of washing she had to do. If she was lucky, she could put them out in the sunshine. Sometimes, it would run onto the carpet. Every day, rain or shine, she had three full beds of linen to wash. God help her if she missed a day.

"There must be something that can help?"

"There's practical things like making sure the boys don't drink an hour before going to sleep. Making sure they are getting enough sleep, cause if they are overtired, then they are more likely to wet."

The doctor was not telling Lisa anything she didn't already know or do.

"So you are saying that there is nothing that will stop this cause it is affecting the boys' social life?" At that point, he looked a bit more interested in the problem. "They can't have sleepovers, and school camps are difficult to manage."

"Well, Plunket do have a special blanket. It has a monitor in it which beeps if the bed gets wet. It will wake the child up so that they can go to the toilet. You will have to book in as there is a waiting list." The doctor said.

"Thanks." With that, Lisa left and got onto the waiting list. It arrived, and they put it on Andrew's bed.

Andrew went to bed, Lisa went to bed, hopeful that they might have a winner. In the middle of the night, the beeper went off. She was out of bed, down the stairs and into Andrew's room. Andrew was sound asleep. Lisa half carried, half dragged him to the toilet. Andrew was still sound asleep and kept falling over. Lisa had to hold him on the toilet.

"Go wees, Andrew, please go wees, Andrew, wake up! Andrew, you have to wake up!" Andrew was still asleep and falling off the toilet. Nothing happened. After a good while, she took Andrew back to bed and tucked him in. Lisa climbed the stairs and went back to sleep. Simon snoring peacefully.

Beep, Beep, Beep.

Bolt awake down the stairs and into Andrew's room. Andrew still fast asleep, beeper going nuts. Bed sopping wet. Lisa looked at the child, who was sleeping soundly and thought 'fuck it', She would sort it out in the morning. Turned the beeper off and went back to bed

Next day, Lisa washed the blanket and remade the bed.

That night, Andrew was tucked up in bed again, and Lisa went to bed. Beep, Beep, Beep, Beep. Back down the stairs, Andrew was dragged to the toilet, still sound asleep and pleaded with. Nothing. Andrew simply would not wake up. After four days of this and sopping wet beds, Lisa gave up. She was getting no sleep and still working full-time on the farm. She was a walking zombie and couldn't continue with it.

After a week, Lisa tried it on Jim's bed. Lisa explained to Jim how it worked. Jim nodded and seemed happy about it.

Beep, Beep, Beep

Wide awake, back downstairs into Jim's room. Bed sopping wet. Jim was awake. "Go to the toilet, Jim?"

"No, I don't need to."

"You never know. You may still have some left."

"No, I'm good."

"The beeper woke you up, didn't it? So why didn't you go to the toilet?"

"Well, it was wet, so I didn't see the point of going to the toilet for the rest."

"Jim, why the hell not? It would be less mess." Lisa changed the sheets and Jim's Pyjamas, put Jim back to bed and went back upstairs.

Lisa had hopes the next night. After all, Jim had woken up, and now he knew how it worked.

Lisa slept peacefully through the whole night. Not a sound.

In the morning, she woke the boys up for breakfast and school. Jim had a slopping wet bed.

"Jim, didn't the beeper work? It should have gone off when you started to wet the bed."

"I turned it off."

"What, Why?"

"It woke me up, and I didn't like that, so I turned it off. I don't mind a wet bed." Oh God, what the hell was she supposed to do with that?

"Jim, when you wet your bed it affects you staying with your mates. Why wouldn't you use the beeper?"

"I don't like being waken up by the beeper."

"Jim, a wet bed makes a mess, and I have to do more washing."

"Mum, you have to do the washing for Andrew and Daniel anyway."

At that point, Lisa knew she was beaten. Jim didn't give a shit whether he wet the bed or not. Lisa looked at him and thought of trying again. She didn't see the point. Jim was simply going to turn it off again.

Andrew was such a deep sleeper he never woke up. A bomb could go off, and he wouldn't have noticed.

That left Daniel. Lisa wasn't sure she could cope with putting it on Daniel's bed. Being only three, he was probably a bit young. The blanket had to go back to the Plunket for the next family to use.

Mary found out about the blanket and proceeded to tell Lisa that she didn't need to use it.

"When the boys stay with me, I wake them up before I go to bed and they all do wees on the toilet. I then set my alarm for 2 am. I take them to the toilet then. In the morning, they all have dry beds. If you did that, then you wouldn't have a problem. It's quite simple to manage."

Lisa just looked at her. She knew Andrew wouldn't wake up, so how she managed to carry Andrew to the toilet was beyond her understanding. Jim probably would have gone, but Lisa needed her sleep as she worked full-time. Waking up every night at 2 am to spend at least an hour getting them all to the toilet was beyond her.

Lisa just had to carry on managing it as best as she could. The boys didn't stay at their friends' houses, which made the other parents wonder why. When they had friends staying, she would have to dream up a reason why they had to be in another bedroom.

When Daniel was about five, he went and spent a day with his friends. The plan was he would stay the night. Lisa got a phone call from Daniel about 8 pm at night. He was sobbing down the phone. "Can you please come and get me?"

"Daniel, you were going to stay the night. What's wrong?"

"Please come and get me."

"OK, I will come now. I will be about half an hour."

She drove over to where Daniel was staying and collected him up. The other parents couldn't understand why Daniel didn't want to stay. Lisa had a good idea what the problem was but couldn't tell them and just made a vague excuse. "Why did you want to come home?" She asked Daniel in the car.

"I was scared I would wet my bed, and they would find out."

"Oh." The two lads at the other house were very critical of other kids and would probably have given Daniel a hard time about the bed-wetting. Lisa quite understood Daniel's problem. She got him home,

411

and he went happily to bed. Daniel stopped bed-wetting when he was about six. Still had the odd accident, but most nights, he was dry. Thank the lord.

Chapter Seventy-Six

Friends

L isa quite often got someone to help her with the docking, as Simon would complain about being asked to help. Liam, Rose's son, did the docking with her the year he stayed. Simon made the lunches and bought it out in the Ute. One day after a week, Liam got fed up with the lunches Simon made. It was the same every day. Lettuce, tomato and cheese sandwiches.

Liam said to Simon, "Can't you make something different?"

"I have. Yesterday, you had lettuce, tomato and cheese. Today, you have cheese, lettuce, and tomato."

Liam wasn't impressed. They were docking the replacement ewe lambs, and they were being tagged so Lisa could choose her replacements from the twin mobs. It made docking slow as the tag gun had to be loaded.

Liam said to Simon, "You will stay and load the tag gun for us?" Simon replied, "I have to go and get the kids from the bus."

"You will come back?"

Simon just smiled and got in the Ute.

About an hour later, Liam said to Lisa. "He's not coming back, is he?"

Lisa just shook her head. She didn't expect Simon to come back. They carried on docking.

Liam had a mate in Aussie. Before it was time for him to go back, his mate came and stayed a week. They had a wonderful time. They went shooting, to the beach, had trips through caves and went to the tourist hot spots.

Lisa was pleased to see Liam have a good time. On his last night, she said goodbye to him. Gave Liam some stuff to take home to his mother and wished him luck. Simon was taking them to the airport early in the morning.

In the morning, they had left. Lisa went down to strip the beds and clean things up. The shower was blocked with lumps of soft, squashy things. She didn't have any idea what they were. It was a puzzle.

She fed the boys breakfast, made their lunches and got them on the bus before she went out on the farm.

Simon came home during the day, and that night, she got a phone call from Rose. "Hi, did Liam arrive alright?"

"Yeah, he's here. Liam is ill?"

"Really, why? He seemed fine last night."

"Liam and his mate could hardly walk when they got off the plane. They were really sick. Their eyes were red-rimmed, and they couldn't walk straight. They were still drunk." Rose was not happy.

"Drunk?"

"Yeah. They had no sleep, and Simon put them on the plane drunk."

"What? They were fine when I saw them."

"Apparently, your husband sat up with them that night, and they drank Port all night." Lisa didn't even know that they had Port in the house.

"Port? I am so sorry. I had no idea."

"They are both only sixteen, underage. How could you give them alcohol? A beer is fine, but that much alcohol is excessive. They are only kids." Rose was really upset.

"Rose, I had no idea. Simon took them to the plane. I said goodbye to them last night. I'm so sorry." Lisa got off the phone and went to find Simon.

He was on the computer. "Simon, Rose has just rang me. She is really upset about the state of Liam when he got off the plane. What happened?"

Simon gave a giggle and said, "Oh, we sat up last night and drunk port. They got really drunk. Liam's Aussie mate vomited in the shower."

"Simon, they are underage. You were supplying alcohol to underage kids. You knew they were flying to Aussie. How could you?"

"They had a good time. Stop being such a prude. It was a good experience for them."

"Simon, they could have stopped them from boarding the plane. You could have been arrested for supplying alcohol to underage kids." Lisa was really upset about what he had done. How irresponsible could he get? She walked back to the lounge. At least she now knew what had blocked the shower drain.

As she sat down, she realised that Simon would have been drinking as well. He had just driven them two hours to the airport drunk, then two hours home. It was a wonder he hadn't been pulled over. What the hell was wrong with him? No one with any sense would have done that. He was behaving like a teenager, not a 39-year-old man.

Lisa tried to calm down as there was nothing she could do about it. Talking to Simon was a waste of time. He would blame her and tell her she was being over dramatic. He did the bare minimum around the house and farm, but when it came to the public, he was this charming father and husband who had to put up with a difficult wife. She was so tired of holding it all together.

Chapter Seventy-Seven

Yard Work

Lisa would go up to the house and ask Simon to come down to the yards to push the sheep up the drafting race or the dagging race. Simon was never happy about it, but he came.

One night, Simon came out of the office and said with a smile.

"I need two days' notice of when you need me to help with the stock."

"What?"

"I need two days' notice to prepare myself to be able to come down and help."

"You want me to tell you two days in advance of when I need your help in the yards?"

"That's right. I need time to prepare myself." Simon said in a pleasant voice. Lisa just looked at him and thought, 'Whatever. She could work with that.' "OK." She went back to baking muffins for the school lunches and ignored Simon.

She made it work.

"On this day, I need you in the yards at 9 am." Simon would come down and help. No arguments. In fact it was quite peaceful instead of the usual drama.

Chapter Seventy-Eight

Xmas in the New House

The shearing was done for the season. Quite often, their final day of shearing would be on Xmas Eve. They would then go down to the Xmas parade and see all the locals, including the guys who had been shearing that day in their woolshed.

The Xmas parade was part of the Xmas tradition. The boys watched the local floats go up and down the street, rush to collect the lollies thrown by Santa from the fire engine and then ride on the swings or play in the bouncy castle. The next day would be Xmas. They had a large Xmas tree by the fireplace. Due to the vaulted ceilings, the tree was 12ft. tall, and they needed a ladder to decorate it. It looked spectacular with all the lights flicking on it. On the verandah, they had icicles and coloured lights.

On Xmas morning everyone opened their presents. The boys had the Xmas stocking with all the little surprises like bags of nuts, lollies, little dinky toys etc. Their big presents were Lego. The boys loved Lego and they each had a theme which they wanted. Jim was into Star Wars, Andrew had lots of farm sets, and Daniel liked building Zoos. Robert and Mary didn't give Xmas presents. Considering the birthday presents the boys got from them, Lisa didn't see that as being a great loss.

For their birthdays the boys got a dollar for every year they were alive, inside a card. So Jim got seven dollars for his birthday this year. One year the boys didn't get any money, instead they got a present. The boys opened their birthday presents from their grandparents and then looked at their Mum, at a complete loss. The boys didn't know what they had been given.

Lisa started laughing. They had been given the complementary bag for first-class travellers. They had a neck support and little slippers.

Lisa gave Simon a book about the history of man. Simon gave Lisa a little box wrapped up in Xmas paper. It was about 4cm by 6cm and heavy. Lisa opened it, thinking it was something special. She was completely dumbfounded when she opened it. It was a box of cutters. (Cutters are part of the shearing gear to dag sheep).

Simon started laughing. "You thought it was something else, didn't you?" She just nodded, waiting for the surprise. It didn't come.

"They are the top brand. I couldn't get better." Simon said.

Lisa nodded and said, "Thank you. Simon. They will come in very handy. I was low on cutters."

She then crawled over the floor, through all the wrapping paper, to see what the boys had got from Santa. The boys were real excited about their presents and having fun.

Because they had built a new house, it was decided that the family Xmas party would be in their house. 'Well, OK,' Lisa thought. Simon was keen to show the house off to his family.

Simon's cooking was very basic, when required, it wasn't up to doing a full Xmas luncheon. Lisa had shown him how to make scones, pies and, pasta, etc. When they were married, all Simon could cook was a roast. It went in the oven in the morning with all of the Vegies and sat all day in the oven until he pulled it out that night.

Lisa wasn't looking forward to it since she had all of the farm work to do, plus the shearing. And now fit in the cooking for some very critical guests.

She organised a turkey to cook, ham on the bone, salads and new potatoes. Xmas pudding for dessert, fruit salad, plus a Xmas cake supplied by Mary.

Sarah arrived on the day and offered to help. They had been given some crayfish by some friends, which Lisa decided could be an appetiser. She had cooked them and she got Sarah to finish them off.

Sarah then took the tray around to the family as they sat around talking.

There were 20 adults and 7 children. They all had mismatched plates cause Lisa didn't have a dinner set large enough. Lisa rolled out the silver cutlery set, which had been a wedding present (It was engraved with Simon's initials) and made up the balance with stainless steel cutlery. There was much discussion about the mismatched dinner plates.

Lisa served the dinner and the kids' dinner. Everyone seemed to have enough to eat, and after long discussions, they all went home. Thank God!

Lisa looked around the house at the dirty plates, the leftover food that the kids didn't want to eat and thought, 'Not again'.

Christmas is for the children, not the adults. Why, in God's name, was she knocking herself out cooking food which the kids didn't like? She was stressed trying to get it all cooked and checking to see if it turned out right.

Chapter Seventy-Nine

Cut Out

The shearer's shout would take place at the end of the season. The timing varied, but normally around January before the guys left to shear overseas. The contractor would put on a closed party. All the shearers, wool handlers and some of the farmers would go. It was a big night. This time, it was being held at the local club.

Simon was going. "I could drop you off, so you don't need to worry about driving."

"No, I will drive myself. I'm not some kid who needs his mother to drive him." Simon snarled at Lisa.

"I was thinking about the alcohol and driving. Lots of wives drop their husbands off, so they don't have to drive." Lisa replied in a surprised voice.

"No, I will drive myself." With that, Simon left.

Lisa went back and fed the kids and cleaned up the house. She then went to bed. At around midnight she woke up and found Simon wasn't home. Lisa got worried. The turn-off from the highway onto their road was really dangerous. A lot of accidents happened there, and the fence was always being wrecked with cars going through it. They even had a truck turn over on the corner. Lisa rang the club. They were shut. She rang the contractor. He didn't know where they were. He had seen Simon at the party. He gave her the number of the club manager.

Lisa rang him. He said, "Oh yes, I remember him. I think he's with the group that went off to the other club."

"Thanks." By this stage, Lisa was feeling like an idiot, having to ring everyone at 1 am to see if her husband was alright cause he couldn't ring her.

The other club was about half an hour away in a small district. It used to have a shop, but now just had a club, a school and a sports complex. Lisa rang the club and they put Simon on. He was drunk.

"I will come and get you."

"No. I'm fine."

He put his mate on, "He's fine. We are only drinking out of small glasses, so it's all good." he said as they laughed down the phone.

Simon got back on, and she said, "I will come and get you, so you don't have to drive home drunk."

"No, I am not some kid who needs his mother to pick him up. Leave me alone. I'm a big boy." With that, Simon hung up.

He was very drunk, and he had his mates with him. Lisa sat looking at the phone for ages and decided to stay home. If she went, he would have been really angry with her.

She woke up in the morning to find Simon was home. God knows how he made it home. Judging by his breath, he was rotten. Lisa made a mental note to never ring around again to see if he needed a ride or if he was alright.

Chapter Eighty

Simon's Inspiration

Lisa was out shifting stock and was heading back to the house as it was near midday, and it was getting hot. That humid, heavy heat which just saps the strength. As she travelled up the lane with the dogs on the back of the bike, she heard a lot of high-pitched yelling and screaming. Lisa headed towards the sounds, thinking, 'what the hell'.

An incredible sight greeted her. Simon had parked the Ute up the hill and tied a rope from it to the fence post down in the gully. He had put a pulley on it with a rope tied to it. The boys were hanging onto the rope as they swung over the bank and then were dropping into the pond.

The bottom of the gully had three ponds in a row. The top one had blackberry around it, and then it went through a culvert into this pond. The water was clear and deep, with a lot of rushes and weeds around it. On the downward side, there was a bank with an overflow into the next pond.

The boys were having a ball. It looked like a lot of fun. She went down to see them. They excitedly told her how fast they went and what a big splash they made as they climbed out of the pond.

She noticed some black things on Jim's legs as he came out of the pond. On a closer look, she realised they were leeches. Not what she was expecting. The two older boys didn't care about the leeches; they were having too much fun. Daniel got upset about the them and wanted them off.

Lisa's dogs promptly jumped into the pond and tried to join in. They were swimming around the boys and trying to climb on them. A big splash would suddenly happen next to the dogs, which totally freaked them out. The dogs soon decided that having a boy land in the water from the sky was not their idea of fun. They beat a hasty retreat to the shade under the bank.

Simon was up the hill, sitting in the shade, reading a book. Lisa was completely blown away that he had done this. She was impressed with the effort he had put in and the idea. They had a brief discussion about things. Not long afterwards, Simon packed it all up, and they went home. He never did it again.

Chapter Eighty-One

Dancing

Jim came to Lisa one day and said he wanted to learn highland dancing. Lisa made a non-committal noise and left it. She had no idea why he wanted to learn and didn't know anyone who did it. She just thought it would die a death. It didn't. Jim kept bringing it up and wanted to know why his mother hadn't done anything about it.

Lisa made enquiries and found someone who was one and a half hours away. They could teach it on Friday night, after work. So, on Friday, she took all of the boys to dancing lessons. This made it a very long week for her as the lessons started at 5 pm in a hall and went to 6 pm. They didn't get home till 8 pm at the earliest, by the time she had them all packed up. All three boys decided they wanted to learn.

She then discovered that there were competitions on Saturdays in different centres. This involved collecting the correct attire, which, for boys, is quite hard to come by. Lisa searched the internet, chased up leads and discovered she had to make outfits. It took a lot of time searching for patterns and making the outfits. For the kilts and sporrans, Lisa found a shop, which specialised in Scottish dress. They hired and sold outfits for occasions. Kilts were expensive and hard to find in children's sizes. She had to make the waistcoats as they had nothing in the boys' sizes.

Simon came to the first couple of competitions and then decided he wanted nothing to do with it.

Lisa had a lot of fun taking the boys to dancing competitions. She got quite involved in encouraging them. The girls in the competitions were very good and dedicated. The boys placed quite often but never won. Lisa spent Fridays taking them to lessons, then grocery shopping, and then, on Saturdays, going to competitions. Lisa was tired as she had to get up early to do the stock work.

"Simon, could you take the boys to dancing lessons tonight? I'm really tired." Simon was on the computer. "No, you wanted them to do dancing. You take them."

Lisa left with the boys to take them to dancing class. She was getting very tired with all of the early starts of 5 am over summer, and the travelling was taking a toll. Simon did take them to dancing on rare occasions, but reluctantly. Judging by what was said to Lisa, she thinks some of the locals must have said something to Simon about helping out.

Jim enjoyed the dancing and made progress. He began learning the sword dance and reel. The instructor tracked down some swords for Lisa to take home so Jim could practice. It's a bit surreal carrying swords around.

Lisa organised for the grandparents to take them to a competition on the East Coast in the holidays for the weekend. Robert and Mary had purchased a house over there (They were back to having three houses again), so it worked well for them. Before they had purchased the house Mary had talked to Lisa about visits.

"If we purchased a house on the East Coast, would you come and visit?" Mary had asked.

Lisa was a bit surprised, but the last thing she wanted to do was to travel four hours with three little boys. "No, I won't visit."

"It would be good for the boys. They would associate with the right people."

"Thanks, but no."

They went ahead and purchased the house anyway. They then complained that Lisa, Simon and the boys didn't come and visit.

Lisa sent the boys with all of the costumes, instructions and the competition timesheet.

The grandparents didn't quite understand all that was involved and forgot to put the garters on Andrew. Consequently, his stocking fell down, while he was on stage. Andrew was quite upset and lost marks for presentation. The grandparents were quite surprised about how involved the whole competition was.

Lisa invited them to other competitions when they were closer to them. Robert always wanted to talk about the farm, the markets and what was happening. Lisa explained what they were currently doing on the farm.

Robert looked at her and said, "I wouldn't put up with a wife like you!"

Lisa looked at him and thought, 'No, you wouldn't.' She remembered the time they had told her about how he had walked into their home on the farm down south and had said to Mary, "You had better start packing, old girl. We are moving to a new farm up north."

Mary had no idea he was looking to buy another place, that he had purchased one or what it was like. She just had to start packing. Robert expected a wife to do as she was told. He made all the decisions. Lisa wouldn't have handled that. She didn't reply to Robert's comment.

They seemed happy to come to the dancing competitions, but Lisa always felt like they would prefer it if she wasn't there. They were very jealous of her organising anything with the kids.

Chapter Eighty-Two

Homework

Two years after Jim started school, Andrew went to school. Andrew was a bright, active lad who took great interest in everything. Lisa expected him to slot into school life easily, especially as he had a big brother at school.

It was only a small country school, and he knew most kids from the play centre, so he had lots of friends. At the start, everything seemed good. Andrew was a very good runner, swimmer and competed well at school events. He went to school quite happily.

The boys brought home homework. Mainly spelling and reading books. They did the spelling at the table, and then they went to bed. Lisa would go and listen to them read their story and then read them a story before they went to sleep.

Jim's reading was good. He was progressing well.

This particular night, Lisa did Andrew's spelling, and he did pretty well. Andrew headed off to brush his teeth and hop into bed. Lisa went and sat on his bed to listen to him read. It was a simple first reader with lots of 'the's and they's'. Andrew couldn't read it.

"Andrew, you know what that word is; you just spelt it."

"I can't read it."

"But why not? You read the other books OK. Why can't you read this book?" Andrew, at this point, burst into tears, "I can't read it. I can't read anything at school. I will never be as good as Jim. He can read anything. I try and try, but I can't do it!" Andrew was in tears and flinging himself around the bed, crying.

"Andrew, you can do this. You read the other books."

"I looked at the pictures and guessed."

"Oh, that was clever of you. You are not stupid. Andrew, you are a great kid. You are brainy, and we will fix this." Andrew was still crying, with deep, racking sobs.

She gave him a big hug. "Andrew, it will be OK. Let's try this again. With me holding my finger under the word you are going to read."

"I am not as brainy as Jim; he has no problems at all."

"Don't worry about what Jim can do. He's two years older than you. So, of course, he can do more, but when you are older, so will you."

They progressed slowly along the page, with Andrew getting most words right as long as Lisa's finger was under the word. He was still upset and struggling to read the words.

"Andrew, we will find out what the problem is. It could be something with your eyes. We will get them tested. What story do you want me to read to you tonight?" Andrew settled on a cowboy story. Andrew loved cowboy stories. Lisa went into Daniel's room to read him a story, thinking about Andrew. The next day, Lisa started by ringing the school. The only thing they could suggest was that she contact Kip McGrath for help. She wasn't impressed; surely the school would be able to direct a concerned parent to the right channel. Apparently not.

The lady at Kip McGrath was helpful once she explained what had happened. They directed her to a child education psychologist.

Andrew and Lisa sent off a fortnight later to see her. She was lovely, calm and down to earth. She had this folder of tests for Andrew to do. It was simple stuff like reading numbers or letters. They got to the second page. Andrew had to read columns. It was a complete shambles. Andrew read out numbers from all over the page. He didn't come anywhere close to reading a column.

She closed the folder, "It is pointless continuing with the tests. He hasn't even made it past the first test. You need to get his eyes tested. Andrew cannot focus on one point, stay on a row or column."

"OK, so what do I do now? Where should I go?"

"In the main centre, there is a very good eye specialist. He works with children regularly and has very good results."

At least they knew that something was wrong with Andrew's eyes and Andrew seemed quite happy and more relaxed about the whole situation.

Off they went to the eye clinic a month later. The clinic had exciting toys in the waiting room, like throwing little bean bags into holes. Andrew had fun.

Once in the room, Andrew sat in the chair and was asked to do all the normal eye movements, close his eyes, look up, down, etc, while he changed lens. It didn't take long.

"Andrew has a lazy eye. When you hold a finger in front of Andrew and then moved it closer to his nose, one eye will suddenly turn in another direction. Both eyes should have stayed focused on the finger." The specialised explained.

Lisa nodded.

"Is Andrew scared of heights?" He asked.

"Andrew isn't happy about being up high. He hugs the wall and gets upset about where he is."

"That's normal for his condition. Every time he blinks the world has changed. Andrew has a very bad case of it. There's no way he would be able to learn to read cause the words would be moving all over the page. They would never be in the same place on the page."

"Oh, that would make it hard. So everything in his world is unstable?"

"Yes, he will never be sure of where anything is."

Lisa tried to understand what it would be like living in a world, which constantly changed. It would be so scary. "Can you fix it?"

"Yes, it's about retraining his body. There's a set of exercises called floor dancing. You need to retrain your brain to coordinate the muscles."

This sounded interesting but it did make sense to Lisa, mainly because her mother had talked about her work as a speech therapist. Children who went from sitting to walking and completely missed the crawling stage had trouble with speech. Apparently, if a baby didn't learn how to crawl, then a process of learning didn't happen in their brain. This had side effects like speaking. Otherwise, it seems a bit far-fetched, as they appear to be completely unrelated. How could getting coordinated muscles affect your eyesight?

They went home with the booklet of instructions. Andrew had to spend 10 min every night doing the marked exercises. The first ones were reasonably easy, and then they got harder. It sounds easy to lie on your back and lift your left arm and right leg, then put down your right leg and lift your right arm and then lift your left leg and put down your left leg. As they progressed, Lisa read out the instructions, and Andrew had to follow along in the right order. It got quite complicated and she would have to stop as Andrew sorted out which leg was up and which arm was down. It was a lot of fun.

Andrew, when he was younger, had always fallen over. They would be walking along, and for no reason, Andrew would fall over. Lisa had taken Andrew to the doctor to see if anything was wrong. The doctor had, had a look at him and said, "As children grow, their hips alter to allow for walking. His hips have not fully moved yet, so that is why he keeps falling over."

Lisa had accepted that as being a reason at the time. Andrew did stop falling over as he grew. Now she was wondering if some, most, of the problem was the fact Andrew couldn't see. It would be hard to walk when you never knew where the ground was.

So once a fortnight, they travelled two hours to the clinic and spent half an hour doing new exercises. On the way home, they stopped and had afternoon tea. Andrew was uncomfortable the first few times they had afternoon tea in the mall, As they didn't normally eat out or take the kids to cafes. Andrew sat in his chair, looking around at all of the people.

After a while he started to be more relaxed. They then cruised through the shops in the mall, mainly the bookshop, then grocery shopping on the way home. It became a special time between Andrew and his mother. Being the middle child he didn't have much time spent, where it was just him.

Once he got better at the coordination, they moved on to eye exercises. Again it was look up, down, left. One eye shut, one eye open, etc. Andrew made good progress and started getting better at schoolwork. He could now read along a row or column.

Lisa missed it when they stopped going to the sessions. It had been a break for her from the routine of farm work, cleaning and general work.

Chapter Eighty-Three

Xmas

Another year rolled around, and Xmas arrived again. This year they were having it at home and didn't have to visit any family. Lisa and the boys were delighted. After the previous Xmas with all of the extended family and Xmas food Lisa decided to do it differently.

She sat the boys down and asked, "What do you want to eat for Xmas? You can choose anything you want, no restrictions."

They looked at each other, laughed and the demands came thick and fast. Cheerios, pizza, lollies, ice cream, nuts, chips and big lolly pops. So that's what they had. They started eating what they wanted in the morning and grazed all day. Lisa was not stressed, and she could spend time with the boys. The preparation was easy. They had a great Xmas.

Lisa was out in town and saw a local who asked, "What did you have for Xmas?"

Lisa explained what they had done.

"You can't do that. It's not Xmas if you do that. You got to have the proper Xmas food."

"Why? The boys are happy, I was happy, and no one was stressed." They walked away, shaking their heads; they did not approve.

Lisa was very happy with the arrangement and couldn't understand why she hadn't done it sooner. The boys liked it, too. Weeks out before Xmas they would be making suggestions as to what they wanted. Ideas would come and go leading up to the final choice. It was part of the highlight for them.

Chapter Eighty-Four

Cross Roads

Lisa ran the bulk of the farm. They had, over the years, applied massive amounts of fertiliser, regrassed, put in tracks, developed a 186-hectare block of gorse, fenced and now had a very productive farm. Simon was still running the flats down below the house. Lisa didn't go down there or have anything to do with it. Simon, over the years, had complained about her taking over and interfering in what he was doing.

Simon went to the club every Friday night and came home drunk. Tonight, he came home earlier than normal. Lisa was in the office doing the accounts.

"I caught up with the fencer tonight." Simon said in a chatty voice.

"OK, so how is he?"

"Oh, he's good. He took me aside to have a chat with me." Simon said in a very smug voice.

"Oh, what about?"

"He is very concerned for me. He asked if I was alright 'cause living with you must be very difficult."

"What?"

"He was concerned for my mental health cause you are so difficult."

"Really." Lisa was thinking frantically of anything that might have given him that idea. She thought she got on alright with him.

Simon smiled and went into the kitchen to make himself a coffee.

From the house, Lisa could hear cattle bellowing. Cattle only bellow when something is wrong. No water or feed. Lisa could see bits of the bottom flats from other parts of the farm. It looked like they had feed and water was OK. The next day, the cattle were still bellowing. Lisa knew that if she went down there, Simon would have a row with her. She would be interfering, and he would have a major row. It would be her fault, and it would give him another reason to blame her. She would never hear the end of it.

The next day, the cattle were still bellowing, and Lisa was having an argument with herself about going out to see what the issue was, compared to how Simon would behave.

She was in the kitchen on the third day, and she could still hear the cattle bellowing. She wasn't sure what to do. Either way, she was going to end up in the shit.

At this point, Simon arrived up at the kitchen door and yelled at her, "I don't want to have anything to do with the bull unit. You can take it over."

"Simon, are you sure?"

"Yes, you take it over. I want nothing to do with it." With that, Simon disappeared down to the garage.

Lisa dropped what she was doing. Turned the oven off and shot out the door. She went down to where the cattle were bellowing to find they had no grass.

Simon had them locked up in a paddock. Lisa moved them into the next paddock and went around the whole unit. It was a bloody mess.

Posts and wires were broken, drains were overflowing, cause they hadn't been cleaned out. The electric wire wasn't working and was shorting out from vegetation and touching the permanent fence. Lisa checked all of the stock. Figured out a plan and decided it was over-stocked. The mob of steers, which had been bellowing, probably needed to be sold.

Lisa got home and rang the digger operator. He enquired on the phone how long the job would take. Lisa said probably over a week at least. Could be two weeks. He was surprised and thought it would be less time.

That night, after tea, Simon went into the office to play on the computer. While the boys were having showers Lisa went and talked to Simon.

"Simon, don't you want to run anything on the farm?"

"No, you can do it all. I don't want anything to do with it."

"Simon, you are part of the partnership and the trust; the farm is in your name."

"It was always my father's dream that I take over the farm. I never wanted it. I always wanted to dig up fossils."

"You can still do that. Do some papers at Massey."

"No, it's too late for that. Do you know what I did the night after Dad signed the farm over to me?"

"No? We came home and had tea."

"I went up the hill in the dark and howled my eyes out. I just sat up the hill and cried and cried. I could hear you down at the house doing things and I just thought he's won. I have to do it. It was the last thing I wanted. I was going to spend my life doing something I hated. A future of slowly being strangled stretched out in front of me."

"But Simon, we talked about you and farming. You said that was what you wanted."

"I did it because of you, and I didn't know what else to do."

"So you want nothing to do with the farm?"

"No, I don't want it."

"Ooh." Lisa was having a hard time understanding. To her, he had so many opportunities and options. She knew a lot of farmers committed suicide, and some of that was due to family expectations.

"Why don't you do some study with Massey? They have a lot of courses. I need you to help with things on the farm like dagging, etc, but the rest of the time, you could study."

"It's a waste of time."

"Well, have a look anyway. What have you got to lose?"

Lisa could hear the kids making noises. They were ready for her to put them to bed, so she went and organised them.

She hoped Simon could find something, which would grab his interest. Lisa struggled to understand Simon's problem. Everyone has to do things they don't like. He had three sons, a good house, a very large asset and time to do what he wanted. He could join any club, read books, and study. Why couldn't he make it work for himself? Why couldn't he just figure it out and do it?

The digger came out, and he was down there for three weeks. They replaced the broken posts, cleaned out the drains and had a discussion about the drains and water. They decided that the wettest paddock, they would install tile drains. As it was, they couldn't even regrass the paddocks cause of the many drains.

All the drains were cleaned out and left to dry out before the tile drains were to be installed. Doug, the operator, had a measuring wheel. Lisa ran this along all of the drains to find out how much nova flow and drainage metal to order.

They started. Lisa had to roll out all of the coils of drainage pipe along the drains and make sure they had a slope on them. That means if the drain had a dip in it, Lisa had to fill it in or dig it out so that the water flowed evenly. If it didn't, then it would silt up and block. It was a lot of work climbing in and out of drains and fighting with the coils of pipe. Simon stayed up at the house. He didn't come down at all.

After some discussion they decided it would be a good idea to put in inspection holes. This would allow the surface water to flow into the drains, plus they would be able to see if there were any problems with the pipes. Lisa had to cut up plastic culverts to the right length and drill holes in them for the pipe. It was quite difficult to do. She asked Simon if he would help. He refused.

She managed to get them done and back to the paddock. Once the pipes were all in, the subsoil was pushed back and then the topsoil. It looked wonderful. A tidy, usable paddock to be regrassed. The productivity went up, as they didn't have water lying on the paddock, and it was easier to manage. Lisa was very happy.

She then looked at the next paddock and decided they needed to be done as well. A plan was formulated to do a paddock each year. The budget had to be reworked, and it put them under financial pressure.

Lisa was busy running all of the farm and doing the development work. They had more fencing to do. The gang came out and started work on a new paddock. Lisa, who was still flabbergasted about the fencer, had decided to ask.

"I hear you caught up with Simon the other night at the club?" Lisa asked.

"Yeah, we had a chat." Pete said.

"Simon told me that you were really concerned about his mental health."

"No, I never mentioned that." Pete replied in a confused voice.

"Simon said you were concerned about his health because I am so difficult to live with."

"No, That's not right. I took Simon aside and said he can't keep treating you the way he does. He has to help out more. You can't keep doing all the work. You will break down or have an accident." Pete looked at her with concern. "You need a break, and he does nothing."

"Oh. Thanks. Simon doesn't want to do anything." Lisa was not sure if she should say more. It was a small community, and anything she said would travel like wildfire. If it got back to Simon that she had said anything, he would have a horrendous row with her. Lisa had been taught by her mother that you didn't discuss family issues with outsiders. It was disloyal.

Simon stayed in the house, went to the club, took the kids to school, coached the kids hockey during the week and enjoyed attending his lodge.

One night, Lisa was in the kitchen cooking tea when Simon came out of the office.

"Why don't we sell everything and go live in the south of France?" Lisa just looked at Simon in bewilderment. "What?"

"We move to South of France."

"Why?"

"We just go and live there."

"And do what?"

"I don't know. We could just live there and travel. We could travel all round Europe."

"What about the kids, school, income? You can't just move to another country without a plan."

"Why not?"

"Well, it's not feasible. What would we do? No, don't be daft. That's a stupid idea. We have everything here."

"You are so closed off." Simon stated angrily and stalked back to the office.

Chapter Eighty-Five

Wedding Ring

The covered yards on the farm were attached to the woolshed. It was where the calves were reared and where they held the sheep before shearing. Being on the West Coast, they got a lot of rain, so being able to hold 1400 sheep undercover was important. Especially for the winter shearing.

The fog in the morning could keep the sheep wet all day with the short sunshine hours. The trouble with the yards was that they had no sides on them. This meant the rain blew in, and all sheep in the side pens got wet. They lost the ability to hold 3 to 400 sheep under cover. It was very frustrating so Lisa decided to fix it before the winter shearing. She got the local engineering company to come and put up an angled side, which only came down a third of the way. The roof was on a slope, so they had to adjust the frame to make it fit. She had been in town with her youngest, Daniel, grocery shopping when she remembered her wedding ring.

Lisa always took it off when dagging. The tooth of the comb can get caught in the ring, which can cause a finger to be lost. She always left it hanging on a nail by the dagging plant. She went over and got the ring and had a look at what they were doing. It was coming along very nicely. She walked back to the car and started putting on the ring. She was looking at it as she got into the car. She took the ring off and just sat in the car, looking at the ring. She wondered why she was wearing it, as she didn't have a marriage. They were just two people living in the same house.

She put the ring in one of the little compartments in the car and drove home. For the next few weeks, she thought about the marriage and what options she had. Simon carried on playing on the computer, making lunches, hanging out the washing and going to the play centre with Daniel. He liked going to play centre as he was the only father there. The other mothers all thought it wonderful he was there and fawned all over him. He helped out on working bees and did little projects for them.

Lisa and Simon didn't talk.

Sarah

Lisa caught up with Sarah at the family Xmas party. They were sitting in a quiet spot while the boys were swimming in the pool.

Sarah proceeded to tell her about her latest exciting situation. By this stage she was living in America for about six months of the year. Sarah had learnt to surf and was part of the surfing scene. She had a new boyfriend Sam, who Lisa had never met. He was a New Zealander but spent a lot of time in the States.

He was away somewhere for a couple of months working, and Sarah was staying on her own. In her round of social events, she met an Italian fellow. Sarah didn't speak any Italian, and he didn't speak any English. It was all hand signals and gesturing. According to Sarah, they enjoyed torrid love-making sessions for three weeks.

"It was getting a bit frustrating with it all having to be hand signals. He was great in bed, but it was time for him to go back."

"I suppose you miss him." Lisa replied.

"Oh no, it was time for him to go. I took him to the international airport to fly back to Italy, and then I went round to the domestic airport and picked up my boyfriend, Sam. I felt so bohemian. It gave me such a high being the woman about town."

"Ooh, that's impressive." Thinking about the emotional drama she had brought down on everyone's head when she caught her boyfriend with another girl.

Apparently, the rules only applied one way.

"Yes, I took my boyfriend home, and we had a lovely afternoon in bed. He was so attentive."

Lisa just smiled and nodded. This lifestyle she would never have coped with.

Morality didn't seem to exist, and Sarah was so pleased with herself.

It gave Lisa something to digest for the rest of the Xmas party as everyone made a fuss over Sarah and how well she was doing.

Chapter Eighty-Six

Skiing

Simon had done a lot of skiing when he was a kid, and Lisa understood from his father that he was a good skier. She had never been skiing or been up the hill when Simon was skiing.

It was the school holidays, the mountain was open, and being just down the road, Lisa suggested that Simon take the older boys skiing. Sarah had given them ski suits a couple of years earlier. She had been working for a company and had obtained/been given them.

They set off in the morning armed with hats, gloves, goggles and suits. They were going to have to hire boots and skis.

They came home tired but very happy, excited lads. Simon had a sore leg and was limping. Lisa never really understood what happened, but he fell somehow. Simon complained about the leg for some weeks. He couldn't do anything cause the leg hurt. Lisa wasn't sure what the issue was or if it really was a problem. Simon finally went to the doctor. He had broken a bone in his knee and had to be rested for weeks; could take months.

"Simon, why don't you sign up with Massey and do some papers? The semester starts in a month. Have a look at the options. You could do two or three papers."

"Yeah, I suppose. I can't do much else."

"You could set it up down stairs, have a study area."

Simon went ahead and built a desk with shelves above it. Set up a lamp, a computer and got himself an office chair. It was well organized. He had signed up for two papers.

Lisa thought this was wonderful as it would give him an interest. He could do what he wanted.

Mail arrived. Simon spent time downstairs, and then it seemed to die a death. Simon would be lying on the bed asleep.

"How's the study going?"

"It's not what I want to study. I want to study Neanderthal man and Bog man."

"Well, perhaps you have to do this study before you can study those. Most degrees have the general study before you get to the really interesting stuff."

"It's not what I want to do."

"Well, complete the papers, then you can look at other papers."

Simon didn't. It died a death, and nothing happened. Lisa was busy on the farm with spring, lambing, calving, docking, and shifting stock.

Chapter Eighty-Seven

Coaching

Simon used to play hockey at school and Lisa understood he was pretty good. During the week, there was a hockey competition in the local town, which the parents coached and refereed. The boys wanted to play, so either Lisa or Simon took them in.

They asked Simon to coach the team that Daniel played for. Simon was very happy to coach and would go into the local school to coach and then travel to the main centre for the games. He got on well with all of the parents, and they seemed to have a lot of fun.

Lisa would travel in to watch some games and see Simon coaching. Simon never liked it when she came and would ignore her. It made Lisa feel excluded and in the way. Many of the other parents ignored her but made a great fuss over Simon. How impressed they were that he found the time to come in and coach. How much the children liked being around him.

Lisa went in for the final games. She watched the older boys' games and then watched part of Daniel's game. Simon was the referee and was chatting to the parents. Lisa watched the game and went over to talk to Simon about shopping before going home.

"You will take Daniel home with you." Simon stated.

"Won't you take him home with you? I have the other two boys to pick up."

"No, the parents have organized a 'Thank you' for me at the local café."

"Ooh, that's nice. We could come as well."

"No, it's not for you. They have done it for me." Simon replied in a very firm voice.

"Ooh."

Lisa collected the excited boys and all of their uniforms. She saw one of the parents whose son was in Simon's team.

"The team did well." Lisa said.

"Yeah, they have. Simon is a very good coach. We are so pleased that he made the effort to come in."

"I hear they have organized a thank you tea for him."

"Yeah, we have. It's the least we could do. It's for him and the parents only."

"I could stop in on the way home." Lisa said

"No, it's not for you. It's for Simon. It's just a small gathering."

"Oh." Lisa said.

Lisa went and loaded the boys in the car, did the grocery shopping and drove past where the parents were gathering to thank Simon. She could see him through the window. She felt isolated, insulted and not appreciated. She did all of the work, which allowed Simon time to do the coaching. It felt like a real slap in the face. Lisa drove home wondering what Simon had said to the other parents for them to behave like that to her. He must have really made himself out to be the unappreciated father.

Chapter Eighty-Eight

Surprise

Simon came out to the kitchen and said, "On Wednesday next week, I need you to come to town with me."

"Why? You know I am busy."

"I just need you to come to town. It won't hurt you to come to town with me. The boys will be at school, and we will be back before they come home."

"I don't understand. Why?!"

"Stop being so difficult. I want you to come to town. Why can't you do that?" Simon was getting angry. He seemed to have something organized.

"Alright, I will come." The arrangements were made. The boys were put on the bus in the morning, and they left to drive two hours to the main centre. Once they reached the city, Simon pulled up at a medical clinic.

Lisa was surprised, "Why are we here?"

"You'll see." They went inside, and Lisa discovered Simon had an appointment. Once in the room, the doctor said, "I'm glad you came. Your husband has requested a vasectomy. We won't carry out the procedure unless the wife agrees as well. You may want more children, and the reverse does not always work." Lisa just sat there staring at Simon. He was watching Lisa's face intently. Bloody hell, she wasn't expecting this. They had, had no discussion about it at all. She didn't even know Simon had been to town to meet with the doctor.

Lisa couldn't believe it.

Simon quite obviously didn't want any more children. This from the guy who said he wanted four children. But then he did have four sons.

Simon had gone to a lot of trouble to organize all of this. It seemed pointless to say no when your husband wants it. If she said no Simon would have had a major row with her. Considering how the relationship was and the amount of work Lisa was doing, more children probably wasn't a good idea. If the doctor hadn't insisted that his wife be asked, Lisa mightn't have even known that he had got one.

"No, it's fine. He can have a vasectomy."

They got up and drove home. "Simon, why do you want a vasectomy?"

"Thought that was obvious. I don't want any more children."

"When we were first married, you said you wanted four children."

"Oh, I had this picture in my head of the children getting off the school bus. It was a sunny day, they were laughing, and the birds were singing. "

"So you had this perfect picture in your head not related to reality?"

"That's right. I had no idea how much work kids were."

"Oh." Who doesn't know how much work kids are? You only have to look at stressed Mums in the supermarket.

They got home and collected the kids. Simon disappeared into the office, and Lisa organized the kids.

Chapter Eighty-Nine

Stockwork

“ “S imon, I am going to need you to help with some dagging in two days time.“

“No, I am not going to help any longer.”

“What? You said you needed two days' notice, and that's what I am giving you.”

“No, I am not going to do it. You want to farm, you can do it on your own.” Lisa just looked at him. He benefited from her work; his asset benefitted from her work; why wouldn't he help?

“Simon, you know it's a lot faster with someone pushing the sheep up.”

“You can do it on your own.” Simon snarled at her and went back to the office. Lisa just stood there thinking, ‘Bloody hell’. It was going to make her life harder and take more time. The boys could help when it was the holidays, but for the rest of the time, she was going to be on her own.

Simon started going to the club regularly and would come home late. Lisa knew he was drinking and driving. After her offers to drop him off and pick him up she stopped offering. He never accepted anyway.

Lisa lay in bed wondering if he was alright. It was emotionally hard thinking that he might have an accident. She also knew that if he was drinking, there would be no insurance on the Ute. She tossed and turned, thinking over what would be best.

She played with the idea of ringing the police and telling them that he would be driving home drunk. He would lose his licence as he would have been well over the limit. If she did that, Simon would never forgive her. It was a small town, and everybody knew everybody. What if Simon killed someone on the road? Lisa thought he would be alright in the Hilux with bull bars on the front. What if he hit a truck? Lisa lay in bed playing out all of the scenarios. This went on for some weeks and she was feeling sick about it all.

After weeks of worry, she reached some conclusions. Simon knew the risks. Simon was an adult. Simon had turned down all of her offers. If he wrote the Ute off and there was no insurance, it would be hard, but they could cope. If he killed himself, there was nothing she could do about it. If he killed someone else, it was a risk, but nothing she could do about it. Lisa just had to accept his decision.

Once she had accepted the situation she relaxed about it. Simon would always come home, and he would smell rotten in the morning.

She would leave at daybreak to shift stock before the heat of the day. Some mornings, Simon would still be asleep in the Ute as he had been too drunk to get out. She would see him as she drove past on the bike. Other mornings, he would be asleep downstairs as he couldn't make it up the stairs to their bedroom. Lisa never said a word to him about it. This was what Simon wanted and she left him to it.

Simon got more and more depressed.

What Lisa could not understand was why Simon never got caught for drinking and driving. He would have lost his licence if he had been stopped. He drank at the lodge meetings, he drank at the club, he drove all over the place drunk and not once was he stopped or involved in an accident. It was like God was looking out for him. Amazing!

One night Lisa went up to their bedroom to find Simon sitting up in bed with the light on. This was unusual. She had a shower and got into bed. By this stage, she had developed the habit of lying on her side facing the wall, right on the edge of the bed.

As soon as she got into bed, Simon said in a quiet, firm voice. "You have ruined my life…" A long pause. "I can't stand being around you.." Long pause. "You are nasty and have no patience…" Long pause. "You are too aggressive…" Long pause. "People don't like you…" Long pause. "The locals feel sorry for me, being married to a bitch like you…" Long pause.

Lisa was looking at the green lights on the digital clock by her bed. She was tired from the long hours she had been working, and she really needed to sleep. "You don't look after the house…" Long pause.

Lisa lay looking at the clock, thinking, 10 minutes. If he hasn't stopped in 10 minutes, she will go and sleep downstairs.

"You don't do what I want…" Long pause. "You should be spending more time with the boys…" Long pause. "No one likes you, you have no friends…" Long pause.

The green numbers took a long time to click over.

"Your mother warned me about you…" Long pause. "I can't stand going anywhere with you…" Long pause. "You embarrass me…" Long pause.

Lisa decided that she wasn't going to wait for the 10 minutes. The clock was so slow. She got out of bed and went into the storeroom off the en suite. She got a sleeping bag and headed back out to the bedroom.

"What are you doing?" Simon asked in a surprised voice.

"I am going downstairs to sleep. I need to sleep, and you don't need me here for this. You can carry on without me."

"Don't be so stupid. Get back into bed." Simon said in a shocked voice.

She looked at him sitting up in bed and got back into bed. He stopped going on about her. Lisa went to sleep.

In the morning, Lisa got up and went about her day. Nothing more was said.

She had previously thought long and hard about the marriage. They were living separate lives, which is what Simon wanted.

For her, marriage was about two people working together for a common goal. The children and their futures came first. She wasn't expecting a marriage of fluffy ducks, romantic nights, gestures or an exciting social life. For her, it was about working hard and making a future for the children. Her priority were her children. She loved her sons and was jealous of missing out on any experience with them.

When they married, she thought Simon had the same values as her and that he would never beat her. That was a thought Lisa actually had when they were going out. That he wouldn't beat her. After her experience with her brother it was an important factor for her.

They had done a lot of work on the farm, built a new house, not that she got to spend much time in it, and the boys were happy. They had good friends in the district, and Lisa enjoyed the farm life when she wasn't overworked.

She decided that when all of it was taken into account, she would stay. Simon could carry on with his life and she wouldn't interfere in it. If he wanted to stay up all night on the computer, then that's what he did. If he wanted to go to the club and stay all night, then drive himself home, that's what he did. It was a bit hard with the lodge cause three or so days per week he would be away. He would go to the main city for some occasion, fly to the south island for another, go to a local one and then travel back up to the city. He was never home.

Lisa asked, "Could you stay home tonight? You are out all the time. It would be nice if you spent some time with the boys."

"No, I'm going. You just want to stop me from having fun."

Simon left. Lisa heaved a sigh. It was going to be just Lisa and the boys, so she had better figure out a way to make it work.

463

Simon came back from a night at the local lodge meeting. "I have decided to leave my life insurance policy to the lodge."

"What?"

"The lodge does a lot of good work with struggling families, and they will benefit from my life insurance." Simon said in a very positive, energetic voice.

"What about your children? The policy is for them if something happens to you."

"They don't need it. The lodge needs it."

Lisa followed him into the office and said, "Simon, that money is for your sons' future. You can't leave it to the lodge."

"You don't care about other people. All you think about is yourself. I will do what I want." Simon said as he dropped into the chair and glared at Lisa.

She went back to the kitchen, wondering where his head was. Surely, their sons came first.

She was in the supermarket doing the grocery shopping, and she had nearly finished the shopping when it occurred to her that she didn't have any cream. Lisa had to get some cream. What could she make with it for pudding? Lisa headed back to the dairy section to get the cream.

Lisa stopped and thought, 'That's strange you didn't use to make rich fatty puddings; why now?'

On the way home, Lisa thought about the cream for pudding. She served dinner and then a creamy fruit pudding, which the boys and Simon loved. Andrew had something else due to his lactose allergy.

Simon scraped his plate clean, "Simon, have some more; there's plenty,"

Simon served a second helping. Lisa was sitting next to him watching, thinking, 'have some more,' and then it hit her. She was trying to kill him. She was actually trying to make him so fat that he would have a heart attack.

She hadn't consciously planned it; she hadn't made a plan. She had been doing it subconsciously. Simon was so depressed, negative and mentally draining that she had reached the point where she wanted to escape. Removing Simon was the key.

After tea was finished Lisa went up to have a shower to think about it. The next day, around the farm, she thought about it. She decided that it was quite scary. If Simon left, then she would be happy. The boys would be happy. Simon was really critical of the boys, wouldn't spend time with them unless it was seen by the general public and was depressed. It was affecting the boys. It was affecting all of them.

If she was trying to kill him subconsciously, then what would she do if Simon pushed her too far? Something had to change. This situation couldn't continue. She had to find a solution which had a positive outcome.

Lisa was running all of the farm with some outside help. Simon was taking the kids to catch the school bus, making lunches, having a social life and being seen around the district. He would help now and then, but only occasionally.

It was summer, and Lisa had been putting in long hours. Most mornings, she was up and gone by five am just as the first sunrays touched the top of the hills. The sky in the east would be a riot of yellows, oranges and pinks. The air would be cool on her face as she rode the bike onto the farm. Lisa knew she only had a limited time before the heat made shifting stock impossible.

The dogs loved the morning work, but once the heat hit, all they wanted to do was sit in the shade. She then did maintenance or paper work in the midday heat and shifted stock again in the evening. Some days, Lisa had to do stock work during the day. Dosing lambs, ewes, weighing cattle, loading trucks.

Today, she was tired as she had had a long month. She had asked Simon to do a small job for her in the morning. She stopped at the house on the way past to get a drink about mid-morning. She was at the corner cupboard getting a glass and Simon was in the kitchen wrapping something up in glad wrap. Jim was on the other side doing something.

Simon was laughing and said, "I have been thinking about what you asked me to do. I don't need to do it 'cause if you went the other way around the farm, you could fit it in when you go past."

Lisa couldn't believe it and it just added to her already stressed day. She threw the glass she had in her hand across the kitchen on a downward slope, and it smashed on the floor. She turned away to go back outside.

Simon grabbed Lisa and hauled her into the office so fast she didn't know what was happening. He then held her up against the wall with an arm across her throat. He had her pushed so far up against the wall that only her toes were on the ground. He shouted abuse in Lisa's face. She wasn't really listening to what he said as she was still getting over the shock of Simon's reaction.

A few things that Simon said did penetrate her brain, like 'not putting up with that shit. She had no right to behave like that, and he wouldn't stand for it.'

The rest was just abuse. He then threw her across the room, and she landed in the corner of the office. Simon then flung himself out of the office, slamming the door.

She hit the carpet-covered concrete floor hard with her bottom. She felt a rolling force of energy move up her backbone and shoot out the side of her neck. Her head snapped sideways. Lisa sat stunned in the corner for a while and then slowly stood up. She slowly tested her body to see if it was OK. It hurt to move her neck. It was fixed sideways, with her ear nearly touching her shoulder. Any movement hurt.

Lisa left the office and went back out on the farm to carry on with her day. She had trucks coming, so she couldn't leave it. She came home in late afternoon to ring the Physio. Simon and her didn't speak about what had happened.

The Physio was a local woman, Karen, who had a small clinic in the local town. She was booked up for two days. Lisa carried on working until she could see her. Simon drove her in.

As soon as Karen saw Lisa, she said, "You are in a bad way. How did you do it?"

"I was out on the farm when I hurt it."

It took quite a few sessions before it came right. Lisa stopped asking Simon to do anything on the farm. She just avoided him where she could and was quietly polite regarding any discussion. Simon spent most of his time playing on the computer and ignored her. He played video games.

They happened to be at a local school event when she overheard Simon talking. He was explaining to some locals that she tended to get worked up and over-excited about things. He just needed to sort this out, and then she calmed down again. He was laughing about how he managed to control her.

Lisa thought he was right from his point of view. She did go quiet. What he didn't understand was that she just withdrew from him. Lisa was isolating him from her life.

It was mid-afternoon, and Simon was yelling at her. He was really angry about something. It wasn't anything major, but he was telling her that she should have done it differently, and it was her fault that it had gone wrong.

She tuned most of it out and was concentrating on the floor pattern, as he went on about how she had 'ruined his life and it was her fault that he was unhappy. She was just like his father'.

He was also yelling at her 'that people didn't like her and Lisa was a horrible person. The locals felt sorry for him being married to her'.

She raised her head and was just looking at him waiting for him to finish so that she could carry on with her day. As she was looking at him, she heard a clean, crisp snap in her chest. Lisa wondered what it was as nothing seemed to hurt. She then looked at Simon as he yelled at her and thought, 'I don't care any longer'.

She left the house to do things on the farm.

Chapter Ninety

Summary Holiday

Lisa had a bach at the Nelson lakes they could use. The boys loved it, and it gave them a good break. They had the 7 am ferry to catch on Xmas day, so they had to leave at midnight. Lisa had put in some very long hours for weeks with the farm. The shearing was done, and all the stock moved to long-term paddocks. The neighbour had been over and agreed to shift the bulls, feed the dogs and generally keep an eye on things.

Simon was home with the boys. She got home about 5 pm to find Simon in the office and the boys playing in the lounge. The kitchen had dishes all over it. The dirty meat dishes, the gas top was dirty, the fridge was full of food, which would go to off. The boys weren't packed, dinner wasn't done, and no food was organized for the trip. She knew it was a waste of time to ask Simon to do anything. It would just result in a row, and she would have to do it all anyway. Lisa started; she cleaned, she cooked dinner, she fed the boys, she found food to take with them in the car. She packed the boys, she packed herself, she got the boys ready for bed and in bed.

Lisa was exhausted. Simon stayed in the office.

At 11 pm, Lisa got the boys up and in the car with pillows and blankets. She had the drinks and food and all of their bags in the car. At midnight, they were all sitting in the car, ready to go, with no discussion with Simon at all. He hadn't come out of the office once, not even to have tea.

Simon came out of the office. His bags were sitting by the door where he had left them.

"What are you doing?" Simon asked.

"We are waiting in the car for you."

"Well, the least you could do is help me put my bags in the car." Simon said in a peeved voice.

Lisa got out of the car and walked round to the boot, which was open. She picked up Simon's bag and asked, "Do you want me to put it here, or would you like me to put it over there?" As she moved the bag from one side of the boot to the other.

"Ooh, just leave it alone." Simon muttered in a strained voice.

Lisa went back and got in the passenger seat.

"Why aren't you driving?" Simon asked.

"I am too tired to drive. I would drive us off the road."

"I don't want to drive."

"Simon, I am too tired, you will have to drive." Simon got in the car, and they were off.

The trip was a blur until they got to the town an hour and a half from the ferry. All Lisa remembers of the previous five hours was being flung against the car door occasionally and Simon saying "Why can't you drive?"

"I am too tired." was her reply as she tried to sleep.

In the town, the boys came awake. "Mum, we're hungry."

"I've got some muffins for you and a drink." Lisa fished them out of the bag. They stopped at the local toilets and stretched their legs.

Once they got to the ferry, Simon got out of the car and disappeared. The boys and Lisa went and walked along the seaside and watched the ferries.

Once they were on the ferry, Lisa found a spot to go to sleep, and the boys watched a movie.

The ferry docked, and Lisa drove to the bach. They pulled up at the bach, and Simon got out of the car without a word and disappeared. Lisa knew he had a mate down the road, so assumed that's where he went.

Judith met them and they got the boys inside and sorted. They were really excited about the lake and what they were going to do.

Judith offered to do all of the cooking, which was wonderful and meant Lisa had a holiday as well. The boys went swimming in the lake; Darren took them out on the boat; they took walks around the lake and played games.

Simon came back to sleep and then disappeared again. One day, he arrived back in the middle of the day with a trout. He put it in the fridge and said, "This is my trout. No one is to touch it."

Lisa just nodded. Simon walked back out the door again.

Judith saw the trout that night and said, "It needs to be cooked. Leaving it in the fridge like that will deteriorate it." Judith, being married to a fisherman, knew about fish.

"Just leave it. Simon wants it left alone."

Judith looked at Lisa with raised eyebrows and nodded.

Two days later, Simon came back and said, "Have you touched my fish?"

"No, it is exactly as you left it."

Simon looked in the fridge, took it out and cooked it. Sat down and ate it as he watched Lisa in the house. Then left.

Lisa and Judith organized to take the boys to the rock pools an hour and a half away. Judith thought Simon should come as he had done nothing with the boys. Simon refused.

They had a wonderful sunny day in the rock pools. They found shellfish, little fish and mini octopus. The surf crashed on the rocks below them, and the sea breeze kept it cool. They then had fish n chips for tea before going back to the bach.

On another day, they took the boys to the wave pool. It was awesome, with little channels that could be floated around. A deeper pool where they could do laps and a wave pool with incredible waves. Jim loved the wave pool. He had a ball. Daniel and Lisa swam around the little channels with Andrew. Andrew was spending most of his time watching Jim wistfully. He wasn't big enough to be allowed to go on the wave.

Judith became concerned that Simon and Lisa weren't doing anything as a family. Judith encouraged them all to go to Takaka for a day trip. She must have talked to Simon.

They all travelled over the hill on the winding road with Simon driving. Partway up the hill was a lookout point. The boys and Lisa all got out to look. Simon didn't cause his leg hurt to much.

The hill is made of marble, which has weathered into many odd shapes. Quite a sight. In winter the hill quite often has snow as it is 791m high. From the top, there are panorama views over Nelson, the bays, Motueka and Golden Bay. The very top of the hill has limestone outcrops, which has Tomos and contains a cave system. It has a spot where guided trips of the cave are organized. They all went through the cave, looking at all of the calcified stalagmites and stalactites. Simon really enjoyed going through the cave.

Once off the hill, they went to the Pupu Springs. Their proper name is Te Whaikoropupu Springs. They walked on a track through the native bush on the way to the springs and came to a clearing along the edge of incredibly clean water. From the viewing platform, they looked down into the crystal clear water bubbling up from the spring. It is so clear they could see the rocky bottom with shades of bright blue glittering amongst the rocks. The rocks look like they could be touched, being just below the surface. They are actually really deep. The different shades of green glide in the water with the movement of the water plants. Tranquil, natural, pure water. Once it has bubbled up, it then spills over the river rocks to find its way to the sea.

It is memorizing watching the water plants move with the water. The boys were lucky as they saw a trout and little crustaceans. They were fascinated watching the water and the fish glide amongst the plants. The walk back to the car park was quiet as everyone was in a peaceful mood, with bird songs as company.

They carried on, and Lisa saw a sign about a salmon farm. Simon didn't want to go but eventually gave in. The farm allowed visitors to catch a fish. They all collected fishing rods and headed to the lake. Jim, Andrew and Simon all caught a fish. For some reason, Daniel was having trouble getting one. Simon and the other boys started to head back, leaving Daniel behind. He was getting a bit upset about missing out. Lisa stayed and helped Daniel to catch a fish. Daniel was so excited to have caught one.

They got one fish, smoked and ate it at the farm. It tasted heavenly. Moist, warm, pink, flaky salmon. The other fish Simon gave to the operators.

On the way back, they stopped at the beach, and the boys and Lisa went swimming in the surf. As they swam, they could feel something brush past them. The first time it happened, the boys and Lisa freaked out, trying to see what it was. When they looked carefully in the water, they saw a shoal of little fish swimming around them. Once they realized what it was, it was so cool.

At the end of the day, they headed back to the bach with three very tired boys. Once they pulled up at the bach, Simon got out of the car and disappeared.

The holiday flew past, and it was time to head home. They packed up, said their goodbyes and were ready to catch the ferry. No sign of Simon. Lisa had some friends visiting who were standing by the car saying goodbye. No sign of Simon. Then Simon arrived. Lisa's friend said, "That was deliberate. He arrived late deliberately."

Simon got in the car, and they left with Lisa driving. As they pulled away, she thought about what she had said. It hadn't occurred to her that Simon was deliberately late. What did he gain from that? The only thing he gained was trying to make Lisa worried about being late. Was that what he was trying to do? Cause Lisa concern. If so, that was petty and pathetic. She started thinking about what sort of person would do something like that. It gave her something to think about as she drove to the ferry.

It was a lovely summer's day. The crossing was smooth, with the water looking like glass. It was beautiful sailing through the sounds, watching the land, the fish farms and the boats servicing them slide slowly past.

Once they landed, Lisa drove. They went up the West Coast 'cause that is what Simon wanted. The trip is slightly longer that way. Two hours from home, Lisa stopped at a toilet so that they could all relieve themselves.

When Lisa got back to the car, Simon was sitting in the driver's seat. "Give me the keys."

"Simon, you said you didn't want to drive. It's only two hours to go, and I can drive."

"Give me the keys. I am going to drive."

"Simon, you said you didn't want to drive."

"I'm driving. Give me the keys." Simon said in a tight, angry voice. Lisa gave him the keys, and he drove the last two hours home.

Once home, Lisa unpacked, fed everybody, put the boys to bed and rang the neighbour to see how things had gone.

Simon was on the computer.

Lisa had hardly seen Simon on the holiday, and neither had the boys. He had avoided them as much as he could. Simon really didn't want to spend any time with his family.

Judith rang to catch up two days later. They had gone home a day after Lisa's family had left. In amongst a general catch-up, Judith told Lisa about a conversation she had.

"I was down at the shop getting some milk when I got talking to a local. She asked me where I was staying. She knew the bach and said, 'Oh yes, I met the owner of that, such a nice guy.' I replied it belongs to my sister. She then said "Oooh no, he was quite clear he owned it. He has a large farm on the North Island, and it was so nice for him to get away for a few days from all of the stress of running it.' I corrected her and made it quite clear that he didn't own it.

"Oh, thanks. I wonder why he said all that?" Lisa couldn't understand why Simon had to take ownership of everything.

Chapter Ninety-One

Ducks

February is normally a hot, dry month, and Lisa had a summer crop in the paddock next to the duck pond. The pond was Simon's main duck shooting pond, being over one hectare in size. Simon and his mates would spend all opening weekend down there shooting and drinking. They would get in excess of 100 ducks, sometimes 200 ducks. The pond was in a small valley and had mature trees around it. It also had nesting black swans on it. A creek ran out of it and joined the other creek, which ran into their property. It then ran through their paddocks, then crossed the boundary again at the back, back into the neighbors before it flowed into the river. Simon's mates had built a Maimai (A small hut) in the trees where they stayed. When they weren't duck shooting, they went pheasant and deer shooting.

This year, the ducks had picked this pond to moult in. Lisa had over 300 ducks in it. They would sit on the pond all day and at night, walk into the paddock and eat the crop. She was losing an incredible amount of feed to them. Lisa rang up Fish and Game and asked what could be done. Could she shoot them? They replied, "No, it's illegal to shoot them out of season."

"Well, I have to do something. I am losing my lamb feed."

After some further discussion, they said she could use their airgun. It's a large pipe structure which works on a timer. The gun goes bang at intervals to scare the ducks. It worked for a while until the ducks figured out nothing happened. Lisa was moaning about the ducks to the stock agent. He laughed and said, "You should do what the local farmer did."

This farmer was a character who was quite aggressive in his dealings. He had set up a blind in his paddock and was shooting them. The Fish and Game warden found out and rang him up. He was told he couldn't shoot them, and there was a fine. He had to stop.

The farmer replied, "Do you own the ducks?"

The warden said, "I suppose I do."

"In that case, I will be sending you a bill for grazing them. What's your address?"

The warden apparently said goodbye and nothing else happened. The farmer carried on shooting the ducks.

Lisa wasn't quite that brave, but she fully understood his position. She basically lost the crop. What they didn't eat, they soiled. This reduced feed for her lambs at a time she really needed it.

Lisa had the ewes in the paddock below the dam. She was feeding them up for tupping. That's when the ram goes out. Lisa went out there to shift them and found 22 dead ewes. Big fat ewes all with the same watery green discharge. She rang the vet.

The vet came out, looked at them, took some samples and said, "I think it's salmonella. I need to wait on the results to find the source, but it could be the bird strain. In the meantime, you need to vaccinate. Destroy the carcasses and use gloves. You could catch it."

Lisa couldn't believe it. She had never had this before. Her heart dropped as she realized just how much work she had ahead of her. All of the ewes had to be vaccinated; all 2,500 ewes. They had to be dagged and dosed anyway, but the vaccination was going to make it so much harder. She bought the ewes closer and collected the expensive vaccine.

Gary from Aussie was staying with them. He was working for the local shearing contractor, getting ready for the show competition. The Aussie shearers like to come over a couple of months beforehand, to get used to New Zealand sheep for the show. When it was wet, he couldn't work, so he helped Lisa on the farm.

Lisa got the ewes in and found another 7 dead ewes.

Gary had some days off, so he helped Lisa with the vaccination. It was slow work. He vaccinated and dosed. Lisa dagged and pushed them up. Simon spent his time at the house in between taking Daniel to the play centre.

They started work in the morning. About 11 pm, Lisa had a visit from the Ravensdown rep. She was leaving and had bought out her replacement. They had a brief chat, and Lisa said she had to get back to work. Simon turned up from the play centre, said hi, and Lisa left him talking to them.

Gary and Lisa carried on with the ewes. At midday, they went up to the house to have lunch. Simon was up at the house laughing and chatting to the two women over biscuits and cups of tea. Lisa was surprised as she thought they had all left. Lisa got Gary and herself lunch as Simon hadn't done anything. She could see that Gary was really angry.

Lisa rang the vet, and the answer came back it was the bird strain. All those bloody moulting ducks in the pond. She could not use any of those paddocks where the stock had access to that stream. Damn, expensive ducks!

Lisa and Gary left and went down to the shed to carry on. The next day, they did the same thing. Lisa was so thankful that Gary was there 'cause, on her own, it would have been a nightmare.

Gary said, "I went to the club last night. It's amazing what you find out if you ask the right questions."

"Oh?"

"Yeah. I asked what people thought about you and Simon."

Lisa was curious and enquired.

"They have no time for him. They said he does no work, and you do everything."

"Oh. I thought they all liked Simon 'cause he's always telling me how popular he is."

"No. When he walks into the club, they will all greet him, but they have no time for him."

"Oh. They always seem happy when he's around."

"No. They think he's lazy, and they have no respect for him. They don't know how you manage everything."

Lisa needed to talk. She talked and talked. She told Gary about the household, what Simon did, what he didn't do, about the porn she found, about him complaining. About how little he did with the kids. She talked and talked. Gary listened and made comments. At one point, Lisa said, "You must be fed up with this."

He replied, "No, I am finding it really interesting. I am seeing things from a woman's perspective. My first marriage failed, and I didn't understand why. I am now starting to get it."

Lisa was surprised. His current partner was a vet, and he seemed very happy with her.

After three days of talking it all out, Gary said, "You can't stay. You have to leave. If you stay, you are going to go mad."

She just looked at him and thought about all the effort she had put in and the boys.

"You really can't stay. It is toxic. It's bad for the boys as well. I see what it's like at the dinner table. He's depressed, negative and won't help himself. Things have to change."

By this stage, they had finished the mob. Gary then got onto the subject of the sheepyards and how to improve things. He had a very good eye for planning and building. He offered to make the changes when he wasn't working.

The race was pulled apart and a curve put in so Lisa didn't have to walk so far. A platform was made for her to stand on to dag. It was wonderful. The boys came down and helped to sand the timber. They talked and laughed about things with the boys. It was light and fun. Gary made all those changes out of the timber they had lying around the farm.

Simon came down and got really angry about it. He yelled and said, "It was a waste of time." Then he went on about the screws being the wrong sort. Lisa was at a loss as the screws worked fine, and why was he angry? It was an improvement and he didn't have to do anything.

Gary said, "I understand why. You are down here with me and I am fixing up things. I am making him look bad, so he has to make complaints about me."

"Really? Cause he never wants to help and never fixes anything."

"Yeah, but now it's reflecting on him. He doesn't like that."

Dagging for Lisa got easier. Not as easy if someone was helping, but still easier. Gary headed back to Aussie and life continued on.

Lisa thought about Gary and what he said for sometime. She had needed to talk to someone and he had made her look at the whole situation. She had, in desperation, been asking for help from the universe for some time as she lay in bed at night, wondering what to do. She knew things were not good, but what was the answer? Gary gave her a chance to get an understanding of her situation and what options she had. What should she do?

The boys came down and helped with the yard work when they could. They could see their Mum struggling on her own. Lisa and the boys had finished the mob, and they were standing around talking. Jim bought up the time when they had been playing in the hay shed on top of the stacked timber. Lying on top of the timber were some old windows. Jim had walked on the glass, which promptly broke. Jim wasn't hurt as he just landed on the timber a couple of inches below. Jim said, "Dad yelled at us, and then he got a polythene pipe and whacked me around the legs." Jim's brothers were all nodding

"Really? I didn't know he hit you, Jim."

"Didn't you? We thought you did."

"No. I had no idea. He never said anything. I thought he just yelled at you. I was busy dagging."

"No, he hit me, and it hurt."

"I'm so sorry, Jim, I had no idea. You wouldn't have known not to walk on the glass." Lisa gave Jim a hug.

Lisa was shocked that Simon had hit Jim with the polythene pipe. That was really violent and abusive. Jim didn't deserve that, and what possessed Simon to do it?

Chapter Ninety-Two

Simon's Holiday

Simon was depressed. Overweight and depressed. Everything in his world was negative. It was affecting the whole family. He was abrupt with the children, critical of Lisa and wanted nothing to do with any of them.

At the dinner table one night, Simon suddenly got really angry with Jim. Simon didn't like the look Jim had on his face. Lisa sat there watching in shock as Simon leapt out of his chair, flinging cutlery on the floor, to tower over Jim while he yelled and threatened him. "Get that look off your face, or I will wipe it off your face for you."

Jim was sitting there with his head down, looking really scared and lost, wondering what he had done. Lisa just looked in shock, thinking, 'It's exactly the same look you have on your face, Simon.'

Simon then sat down and carried on eating as if nothing had happened. Lisa and the boys all looked at each other, wondering what had set him off. Simon was becoming unpredictable and abusive over the silliest of things.

Simon spent most of his time on the computer or away at lodge meetings. Lisa was struggling to know what to do with him. It had got so bad that something had to alter.

Lisa avoided having sex with him as much as she could. She knew that sex was important to Simon, but she just didn't want anything to do with him. She came up with every excuse she could find. However, sometimes she was trapped. Either she would have to have a major row or give in. He would wheedle about how he needed to be loved and how about it. If he didn't get his way, the next few days would be just awful in the house, and Simon would be horrible to the boys.

It wasn't a loving act, though. Simon probably thought so. Lisa would lie there looking at the ceiling as Simon worked away. He would get red in the face, and his sweat would drop onto Lisa as she lay there. She would just be waiting for it to end.

What got to Lisa was the fact that he never seemed to be able to make connections. He wanted sex at night after he had been really nasty to her during the day. She used to look at him thinking, 'Why would I want sex with you now, after everything you have said to me?'

He was turning 40 this year. It occurred to Lisa that if he went on a holiday, it might give them all a break, and Simon might find his passion. It certainly wasn't the family or the farm. If this holiday didn't work, then Lisa couldn't see any future for them.

Lisa went and saw Simon in the office. "Simon, you are turning 40 this year."

"Yea, so what?"

"Well, why don't you go on holiday for your 40th? You could go anywhere you want to in the world."

"I can't do that."

"Why not? It's your 40th If you go in the autumn or winter, when things are quiet on the farm. The kids and I will be alright. In Europe, it will be spring, summer so, a good time to go."

"You mean this?"

"Yeah, it will be a good holiday for you. You could go and see the Peking Man in China or the Neanderthals in Germany."

"I am too unfit to go." Simon said plaintively.

"Well, you can fix that. Do some walking."

"You mean this? I can go anywhere I want."

"Yep, it's your birthday present."

Simon started to look enthusiastic and turned back to the computer.

Lisa carried on with her daily workload. She noticed that Simon was meeting the boys off the bus on foot and carrying their bags home. The bus stop was a 1km from the house so a two km walk. He looked hot, red in the face and sweaty.

Simon got fitter and seemed to be organizing his trip. A new passport arrived. "So, how's your trip going, Simon?" Lisa asked one evening.

"Oh, it's good. I'm going to China first to see the Peking Man. Then I am going to Europe and seeing the Neanderthals in Germany and then France, where I will see your ancestor, who is buried in France's World War 1 cemetery. Then onto Britain and Stonehenge."

"That sounds great. You got your visa to get into China?"

"I don't need a visa for China, just my passport."

"No. I'm reasonably certain you need a visa for China."

"No, I do not!" Simon said in a firm voice.

"OK." Lisa went back to the kitchen. Thinking, 'I really do think you need a visa.'

A couple of weeks passed, and Simon finalized his trip. He was getting excited about the trip and planning it all out.

Lisa was in the kitchen three days before Simon left. Simon came roaring out of the office, saying, "I need a visa to get into China."

"Oh. How long will that take to get?"

"If I apply online, it will take two weeks, and I leave in three days."

"Oh."

"If I go to the Chinese embassy in Auckland, then I can get one within two days."

"Oh."

"I am going to Auckland tomorrow in the car." Simon stated in a firm, slightly panicky voice.

"Oooh, um. You fly out in three days, so you will be driving up tomorrow and back the following day. Then, back to Auckland to fly out. Why don't you stay in Auckland after you get the visa? You could just fly out afterwards and save the extra travel."

"No. I am coming home."

"Why? It's a lot more travel."

"I am coming home." Simon was getting worked up about the idea.

"OK." Lisa replied and went back to sorting out tea.

Simon left early the next morning and drove the four hours to Auckland. He came back the next day with the visa.

"Simon, what time do you fly out tomorrow?"

"In the afternoon. Why?"

"Well, I will take you to the airport."

"No, I don't want you to."

"It's alright. I will take you to the airport."

"No, I am starting my trip here. It's an adventure, and I want to catch the bus from here on my big trip."

"Are you sure? Cause I could take you?"

"No, just take me to the bus stop in the morning."

"OK."

They all went down in the morning to meet the bus. Simon gave the kids and Lisa big hugs, then got on the bus to Auckland with his carry-on bag. After they put Simon on the bus, Lisa went to the garage. The owner of the garage was also in the lodge with Simon. "It's a good thing what you are doing for Simon. He's needs the holiday to relax. "

"Thanks."

"Yeah, Simon needs the time away after all the stress he's been under."

"I hope he enjoys it." Lisa replied as she got into the car. What the hell had Simon been saying for him to think he was under stress? Simon did only what he wanted, and that was as little as possible.

The boys and Lisa settled into a routine without Simon for three weeks. They did everything they needed to plus extra. They all worked well together without the constant negativity and criticism from Simon. They laughed, played and went to the beach. It was as if a big weight had lifted off them. Lisa took the boys to the pet shop two hours away where they could look at tropical fish. They came home with a house dog. A blue heeler pup, which the boys loved.

Lisa had decided that if Simon was going on holiday for three weeks then so could they. She had discussed it with Simon before he left, so he knew that a month after he got back, the boys and Lisa were leaving for Australia.

She talked to a travel agent and they planned a trip to the Gold Coast, then up to the Australian Zoo before driving down to NSW to stay with friends. They had lots of fun looking at travel brochures and planning the trip.

Simon rang up occasionally while he was away to catch up. "Hi, where are you?"

"I'm in a train station in Asia, waiting for my next train."

"How long have you got to wait?"

"The next train isn't for six hours."

"That long? So you will have a look around the town."

"No. I'll just stay here."

"Why? You could look around the shops."

"No. All the locals just stare at me, and the policemen have machine guns. It's scary." Simon sounded like he was really worried.

"I'm sure it will be alright. If the policemen have machine guns, I'm sure the locals won't do anything. It's probably safer there than here."

"No, it's scary. I will stay in the train station."

The conversation then turned to other things, and the boys got a chance to say hi to their father.

Lisa was a bit surprised that Simon found it too scary to walk around the town. He was missing out on seeing all the local stuff.

Lisa worked out that he only rang when he was waiting for a train or bus. When he was busy, they didn't hear from him for days.

Simon came home excited about his trip and all he had seen. He missed out on seeing the Peking Man as the day he was in Beijing, the site was closed. He did see some other sites as he teamed up with an English couple. The trip to Germany was the highlight for him. He got to see the dig site of the Neanderthal man. He came home with T-shirts and replica spear points for the boys.

Simon wasn't happy that they had a house dog when he got back. He did not approve.

Simon said things like, "They replaced me with a dog." in a very aggrieved voice. After Simon had been home for a few days, Lisa found him in the office.

"Simon, did you find what you wanted?"

"Yes, I want to be on the dig site in Germany."

"Well, that's good. So that's what you want to do?"

"Yes, It's where I belong." Simon started to cry. "But I can't do it because of you and the boys." Simon had his hands covering his face as he sobbed.

"Why not? You could go over there for our winter. They don't work in the winter over there cause it's too cold. You would be home for the summer, so it would work really well."

"No, I can't do it." More tears from Simon.

"So you are going to stay here and carry on as it is?"

"Yes. I can't leave." more sobbing.

My God, Simon was making it hard. He didn't like it here. He was depressed, he was hard to live with and critical of his sons. He would not look at or consider his options and was going to slide back into the same black hole he was in before. He would not help himself; she had to hold his hand and lead him down the path.

Lisa didn't want him here. She wanted him to leave or at least change his situation. Why couldn't he take the step to do what he wanted to do and just leave? Everybody would be happier. Lisa couldn't understand why he wouldn't. Simon's attitude made the house depressed. The heavy black weight was descending again, crushing the light and joy.

"Simon, in lots of families, one of the partners will work away from home. Take the mines, for example. The husband works in the mine for a month then comes home for a month. It happens quite often. You could do the same."

"No. I can't do it. It would cost too much."

"Well, you could get a job to pay for it. I'm sure there's jobs you could do over there, which would cover your expenses."

"No. I couldn't do that." More tears.

This was going nowhere. Simon just wouldn't consider it, and Lisa had reached the end of her patience.

"Simon, you don't like it here, and I can no longer live with you being depressed. If you don't want to go and do what you want, then I am going to leave you. The boys and I are going on holiday in June. You have until we get back to decide what you want to do."

"Leave me? You are going to leave me?" Simon asked in a shocked voice.

"Yes, we don't have a marriage, and I can no longer cope with you behaving the way you do. You are depressed, you don't do anything. You just sit on the computer playing games." Lisa walked out of the office, downstairs and went out on the bike to shift stock.

Chapter Ninety-Three

Kids' Holiday

Lisa had spent hours planning the holiday and talking to people as to what were the best options. She had enough points to get access to some of the theme parks on the Gold Coast. Lisa carefully packed the kids and herself for the trip. Each boy had a backpack with their clothes, and Lisa had a bigger one with all of the extra stuff. They were travelling light. She had got three diaries so each boy could write in them each night about the trip. She had taken them out of school for one week for the trip, so she felt they had to do something in the form of schoolwork.

Simon dropped them off at the Auckland airport, and they boarded their plane. They flew for about half an hour. Then the pilot said, "We have an oil leak and need to return to Auckland."

Lisa couldn't believe it. Back to Auckland. All unloaded and had to wait for another plane. It made them two hours late, and trying to entertain three little boys aged 10, 8, and 6 at an airport, who were really excited about the trip, was difficult.

She had organized for them to stay in apartments. It was cheaper and allowed the boys space to move around. The first night, they were going to the Australian Outback Spectacular. It was the only time Lisa

494

could get a booking. Being so late in arriving, the lads were tired. After arriving at the apartment they caught the bus to the show. It was wonderful. The horses, the riders, the whip displays and the lights. Andrew was totally enamoured and couldn't take his eyes off it. The best surprise for Lisa was that the meal was served where they sat.

Didn't have to move the boys or find somewhere to eat.

After the show they caught the bus back to the apartment. All three boys went to sleep on the bus. Lisa woke Daniel up and told him to get off the bus. He promptly sat on the floor and went back to sleep. Lisa woke Jim and Andrew up and started them down the aisle of the bus. Lisa tried to re-wake Daniel, but he wouldn't move. Andrew had collapsed at the front of the bus and was asleep again. Jim, she got off the bus. She then got Andrew off the bus, who promptly sat down on the pavement and went to sleep. Lisa then went back and got Daniel and carried him off the bus. By this stage, the entire bus was laughing at her and the boys.

She got all three lads together and managed to wake Andrew up. With Andrew half asleep and hanging on to her, Jim leaning on her and carrying Daniel they made it into the apartment. Lisa stripped the boys, rolled them into bed and called it a night.

The next day after Lisa had stripped the wet beds and put the washing on. About mid-morning, they went to the Sea World Marine Park. It was a brilliant show. Lisa had arranged for the boys to get a 'kiss' from a seal, which they thought was pretty awesome, smelly, but awesome. Andrew even got the seal to clap for him. Lisa had nothing planned for the next day, so everybody slept in. They walked on the beach and had a look at the local town. It was a nice, relaxing day. Lisa was cooking their meals, so they did a cruise through the supermarket on the way back. The shop had all of these fruits they never see in New Zealand so they gave them a try.

The following day, they went to Wet and Wild. In June, on a rainy day, there are very few people. No queues for the rides. They went down the ride, straight round and back up again. For four kiwis, it was quite warm enough. Daniel, being only six, would start to get a bit blue around the mouth, so back to the heated pools to warm him up and onto the next slide. They had an incredible fun-filled day. At the end, they were all very tired but couldn't stop talking about the slides.

Andrew was still bed-wetting consistently. Lisa had packed an absorbent pad, which she put under his bed and washed it each morning. The other two boys had the occasional accident, but weren't too bad. Lisa put towels under their sheets to absorb any accidents.

They then went up the coast to the Australian Zoo and spent all day there. They could have spent two days there. It was amazing, between the shows and the different animals they had. Lisa didn't like snakes but put on a brave face. They had a large snake enclosure, which the boys inspected, and then they could get a photo with a white Boa Constrictor. It was a cool photo. Lisa reached over and touched the snake, but that was her limit.

From there, they hired a car, and the plan was to drive from the Australian Zoo down to the border of NSW and Victoria on the inland route. Lisa had a map and a list of some things to see. Coming out of Brisbane, it is a four-lane highway. Lisa had given the map to Jim before they set out.

"Jim, you are going to have to navigate." She showed Jim on the map where they needed to go.

Jim looked a bit shocked. He took the map as they set out. Partway down the road, Lisa asked Jim, "Where is our turn-off for the tropical forest?"

"I don't know." Jim replied as he shook the map.

"Jim, you have to tell me. Look at the names on the side of the road as we go along."

"I can't find it, you will have to look." Jim replied in a frustrated, angry voice as he pushed the map at his Mum.

"Do you really want me to look?"

Some muttering from Jim along the lines of 'I can't do it, it's too hard, don't know what to do.'

"Jim, look out the window and tell me if you want me to look at the map." Jim looked up at the trucks beside the car, all the cars in front and said. "No, no, don't look." In a firm, slightly panicky voice. He then started looking properly at the map. The other two boys started calling out place names they saw on the side of the road, which just upset Jim even more.

Lisa only made one wrong turn. Jim got really good at map reading, and by the end of the trip, he could tell them exactly where they were and how far to the next place.

Lisa had nothing booked. The plan was to stop and see anything they wanted and stop when they were tired. It worked well as it meant she didn't have to rush to be somewhere. The boys would ask, "How much further," and Lisa would reply, "We haven't got over the fold in the map yet. Jim, you show them where we are on the map."

They would then go, "Wow, long way to go yet."

At Glen Innes, the boys climbed all over the large sword. They went through the Dubbo Open Plains Zoo stopped at rock shops and Parkes Observatory, where they had cylinders representing the different weights of planets. Some of them were very heavy. They saw many, many aquariums. Lisa got aquarium-ed out. She began waiting at the entrance to collect the boys when they came back out.

Eventually they reach their friends Rose and Ross in southern NSW. They spent a week with them. The boys latched onto Rose's older boys and went wild on the farm.

Lisa went and had a meeting about a job in Australia. Moving to Australia and escaping all of the issues in New Zealand was attractive. She had serious doubts that Simon would change. He wouldn't help himself and just wanted to blame her and his parents for his depression. She bought some new clothes so that she had something to wear to interviews.

They took the train to Melbourne and then flew to Auckland. Their Plane was delayed. They were all very tired so they just sat down in the queue for the plane. Everybody looked at them, but by this stage, Lisa didn't care. There was a family ahead of them with children. They had an incredible amount of luggage which literally included a bath. When they finally went up to the check-in, the guy looked at Lisa in disbelief and said. "Is this all of your luggage? "

"Yep." He smiled, shook his head and loaded their bags.

Simon collected them at the airport and drove them home. The boys slept in the car for the four-hour trip. Lisa walked into the house to find the dining area clean. The tablecloth had been removed from the table so that the hardwood table top gleamed in the light with a huge bunch of flowers sitting in the middle of the table. Beside them was a card. She opened it, and it said congratulations on the scanning percentage of 186%. All your hard work has paid off.

She looked at Simon. "Thank you, that's lovely."

"You deserve it. It was a very good percentage." While she was away Simon had, to do the scanning.

The boys needed to go to bed so Lisa went into the hall towards their bedrooms and fell over this massive pile of washing, which reached up to her waist. It was sitting in the middle of the hall. Bloody hell, Simon has just dumped it here from where the washing pile normally sat, so she didn't see it when she walked into the house.

She got up off the floor and went into Daniel's bedroom to discover the bed hadn't been made. It wouldn't have been unrealistic for Simon to make the boys' beds. Lisa collected the sheets and started making the beds. Simon came into the room and said, "Oh, I suppose it would have been helpful if I had made the beds."

She just looked at him and said, "Yes," and carried on making all three beds. Simon didn't even offer or start making the other beds. He just went back to the office and left Lisa to it.

She had stripped them before they left on holiday. They were all tired, and Simon had left her to sort everything out. She went to bed thinking nothing has changed. Simon, as per normal, has made a visible gesture trying to show the world what a great guy he is, but done nothing helpful.

She went to sleep and caught up on the farm the next day. Back to reality.

They settled back into their normal routines. The boys went to school during the week, dancing on Fridays and playing sports in the weekends. Lisa would often be the one to take them and watch the games, which she enjoyed. She did the farm work while Simon sat in the house.

Mary and Robert came down for a visit. They were keen to talk about the farm and see the grandchildren. Mary was sitting at the table, so Lisa got out the official theme park photos. She opened them up and showed the photos to her, of the boys on the slide and with the snake.

Mary looked at them briefly, looked at Lisa, closed the booklets and pushed them back to her. Lisa had thought that it would have given Mary something to ask the boys about. It would have got the boys talking about what they had done on the holiday.

Mary saw it differently. She never wanted to discuss or acknowledge anything Lisa did with the boys. If Mary or Robert didn't do it, then they never wanted to see what Lisa and the boys had done. Lisa wasn't totally surprised, as that was how Mary normally behaved. They always had to belittle anything she did. Nothing had changed.

Lisa and Simon had discussions about their marriage. Simon wanted to stay married and kept telling Lisa he wanted the marriage to work. At the same time, Simon still stayed in the office, played games, refused to help on the farm and criticized the kids. But Simon seemed different. Something seemed off.

At the sports games, Simon walked off on his own. He would be wandering around, not even watching his sons play. He wouldn't stand next to Lisa and hardly spoke. Funny thing was, he didn't speak to the other parents either and that he normally did.

She couldn't quite put her finger on it, but something was different with Simon. At home, he was behaving the same in between telling Lisa he wanted to save the marriage. But something was off.

Then, one day at school, Lisa met one of the other parents. She was a solo mother who was very chatty and seemed to be quite interested and knowledgeable about Lisa's life. She had no proof, but she came to the conclusion that Simon was having an affair. So he was telling Lisa he wanted to save the marriage while he was having an affair. That would explain why Simon was behaving oddly.

Their 12-year marriage was over. Lisa went and saw a lawyer in another town to find out how to proceed. Simon carried on behaving the same and she carried on running the farm.

Lisa had no idea of the highly emotionally charged roller coaster, they were about to enter. The lies, the manipulation, the isolation and through it all Lisa had to hold it all together for the boys. However, that's a story for another day.

www.ingramcontent.com/pod-product-compliance
Lightning Source LLC
Chambersburg PA
CBHW060757120626
46557CB00001B/3